D1468428

TO PLEA
OR NOT TO PLEA

TO PLEA
OR NOT TO PLEA

The Story of **RICK GATES** *and*
the **MUELLER INVESTIGATION**

DAPHNE BARAK

**CENTER
STREET**®

NEW YORK   NASHVILLE

Copyright © 2019 by Daphne Barak
Jacket design by TK

Cover copyright © 2019 by Hachette Book Group.

All rights reserved. In accordance with the U.S. Copyright Act of 1976, the scanning, uploading, and electronic sharing of any part of this book without the permission of the publisher constitute unlawful piracy and theft of the author's intellectual property. If you would like to use material from the book (other than for review purposes), prior written permission must be obtained by contacting the publisher at permissions@ hbgusa.com. Thank you for your support of the author's rights.

Center Street
Hachette Book Group
1290 Avenue of the Americas
New York, NY 10104

www.CenterStreet.com

Printed in the United States of America

First Edition: October 2019

Center Street is a division of Hachette Book Group, Inc.
The Center Street name and logo are trademarks of Hachette Book Group, Inc.

The publisher is not responsible for websites (or their content) that are not owned by the publisher.

The Hachette Speakers Bureau provides a wide range of authors for speaking events. To find out more, go to www.HachetteSpeakersBureau.com or call (866) 376-6591.

Print book interior design by Timothy Shaner, NightandDayDesign.biz

Library of Congress Control Number:

ISBNs: 978-1-5460-8540-9 (hardcover), 978-1-5460-8539-3 (ebook)

Printed in the United States of America

LSC-C

10 9 8 7 6 5 4 3 2 1

CONTENTS

TO PLEA
OR NOT TO PLEA

AUTHOR'S PREFACE

I distinctly remember the time I first met Rick Gates, because I had already known him for a while. At the time, Donald Trump was leading two other candidates—Senator Ted Cruz and Governor John Kasich—but the race for the GOP nomination was aggressive. It was all hands on deck to get Trump the nomination. On April 26, 2016, his son Eric Trump sent me an email:

> This is so fantastic Daphne—we are so happy to have friends on the Trump Team. I have cc'ed Rick Gates who is handling delegates! As always, I am here for you twenty-four seven. —Eric

At this point, Eric's father, Donald, was still facing two other candidates who were trying to secure the GOP nomination for president: Senator Ted Cruz and Governor John Kasich.

Trump was leading, but the race was very aggressive. There was talk that even if he secured the 1,237 delegates, Cruz's people would offer to buy some. So, Trump and his family were happy to hear that longtime friends like me and my life partner, Bill Gunasti, agreed to serve as "Trump delegates."

Others would join up as well, as if we were all stepping aboard a giant cruise ship: excited, energized, and slightly nervous for the long, unknown voyage ahead. And Trump, a political novice, did what he always does when trying to master something new: he recruited the best, those more knowledgeable than himself, and in this case, it was experienced political operator Paul Manafort and his associate Rick Gates. They would run the convention and help steer the ship, hopefully all the way to the White House.

I had talked with Rick on the phone several times, but I met him for the first time a few weeks before the inauguration. It was New Year's Eve 2016, and my family had decided to spend it in Washington, DC. Once he got word from one of the members of the Trump family that we were coming to the city, Managing Director Mickael Damelincourt suggested we try the Trump International Hotel in the capital, which had only opened in September a few months before. Mickael led us, upon arrival, to a four-course New Year's Eve dinner. That night he was also testing the waters for the inauguration night event to take place there in twenty days. Black and yellow 2017 balloons came down from the high ceiling when we celebrated the coming of the new year at midnight. We looked up to the soaring nine-story atrium and concluded that a hotel with such a magnitude and a magnificent aura would require many more balloons than 2017 to make the right impact.

Later that night—or early next morning—as we were coming down the stairs of the BLT restaurant, situated on a large terrace inside the magnificent hotel lobby, someone from the bar yelled, "Hey, Daphne!"

I turned around only to see Laurence Gay, a close friend of the recently fired campaign chairman Paul Manafort. Next to him was Boris Epshteyn. They told me they were working on the inauguration and while we sat down and chatted, another man joined us, but he kept typing on his laptop. At one point, he lifted his eyes and looked at me. "We talked on the phone," he said. "I'm Rick Gates." Then he continued typing.

After Manafort was fired from the Trump campaign in August following media reports about his financial deals with foreign governments, Rick still stayed on the team. He continued to work closely with Trump and his family and was promoted to deputy campaign chair. After Trump's victory, Tom Barrack, a businessman and longtime friend of Trump, was appointed chairman of the Inaugural Committee, and Rick was to be his deputy. Rick then was among the small team who founded the America First Political Action Committee, while continuing to work privately for Barrack.

Although Rick had never sought publicity, never asked for it, he found himself rubbing shoulders with President Trump, Vice President Pence, and some of the biggest supporters, and most substantial donors of the campaign. He might have preferred being in the background, "the Shadow Man" who got things done, but in the world of Trump, Rick Gates suddenly became the ultimate insider.

During the months that followed our New Year's Eve encounter, Rick and I would bump into each other in the Trump Hotel. He would always be pacing around the lobby with a phone glued to his ear. Rick was tall—not quite as tall as Trump, but still not a small man. Even so, Rick has this ability to go unnoticed. A time or two, a friend would say to me, "Rick just waved hello to you."

"He did?" I would look around. "Where is he?"

And indeed, true to a man who likes to be behind the scenes, very few knew his name, despite his key positions. Even fewer knew what he looked like. But as much as he might have wanted to stay invisible, things started to change for Rick the night the first article came out in the *New York Times*. I was hosting a party at the Trump Hotel with friends Dennis and Carol Troesh. At the gathering we were joined by others, including H. R. McMaster, then President Trump's national security advisor, and I had invited Rick to join us as well. He came but sat in a corner, engaging only with my friend Katrina Pierson, who had served as Donald Trump's spokeswoman during his campaign and who was now a spokeswoman for America First. She and Rick were both working on their laptops.

"We are dealing with a crisis," Rick said to me as a way of apologizing. Katrina repeated something of similar nature.

The next day, I would learn from the media that Rick was fired from the America First PAC as a result of the article, which stated that although Manafort was out, Gates was still coming and going from the White House and still working for America First. The article would bring back allegations about Manafort's reported connections to Russia, and a former president of Ukraine—allegations that had been news fodder for months. Katrina and Rick had been working on a press release during the party.

I knew Rick must have been hurt by the firing—he'd told me how fulfilled he'd felt in his role with America First—still he didn't let anybody know it. He immersed himself in his consulting job with Tom, consumed by his work, as always. He still moved in the same circles, still was seen at the White House and the Trump Hotel.

Then, in the fall of 2017, I started to notice a change in Rick's trademark practical and positive demeanor. During a trip to Los Angeles, Rick, who'd always been super busy, tried to push me for a meeting that afternoon.

Daphne, please, let's meet at the Montage hotel for coffee. I'm here until tonight.

I wanted to meet with him, but I wasn't in the city at the time. By then, Paul Manafort's home had already been raided by the FBI, but I didn't quite understand Rick's urgency.

"Something's going on," I told Bill. "He's acting as if he senses that time is not on his side."

The next time Rick suggested we meet was a Sunday in September, at the Trump Hotel in DC. Rick is always very punctual, but on this day, he called at the last minute and canceled the meeting. He told me he'd been stuck in traffic, but his excuse made me believe that he needed to avoid the hotel, which was the flagship of the Trump Organization in the capital. But it was our spot. The informal nerve center where we'd all spent so many days. Was it now too public for him?

Then, in October, came the major breaking news: special counsel Robert Mueller's team was reportedly about to indict two people related to President Trump. It dominated the news cycle and created lots of speculation. Naturally, the names Paul Manafort and Mike Flynn were on everybody's lips. I called Rick and left a message on his mobile.

He called me back. "What do you think is going to happen?" he asked, sounding worried.

"Well," I said, "since they haven't searched your home or investigated you, it's probably not you."

Rick sounded relieved, yet even he wasn't sure. He kept weighing in with me, back and forth. "These two people may be less senior than we think," he said.

I didn't tell Rick, but for some reason, my gut feeling told me that Mueller's first indictments would be significant. We planned to meet the next day, Monday, at 5 p.m. at the Trump Hotel and catch up. Rick confirmed the time, but he acted a bit strange, as if he had a premonition that simple things, like a regular meeting, could not happen any longer.

Hours later, when Bill and I boarded the red-eye to DC, we noticed that our friend California congressman Darrell Issa was on the same flight. He too was wondering who was going to be indicted the next day. We were thinking out loud about Mike Flynn and Paul Manafort.

Up in our suite at the Trump Hotel that morning, Bill was unpacking, and I was taking a shower, when Bill suddenly screamed, "It *is* Rick Gates!"

I came out and saw the words scrolling at the bottom of the TV screen: "Paul Manafort and Rick Gates indicted . . ."

Going down to the hotel lobby later that morning was surreal. Several of Trump's inner circle were in town and two words were everywhere: Rick Gates. Rick was well liked and well known. He'd been staying at the hotel before the inauguration and afterward. In fact, Mickael, the managing director, had told me, "Daphne, you're staying in the same suite Rick has been staying in for months."

I went back to my suite and tried to focus on my work, but I could not get Rick out of my mind. He had been staying here, during the days after the victory, leading to the inauguration. Did he even have time to appreciate the beauty of this old post office? The view of the White House just in front?

That Monday afternoon, Rick Gates was not at the Trump Hotel for our scheduled meeting, and yet he was everywhere. Everyone wanted to know more about what was happening to him, but no one dared to call. Rick Gates, the man whom many tried to contact for invitations to events with America's most elite, had suddenly become radioactive. A photo of him with Trump during the campaign appeared on the big-screen TVs. There was Rick, clean-shaven and smiling, standing behind Trump, the Stars and Stripes draped in the background of both men. Since so few pictures had been taken of the man who stayed behind the scenes, they showed the same photo over and over.

When I heard in the news that he was represented that day by a public defender, I realized how unprepared he was for what was transpiring. Paul Manafort had taken the hard line of fighting the charges at any price. Over the next few weeks, journalists would speculate whether Rick, too, would toe that line or go his own and enter into a plea deal with special counsel Robert Mueller. And then the storm of speculation became a hurricane of head-lines when Rick switched lawyers, the media reporting that his new legal team was known for cutting plea deals.

In the end, I called Rick. I had to. I had not talked with him since that Sunday before he was indicted. It was awkward for the first few seconds, but then he shared how tough and unfamiliar it had been for him. We got to the topic quickly: to plea or not to plea?

"It's not for me or anybody else to tell you what to do," I told him. "It is totally up to you and your family. My only advice is this: tell the truth. I assume they know it anyway, so tell the truth, whether you decide to fight or plea."

It would be months before we met again. We had lunch at a hotel in Georgetown and took a corner booth in the restaurant, so we would have privacy and not bump into anyone. There Rick shared a few moments from the many enormous challenges he had been facing, being in the eye of a political storm. He had always been the listener, but now it was time for him to talk. And it wouldn't just be about the investigation, it was the whole chaotic journey: everything from the colorful anecdotes of the presidential race to endearing moments with the First Family, to Rick's entanglement with Paul Manafort, and of course, his decision to cut a deal. Most important, he wanted his four children to know—for the record—what happened. It was his chance to respond to how history would shape him. And that is why I've chosen to tell his story, in his own words.

—Daphne Barak

PROLOGUE

THE MOMENT MY LIFE CHANGED

t was 1:30 p.m. on Sunday, October 29, 2017. We'd just come back from my youngest brother's wedding. It had been a blissful family weekend. I was at home in Richmond, relaxing with my family. We were playing soccer, watching football, just a regular Sunday afternoon, until the phone rang.

It was my attorney.

On Friday, two days before, several reporters got information regarding two indictments that were on the docket for announcement on Monday. It would be the first time that special counsel Robert Mueller issued indictments. We—and by that, I mean everyone who could've been named as well as our associates—were speculating all weekend. I didn't think it was me because I knew of no collusion. Yet I was nervous after the FBI's raid at Paul's home. But Paul had called me. "I have good sources. It's not you," he had said. I was still nervous because of my proximity to Paul, Don Jr., and Jared Kushner. Their names had been mentioned in regard to the investigation.

"I have got bad news," my attorney said on the phone. "I am sorry."

That is how I found out that I was one of the first two indicted, that the US government was formally charging me with having committed a crime. Technically George Papadopoulos had been indicted earlier that month, before Paul and me. But it was not public knowledge, since he'd offered to collaborate with the special counsel, and his collaboration was kept out of the public's domain for a while.

According to my attorney, I had two options: "Self-surrender, or the FBI can pick you up and bring you in."

My mind was reeling. Even before the 2016 presidential campaign, there had been allegations that the Russian government was interfering with the elections. Russia's activities, such as they were, were disclosed publicly by members of the US Congress on September 22, 2016. A few weeks later, on October 17, agencies of the US intelligence community confirmed that Russia had been up to something, but the details were unclear. Robert Mueller was an ex-director of the FBI who had been appointed by Rod Rosenstein—the US deputy attorney general—as special counsel for the United States Department of Justice. Mueller's job was to investigate what Russia had or hadn't done. What concerned us was the investigation into the allegations that Donald Trump and his staff had colluded with the Russians to win the election. What if someone I'd known and worked with had somehow been involved in some sort of collusion to steal the election?

I went to talk to Brooks, my wife, who was in a different part of the house. Brooks, of course, had been following the news. Naturally she was worried, but at that moment, she became my rock. She was practical, helping me make the necessary quick decisions while being ferociously protective of our young kids. And that has been how she's continued to behave. Of course, we had some breaking points through this long, draining process, but I felt then, and continue to feel even now, that I could not go on without her strong support.

My world changed that day, that moment, but it would take me weeks to get my head around it, to understand what had just happened. Despite all the mounting speculation, I knew—I would have bet my life—there was no Russian collusion.

But I was restless about Paul. I'd worked with him for a long time, but did I really know enough about him? It is normal that he hadn't told me everything. But what hadn't he told me? What hadn't he told me that was important?

Since I was told to appear in court early on Monday, my wife helped me pack a few things, and I drove to DC and checked into the InterContinental hotel. Brooks stayed at home with the kids and tried to act like everything was normal. My lawyer came along, but just as a favor. Tom Barrack, my boss on the Trump Inaugural Committee, who had employed me as deputy chair, had decided to fire me upon hearing the news of my indictment and he refused to continue to pay the lawyer he had hired for me.

I was suddenly left with no defense on the most critical day of my life. After the attorney left, I called Brooks that night. We needed to make some decisions. Nothing prepares you for what you have to deal with when this sort of thing happens. We had no idea what we were facing, but we needed to do some sort of damage control. We decided to prepare a letter to friends and family, to alert them to what was coming and share what we were going through. It's no easy task, to think clearly when your future is on the line. To put such volcanic emotions into logical sentences

when you have more questions than answers, and people are looking for answers you can't give. In the end, we came up with the
following letter:

> I wanted you to hear it from me directly and it is with
> much disappointment that I tell you that at some point
> on Monday you will hear that I am one of the individu-
> als that will be brought in as part of the ongoing special
> counsel's investigation related to the election. Unfortu-
> nately, I have no details other than being notified of the
> event but am absolutely resolute that I did not participate
> in any activity involving collusion with any Russians, and
> I am unaware of anyone else doing so.
>
> Much has been written about Paul Manafort and his
> companies. The distorted narrative of him created by the
> media is unfair. It is clear that this investigation is highly
> politicized and an assault on those who helped elect a
> President that was not favored by many. I suspect that the
> media coverage will be nothing short of a frenzy today
> and in the days ahead with many opinions being writ-
> ten. But at this time, I would like to ask that you pray for
> Brooks and the kids most importantly—they have done
> nothing except support me throughout the election and
> beyond. Thank you most of all for your thoughts and
> prayers as we navigate this difficult time.

I sent it on Monday at 7:55 a.m., just before I went down to
DC. When I got there, I was picked up by the FBI in the hotel's
garage. I was relieved that nobody had gotten a photo of me walking in. It may not sound like much, but at that point, I was thinking about my children.

When I appeared before the judge, I was not shown the indictment because I didn't have lawyers. I pleaded not guilty without even seeing the charges, because I assumed that the charges were about collusion, and I knew of no collusion. The court appointed me a public defender, which, ironically, was the best thing that happened to me that day. I would have kept him, but I didn't qualify for public defense because of my income.

But when I finally laid eyes on the indictment, my jaw literally dropped. There was nothing about collusion. Nothing at all.

It was all about Paul. Lots of it.

———————

According to Quartz.com, a business news organization that targets high-income readers:

> "Charges detailed in a 31-page indictment also include 'conspiracy to launder money, unregistered agent of a foreign principal, false and misleading FARA [Foreign Agent Registration Act] statements, false statements, and seven counts of failure to file reports of foreign bank and financial accounts,' according to a statement from the special prosecutor's office.
>
> Between 'at least 2006 and 2015, Manafort and Gates acted as unregistered agents of the government of Ukraine,' the indictment says, and of a Ukraine political party led by former Ukraine president Viktor Yanukovych. The pair was paid 'tens of millions of dollars,' then hid those payments from US authorities by laundering them through US and foreign corporations, partnerships, and bank accounts. They lied to their tax preparers, to US tax authorities, and to the Department of Justice

when asked about these accounts, the indictment also claims.

Here is a summary of the twelve counts against Manafort and Gates:

Count One: Conspiracy against the US.
The two, 'together with others . . . knowingly and intentionally conspired to defraud the US by impeding, impairing, obstructing and defeating the lawful functions' of the Department of Justice and the Department of the Treasury.

Count Two: Conspiracy to launder money.
The two 'knowingly and intentionally' transferred money to and through the United States, with the 'intent to promote the carrying on of specified unlawful activity.'

Counts Three through Six: Paul Manafort failed to report his foreign bank accounts with the US Treasury from 2011 through 2014.

Counts Seven through Nine: Richard Gates failed to report his foreign bank accounts with the US Treasury from 2011 through 2013.

Count 10: Unregistered agent of a FARA (Foreign Agent Registration Act) principal.
'Both Gates and Manafort failed to register as lobbyists of a foreign agent, as required under the Foreign Agent Registration Act first passed in 1938,' the indictment says.

Count 11: False and misleading FARA statements.
'Both Manafort and Gates lied in statements made to the Attorney General about lobbying for foreign agents,' the indictment says. These include false statements about 'meeting or conducting outreach to US government officials' and false claims that their work on behalf of Yanukovych's party did not include 'meeting or outreach in the US.'

The two also claimed that they could not turn over email correspondence linked to a partnership they formed, because it 'does not retain communications beyond 30 days.'

Count 12: False and misleading statements.
The two lied repeatedly to the DOJ [Department of Justice], the count says, in statements submitted in November 2016 and February 2017. In addition, they also had other people 'falsify, conceal, and cover up, by a scheme and device a material fact,' make 'false, fictitious and fraudulent statements,' and use 'false writing' and documents."

———————————

After my five-million-dollar bond was posted, I was ready to get back home to Richmond, to normalcy. How naive that thought seems to me now. As if there was ever a way to return to what was before.

Even though we live on a private street, Brooks had told me there was media swarming the front of the house. I braced myself to face them, but fortunately, by the time I got back, the neighbors had called the police and gotten the cameras kicked out. Most of our neighbors were very supportive and saddened by what happened to us. It is a mostly Republican neighborhood, a quiet one. Some brought us meals and others came to see what we needed. I was truly touched by all the kind gestures. I would have broken down and wept, but I had to keep up the front that I had everything under control, even though inside I was beginning to feel a profound sense of violation, of outrage.

The red leaves were already falling from the trees and it was chilly, but pleasant. I usually love this beautiful scenery, but this time I just stared blankly before heading inside. I attended to the kids. It was strange, trying to behave as usual.

Daddy's home. That simple truth emphasized the unknown and made it all the more surreal. Daddy wasn't usually home at this time of the day. Would I be able to be home for them at all in the near future?

I sat down. I was filled with anger. I felt betrayed. Life had been moving so quickly there'd never been time to reflect. It was as if I were watching the last couple decades of my life on a film reel: the strange, fascinating, and hectic days I spent with Donald Trump, the fiascoes and pitfalls, my start with Paul Manafort and my early career. All of the twists and turns that brought me here.

ONE

MY ROOTS

S omeone asked me recently about my childhood. This person, who met me later in life, was curious, in light of the headlines, how my upbringing positioned me to be a key player in domestic and international events. But my background is quite normal, so far away from what someone influenced by media reports might imagine.

I was born at Fort Lee military base in Virginia. My dad was a career military officer. I am the eldest of three boys. My middle brother is two years younger and my youngest brother is ten years younger than me. My mother was a nurse, but as an officer's wife, she quit working when we were born. After we went to school, she went back to work in an emergency room. We moved about every three years. In the United States, two of my favorite places were Kentucky and North Carolina.

Later on, we moved to Nuremberg, Germany. On the one hand, it was difficult for me and my brothers. I felt what so many army brats feel: the vicious cycle of impermanence, of castles on sand. I started life over every few years. Left behind friendships, built new ones, then left those behind. For a child, this can be exhausting, and no doubt, it shaped my personality.

But there were benefits to the constant waves of change. My eyes were opened to the big world out there. Many Americans don't get the opportunity to experience life in other countries. When we lived in Germany, we took vacations in Holland. It got me interested in foreign countries, and later on, in foreign policy.

I also developed more European hobbies, like playing soccer for a German team. I was quite good at that, and I follow soccer to this day. In Germany I attended an American school. Most kids, like me, were from American families working overseas. I didn't know another kind of childhood existed. Life on a military base was what I had known. All houses looked alike. All fathers served. That was my world.

My father's last station was at the same Fort Lee, Virginia, where I was born. After he retired, we continued to live in Prince George, a neighborhood nearby. I went to high school there. My dad had wanted my brothers and me to follow in his footsteps, but he did not pressure us. I ultimately joined the military—the reserves—and served six years. I attended the College of William and Mary in Williamsburg. I was fascinated with history and political science, and these topics would dictate my academic choices.

When I was in my early twenties, we went to see a speech by George H. W. Bush. I was taken by the whole structure of it. The buildup toward the speech, the campaign. These details fascinated me. It was the early 1990s, right at the time when the Berlin Wall came down. I remembered how when my dad was overseas, he'd visited East Berlin at the invitation of the Germans. And then we had come back, and I watched President Bush making a special speech to mark the event. It was a new feeling for me: the beauty and power of politics. I was witnessing history firsthand, and I would mark this event as the first time I wanted to be involved in government and international affairs—to touch history in the making.

Another milestone of my college days was the day I met Brooks. We both served on the Executive Committee at the College of William and Mary. She was studying business and finance. I'd had girlfriends before, but this was different, serious. We dated from the end of our junior year through our senior year and got engaged after graduation in January 1995. The wedding took place in November. We are the proud parents of four great children.

In many ways, this is the story of the average American boy. So what inspired me to take the path I chose? Or prepared me for the extreme ups and downs of the last three years?

I think a large part of my character was formed by my being part of a military family. The change and uncertainty that might have terrified others, for me, was just a way of life. I learned to be outgoing. It became second nature to make the best of new situations and win over new people. I also learned to naturally sense the limitations of my position: don't shine too much, don't upset the already-crowned leaders, don't create new enemies.

In school, I had been described by teachers as engaging and curious, active and happy, helpful and hardworking. But none of them would have used the word "leader." Instead they knew me as a team player, and this quality would define me for years to come.

My parents were always very proud of me, but they were especially so when they learned I was working for Trump. My dad is a veteran and was a Trump supporter from the start, so he was engaged with the campaign, following the rallies and events. After Trump won, and I was the deputy chairman of the inauguration, they were excited on a personal level. Naturally, I invited them to the inauguration as my guests. It was a big moment for them, and what they believed in.

And when that Sunday telephone call came, and I learned I was being indicted, they were worried, but not overly so. It was just the beginning. We did not yet know enough. It was an emotional shock rather than anything that made logical sense. We all thought we could deal with it. At the time, the impact and consequences were still hovering at the surface, and it would be months and months before they started to sink in.

Today my parents are concerned for me, and they are angry. Their main goal is to protect their grandkids. Traveling as kids, relocating every few years, made us a close-knit family. My parents live thirty minutes away from us in Richmond. My two brothers are close by as well. That is how it's always been. I've learned to survive and make calm decisions in part because I have such a united family.

TWO

WHEN I FIRST MET TRUMP

As is sometimes the case in political ventures, my tenure with Donald Trump started before we'd even met. Trump had been leading the polls for months. His undeniable capacity to hold a crowd's attention, his way of speaking the language of the people, and his sheer brute force and energy had already caused many candidates to quit. But the one thing the great dealmaker did not know was the inner political game—the *political* insider's knowledge of who to talk to and what to say (and what to promise) to get the delegates' votes. Some had already predicted Trump would not be able to nail the magic number of 1,237 delegates. But Trump, being Trump, found a guy he thought could get him there. The guy who had a reputation for knowing which buttons to press and when—my boss, Paul Manafort.

So on Easter Sunday, March 2016, Paul met Trump at Mar-a-Lago, Trump's glamorous members-only resort in Palm Beach, Florida. After an hour, they agreed that Manafort would be in charge of getting Trump the delegates needed to win the primaries, and with that, the Republican Party nomination for the presidency. Trump's then campaign manager, Corey Lewandowski, and his communications director, Hope Hicks, joined the meeting. Prior to us joining the campaign, Corey had never advised Trump. He said, "Let Trump be Trump." He did not understand then that the decision was effectively a demotion for him, because from that point on, Paul was going to run the whole show. The next day, Trump officially made Paul his convention manager, to run the delegates, and of course, I would be Paul's deputy.

I had never met the reality TV star before, so naturally, I was curious when, the following Wednesday, I strode through the glass doors on Fifth Avenue in New York. It was only my second time at Trump Tower, and from the way Trump was portrayed in the media, surrounded by ornate interior design, I expected to walk into the sort of room where a Middle Eastern sultan might feel at home. Or, at the very least, I was expecting the stylish, more conservative look of *The Apprentice* boardroom.

So when Paul and I stepped out onto the fifth floor, where the campaign was based, and saw the concrete skeleton, we were shocked. Wires hung from the ceiling. The furniture was a mismatched collection of a scavenged plastic tables and chairs. It was so minimal, so low budget. It looked like a Home Depot rummage sale in an abandoned shopping mall. The fifth floor, I would later learn, was where the production of *The Apprentice* had taken place. By then it had been dismantled and there was nothing left of the glitzy *Apprentice* boardroom that we were so familiar with. We were, in fact, on a TV set, between productions.

It was clear to me, right then and there, how practical Donald Trump was. Since he decided to run for president, and consequently lost the production rights for *The Apprentice,* he immediately switched gears. That's one of the things you quickly learn about Donald Trump. When it's over, he doesn't linger. It's all about dealing in the now. However he might have felt about *The Apprentice*, however much he might have loved it, that part of his life was now finished, and he'd moved on, turning his entire focus to securing the Republican nomination for the presidency.

In complete contrast, each time I went to the boardroom on the twenty-sixth floor, the glamour would hit me at first. That is part of the enigma of Donald Trump, the contrasts. On the one hand, living the life of most rich and powerful, the jet-setting New Yorker, and on the other, eating junk food. It seems inconsistent. You would think it would be all champagne and caviar but having a foot in each world gives him the ability to communicate with the wealthiest people on earth as well as the blue-collar workers.

On Wednesday, I met Corey for the first time in the boardroom, and Allen Weissenberg, longtime chief financial officer of the Trump Organization, joined us. It was clear that Trump trusted him, and for good reason, as I would later learn. It would make news, months later, that Weissenberg was granted immunity by the federal prosecutor in the Southern District of New York, so he could share information in the investigation of Trump's former lawyer, Michael Cohen. These headlines would surprise many. People would criticize Weissenberg, saying he betrayed Trump to save his own skin. But it doesn't seem like that to me now, knowing firsthand the pressure you're under when in the crosshairs of a federal prosecutor.

Trump, in person, is pretty much how he appears on TV—bigger than life, but not unfriendly. As I watched him that day, I realized he was overseeing six meetings in the same room. People were having animated, urgent conversations all at once, each one of them hoping for a few seconds of Trump's attention while the man furrowed his brow, made a snap decision, and then immediately moved on to the next pressing issue. And yet, underneath the constant swirl of activity, there was an order to the chaos, and by some magic, all that intensity turned into action and results. It was scary and exhilarating and irresistibly attractive. And at that moment, I was committed. I dove head-first into the flamboyant, chaotic world of Donald Trump. No questions asked. This was where I was meant to be, and where I knew I could make my mark.

Trump asked lots of questions. Not only about the campaign but also about a wide range of topics—anything that came to his mind at the moment. It was overwhelming. I would learn that was his style while he is processing ideas or decisions. "What would *you* do in this situation?" he would often ask. "What do *you* think about so-and-so?"

So, from that day forward, I ended up doing many more things than I had intended, more things than I'd planned. More things than I'd signed up for. It was like being part of a reality show. You would suddenly get an assignment, and you just had to run with it. Trump sipped a Diet Coke, seamlessly shifting from talking about the campaign to running his business at the same time. Eventually I got used to it—it's actually a sign of his brilliance, his capacity to switch from one thing to another on a dime. There was never a moment wasted. In some of his meetings, he was talking while signing checks.

After the first meeting, Paul and I got situated on the fifth floor. We'd hit the ground running, and we were already working at full speed. For some time, Paul and I had been discussing how we would run the convention, if Trump won. There were two steps before getting there. The first: Wisconsin. We had to win! And secondly, though we'd won Louisiana, some of the delegates were opposed to Trump, so we had to convince them to vote for him.

Paul had been working on getting to Trump from January 2016. He talked with his former partner, Roger Stone, and then with Tom Barrack and had already asked them to put in a good word for him. Paul asked me to prepare documents about how to organize the convention if Trump were to become the GOP presidential nominee and how to win the magic number of delegates. At that stage, Trump was starting to look like he had a good chance. But it was a one-shot-deal. Everything rode on that one shot. If he didn't have the 1,237 delegates on the *first* vote, he wouldn't have made it! The party could have then nominated someone else. Someone who didn't even have a running mate yet. Someone like Ted Cruz. And Ted Cruz was planning on it. You see, Trump was a great candidate. He appealed to billionaires and the middle class. Trump was a man-of-the-people, and "the people" would support him. The people would get him into the White House.

Trump was used to being in control. He was used to being the director. He was used to putting his name on things. But the convention was not a "Trump convention," it was a Republican National Committee (RNC) convention. *They* controlled it. And to win, *we* would have to control it.

The main reason that Paul had been brought in to help Trump was for his expertise when it came to the delegates, so naturally he was put in charge of them. It was April 2016 when then campaign manager Corey Lewandowski was promising: "We're going to win Wisconsin's delegates hands down."

Well, we lost Wisconsin big-time. That's the real reason Corey was sidelined, and Paul moved to the forefront. Corey simply did not have the experience, knowledge, and the expertise needed at that stage of the game. He had been demanding a bigger budget for flights: that is how *he* understood the game. For him, it meant traveling with Trump. We used to call Corey "the body man," or "the purser" (like in a flight crew) because he was always traveling. But Paul, meanwhile, did things completely differently. He chose to stay back at campaign headquarters and was involved with the growing team. And I was doing both. Jared and Paul agreed the person with the most experience should be on the plane with Trump, and at the beginning, that was me.

On Tuesday, April 26, we were facing five primaries: Maryland, Pennsylvania, Rhode Island, Connecticut, and Delaware. After the big loss in Wisconsin, we needed to win badly. Paul's involvement changed the game immediately. That Tuesday we won in all five states! It was not only a great boost to the morale of our supporters and donors, but that victory also saved the Trump campaign millions of dollars. We were off to the races.

THREE

MEETING THE TRUMP "KIDS"

D iving into Trump's world meant getting to know the children, and I would come to understand them as few others would. While preparing them for the convention, I developed relationships with each member of the family, because for all their combined talents and experience, the Trumps were still newbies at politics, and politics wasn't a game you went into unprepared.

The "kids," as we called the three thirty-something children of Trump from his first marriage as well as the younger two, were on the twenty-fifth floor, so for the first few days, we did not see them. Three of them—Don Jr., Ivanka, and Eric—were famous in their own right. They'd taken part in *The Apprentice*. They'd frequently appeared in social pages and in gossip columns. The media likes to make things simple enough for a ten-second sound bite. But people aren't simple, and as I would find out, for better or worse, none of the Trumps were exactly like the media made them out to be.

Ivanka was the first one I met. She came down to the fifth floor and introduced herself. "I am so excited to work with you!" she said. The first thing you notice about her is how well brought up she is. Proper and friendly, but formal. "Centered" would be a good way to describe her. I would learn of her passion for child-care issues and family leave. I give her a lot of credit for her commitment to that issue. Originally, she had not known much about these topics beyond her initial convictions, but she jumped right in, talking with different experts and learning about these important concerns. One thing you can say about Ivanka is that she, like her father, has a talent for absorbing new information.

Ivanka is also persuasive. These types of social issues had not been Donald Trump's passion to begin with, but Ivanka did her homework and got him on board. She was also involved with her father's speeches. Trump usually preferred to talk unscripted, but on the few occasions he agreed to deliver a written speech, Ivanka was a key player in putting together the right words. The first speech that comes to mind that Ivanka had a hand in was in the aftermath of the horrific Orlando shooting massacre. On June 12, 2016, Omar Mateen murdered forty-nine people and wounded fifty-three others in a terrorist attack at Pulse, a gay nightclub in Orlando, Florida. Trump had been perceived as anti-LGBT, so he, as the presumptive candidate of the Republican Party, needed to comfort to the grieving families and the rest of the nation. It was a challenge on a human level.

Ivanka got heavily involved in the editing. She understood that Trump needed to talk directly to the LGBT community and connect with their pain and anger. One can see Ivanka's fingerprints on Trump's speech:

Our nation stands together in solidarity with the members of Orlando's LGBT community. They have been through something that nobody should ever experience. This is a very dark moment in America's history. A radical Islamic terrorist targeted the nightclub, not only because he wanted to kill Americans, but in order to execute gay and lesbian citizens, because of their sexual orientation. . . .

I learned how to work with this father-daughter relationship and obtain the maximum benefit from it. Ivanka understood her father. She also had superb instincts. She knew how and when to weigh in and when to back off. Along with Ivanka, Jared also had Trump's ear and special access to edit his speeches. It was interesting to observe the dynamics between Jared and Ivanka. They are great friends, and they respect each other. While they never argued publicly, they did not always come with one voice. They were both deliberative and were usually in agreement, or at least a mutual understanding, *before* talking with Donald and others. Their proactive, productive strategy was something I could apply in my own work relationships.

I met Eric next. He asked to see me at his office. Friends of the family had been calling and offering to help the campaign, and Eric asked me to call them and sort out how they could be part of it. I noticed right away how serious Eric was. The first impression Eric gives you is complete professionalism. He knows where he fits in the grand scheme of things. He knows what to do and how to do it. That quality is a hallmark of a good executives. But beneath the seriousness, Eric is a man of deep passion and feeling, and he's not reticent to show it.

I saw a perfect example of this at a rally that happened weeks later in Pennsylvania. After it was over, Eric was so moved. He saw the economics. He saw how numbers—the dollars and cents—affected people. How just getting through the day mattered. People came up to him afterward. "We're going to fight for your dad," they said. "We are going to make him win." I witnessed how that moment impacted Eric and engaged him in the campaign. He seemed to realize that if we could win these people over, the big win was a real possibility. And people there were genuinely hoping his father would win. They told him they couldn't pay their mortgages, and this bothered him. He couldn't believe that working people in America couldn't make ends meet. He couldn't believe that things had gotten this bad.

Later on, Eric wanted to do more rallies. He reached out to more friends, made calls to donors. Though Eric's wife, Lara, would become very involved with the campaign, she was not engaged when I first joined up. Not because she didn't want to be; I think maybe she just didn't know the best way. But eventually, Trump suggested involving Lara in campaigning in North Carolina. He asked me if it was a good idea, since she was from there and her family still lives there.

"I think it's a *great* idea," I said. Lara is a very nice person. After she began getting involved with the campaign, she took on more and more, and I felt that she and Eric enjoyed doing that as a couple.

The last of the older kids I met was Don Jr. The media likes to paint him as someone who doesn't quite know what to do with himself, but in real life, that's not the vibe Don gives off. He's a man's man. He's a hunter. He's down-to-earth. He's the sort of guy you can have a beer with. Even so, Don Jr. would interact with me less than his siblings did. He felt that since Paul Manafort was my superior, he would rather communicate with him than me, and that was okay with me. I was so busy, traveling with his father, working on the campaign and then the convention, that I hardly had time to notice what little I had to do with him.

What I did notice was Don's eagerness to show his father how valuable he was to him and the campaign. Don took on any task that might portray him in a favorable light to his father. I would be told later about the tension between Donald and his first son after the messy divorce from Ivana. But when I came along, they had reconciled, and Don Jr. genuinely wanted to make up for lost time.

Then came Tiffany, the only child of Donald Trump and his second wife, Marla Maples. Almost a decade younger than her three older siblings, she's from a different generation. Still young, though not a kid anymore. There is a seriousness about Tiffany as well, as if she knows she has to prepare herself to do important things.

And of course, there's Barron, Donald's only son with First Lady Melania. Since he was underage, his parents sheltered him. They did not wish him to play a role in any part of the campaign. As a father of four children, I supported their decision. I discussed it with Brooks and we both agreed: a kid has the right to be a kid, and politics is a grown-up's game.

Obviously, I'd been familiar with the three eldest kids from the *Apprentice* shows and their media appearances, but there was one more key player in the Trump family I'd yet to meet, the person who would become his senior adviser during the campaign, and later, at the White House. I was headed to a rally with Trump, and there, on the plane, Trump introduced us.

"You know, Rick," Trump said, "Tom Brady could have been my son-in-law. Well, meet Jared."

We laughed. It was clear that Trump respected Jared. That he appreciated how protective he was of his daughter and the whole family. Knowing how Donald Trump feels about Ivanka, it's clear that he wouldn't let his daughter marry just anybody. Jared Kushner was a man who really was good enough for Trump's "little girl."

And just as he had done with his father-in-law, Jared would first capture my attention, and ultimately, my respect. Ever since the surprise victory on November 7, 2016, there has been so much interest in Jared's role and his influence over Donald Trump. *Time* magazine even put Kushner on its cover, suggesting that he was the most influential, behind-the-scenes individual in the new administration. During the later stages of the campaign, Don Jr., Ivanka, Eric, and Lara gave interviews, campaigned, and took the stage at the convention. Yet only a few knew about Ivanka's husband, Jared, and his well-cemented place in the family. There were very few photos of him during the campaign.

Jared defended his father-in-law, in a public letter, after Trump was accused of being insensitive, and even anti-Semitic, during the campaign. Jared's first vocal public address was in front of the White House when he denied the allegations of having taken any part in a "Russian collusion." That was the first time the public ever heard his voice and observed his body language. Social media had a field day. Was Jared playing with the media by operating behind the scenes? Or maybe he just felt more comfortable and productive operating that way? I tend to buy the latter option.

Looking back now, there were obvious ties between us. Like Jared, when my name became an overnight sensation, the media hardly had any photos of me. The public had never heard my voice, and like Jared, I was portrayed as a "Key Man in the Shadows." I'm not an in-your-face guy. It's natural for me to let others take center stage. It felt right, and it allowed me to focus on what I needed to. This is one of the reasons Jared and I got along so well. We had both no problem with the spotlight being on other people.

Although Jared had come from a business background, he understood politics better than the Trump kids. His father, Charles Kushner, a real estate developer, had been involved with politics in New Jersey for years. He was a major donor for the Democrat Party and had rubbed shoulders with American politicians as well as Israelis. It is on the record that he had befriended Israeli prime minister Benjamin Netanyahu, who even slept over at the Kushners' home.

Jared's background might have prepared him for politics more than the rest of the family, and still he was yelled at by Trump as much I was! There was one memorable meeting after polling showed that Trump's numbers were down. The *New York Times* reported on it, which got Trump very angry. He summoned Jared, Ivanka, Don Jr., Eric, Paul, and me to an urgent meeting. "I should fire you all!" he shouted.

We sat in silence, until Jared said calmly, "Well, Donald, four of us are family. You can't really fire us."

In April 2016, after Trump secured the nomination, Jared assumed a more key role in the campaign and became more involved and associated with the Trump agenda. It wasn't easy for him, coming from a Democrat family. His younger brother was on his case, and many of his friends were unhappy with his decision. But Jared was on a mission. He was determined to get Trump elected and make the campaign more efficient. History will be the judge, but I feel that after Trump's presidential campaign, the strategy for winning elections will change forever, and campaigns will never be the same. The Trump presidential campaign was perhaps the first time in history that the power of the internet and reach of social media played an important, even crucial, part. It showed that one doesn't need thousands of people, advisers, and offices in every little town. And it was Jared who played a big role in building a modern, digital, exciting, and above all, *efficient*, campaign.

For example, Jared looked at changing the methodology of polling. He told me multiple times that he believed internet polling was cheaper and accurate enough, and he even had fights with Paul about it. Paul's experience was with traditional polls, so naturally, he vouched for them. After all, they'd helped him win campaigns before. But Jared was adamant that traditional polls were outrageously costly, and we could get similar results with internet ones. He was also critical of traditional TV ads. It was not just that the ads were so costly, but the percentage charged had become a real source of income to the people who placed them. He was so passionate about what he saw as financial extortion that he even described some of these political consultants as "criminals."

Jared decided to reduce the budget we spent on TV advertising, and Trump gave him carte blanche. I also got Trump's approval to go ahead and shrink the campaign costs in direct mail. In any case, we had to deal with reality: we had a very lean, minimal budget, but it was effective. Where Hillary Clinton had more than 200 people on her digital team, Trump had fewer than ten. And Hillary Clinton had more than 850 people total on her campaign, and Trump's employed less than 125.

While Mr. Trump and I began an intense working relationship on the campaign trail, back at the Trump Tower, Paul seemed to be developing a personal relationship with Don Jr. Months later, I would be grateful for being sort of snubbed by Don Jr. and not interacting with him much. Reportedly, Don was lured into a meeting with the Russian lawyer who was to give him dirt about Hillary Clinton. He invited Jared Kushner and Paul Manafort to join the meeting. On that same day, June 9, 2016, I was accompanying Mr. Trump to a fund-raiser at the Four Seasons. We came back to Trump Tower, where oil and gas industry billionaire Harold Hamm had arranged a leadership conference—a great setting of forty or more top business leaders. Trump met them and gave a speech at the conference room. I think we were done there by 2:00 p.m. and Trump left. The attendees then gathered around different round tables and held discussions until around 4:00 p.m. I thought it was a great idea of Hamm to bring these people together, and the meeting was well executed, which meant that it had been effective. People were making things happen.

Paul had attended our fund-raiser earlier in the day. He mentioned to me briefly that he had a meeting that afternoon with then Republican National Committee chairman Reince Priebus in the conference room, and that he would stop there earlier, around 4:00 p.m., for a meeting that Don Jr. was arranging in the same room. Don Jr. had told us that he was about to get important information against the Clinton Foundation through an overseas source. He shared it with us in one of our "family morning meetings." Paul immediately warned him not to take such sources too seriously.

The rest of what happened in that room on that day would occupy the special counsel and congressional investigations, as well as media headlines, for months. Referred to as "the Trump Tower Russian Meeting," it would put the first years of Trump's presidency under a cloud.

FOUR

THE SPEECHES

I want to set up a weekly meeting with the family, in order to prepare the kids for the convention," Paul told me.

We both agreed that the kids were assets to the campaign. Trump, at that point, did not care as much about how the convention would go. He was still focused on campaigning, but it was our job to keep our eyes on the finish line, to be three steps ahead. So, we started "family meetings" first thing every Monday. The meetings included Paul, Ivanka, Jared, Eric, Don, and me. Sometimes Corey Lewandowski joined, but there was tension between him and the family, especially Don Jr., so he didn't come often.

We asked each of them to be available on a few dates to help support the campaign. They could not do all of them. Ivanka explained that she had to take care of her business, but she gave us some dates, as did Don, and Eric gave us the most. To be fair, the kids had to take over more of the family business because their dad was campaigning. That all changed when Donald Trump became the presumptive nominee. At that point, the stakes were much higher, and the kids made themselves available and worked hard to help him win.

During the meetings, we went over the weekly agenda: campaigning with their dad, making fund-raising calls on his behalf, etc. Then, after we got the 1,237 delegates, we started working with each one on their speeches. It was so interesting to witness how they each took the structure we gave them, and on their own, created uniquely different speeches. Then it was up to Paul and me to order their spots. Ivanka—it was a no-brainer—would introduce her father. It was not important which night they spoke; what mattered was that their speeches got them on prime-time TV.

Eric Trump's speech was heartfelt and personable. He highlighted his foundation, a charity for children battling cancer. He appealed to voters in need and those who felt forgotten:

> When I was twenty-two years old, I founded the Eric Trump Foundation, to benefit St. Jude's Children's Research Hospital, an incredible, incredible organization. I run my foundation based on the principles my father taught me: honesty, integrity, and values.
>
> I expect other charities to be run by the same moral code, not serve as conduit for personal enrichment, not become a beacon of corruption and scandal. To whom much is given, much will be required. This is the very belief that compelled my father to make this great sacrifice, to run for the most powerful yet unforgiving office in the world. There is no greater calling, there is no more selfless an act.
>
> To the unemployed voter sitting at home watching me right now, wondering how you're going to make your next

mortgage payment, or rent payment, my father is running for you.

To the veteran tuning into this speech from his or her hospital, who has been ignored and disrespected by an ungrateful system for far too long, my father is running for you.

Don Jr., like his brother, was also a huge success. He appealed to the charged crowd in the room, through the cheers, saying:

To this day, many of the top executives in our company are individuals that started out in positions that were blue collar. But he saw something in them, and he pushed them to succeed. His true gift as a leader is that he sees the potential in people that they don't even see in themselves. . . . He's promoted people based on their character, their street smarts, and their work ethic, not simply paper credentials.

His message was clear: everyone would have a chance under President Trump.

And then there was Tiffany. It was Ivanka who said to me, "Make sure you loop Tiffany in regarding the convention."

And then Trump followed it up, asking me, "The kids are going to speak, right? Even Tiffany?"

"Yes," I replied.

"Great!" he said, a pleased look on his face.

After Trump had secured the delegates, I spoke with Tiffany about the convention. She was nervous, but she wanted to support her father. Tiffany asked me what her siblings were going to talk about, and then she began earnestly working on her speech. She called me several times before the convention, or I called her to check in. It was a good working rapport. We needed to do some dancing around her mother, Marla, who, of course, wanted to attend her daughter's speech. Marla stayed at the Westin hotel, where we reserved rooms for the Trump family and the campaign, but we had agreed she would stay only one night. Trump and Melania were there the night before, when Melania delivered her speech, but they'd already left.

Tuesday was Marla and Tiffany's night. Tiffany used Ivanka's hair and makeup artist. Having her older sister involved definitely gave it a nice family feel. Don and his wife, Vanessa, Ivanka, Jared, Eric, and Lara were in the family box, pleased with their younger sister's warm reception.

Instead of hiding how nervous she was, Tiffany made a smart decision, opening her speech by sharing her nerves with the crowd:

> Please excuse me if I'm a little nervous. When I graduated college a couple of months ago, I never expected to be here tonight addressing the nation. I've given a few speeches in front of classrooms of students, but never in an arena with more than ten million people watching. But, like my father, I never back down from challenges, so here I am, a little new to the convention scene but incredibly honored and very confident in the good man that America is coming to know.

She won them then and there. After her speech, I met her in the back room. She asked me for feedback, and I told her how well she did. The other kids were complimentary as well. It was a bit weird, because Marla was there. It's no secret there's been tension between Marla and the kids for years. But to her credit, Marla stayed in the background and kept the night about Tiffany.

When it was Ivanka's turn to talk, we all got the flawless speech we expected. She included some policy issues like health care in her speech.

> This has long been the philosophy at the Trump Orga-
> nization. At my father's company, there are more female
> than male executives. Women are paid equally for the
> work that we do and when a woman becomes a mother,
> she is supported, not shut out.

> Women represent 46 percent of the total U.S. labor
> force, and 40 percent of American households have
> female primary breadwinners. In 2014, women made
> 83 cents for every dollar made by a man. Single women
> without children earn 94 cents for each dollar earned by
> a man, whereas married mothers made only 77 cents.
> As researchers have noted, gender is no longer the fac-
> tor creating the greatest wage discrepancy in this coun-
> try, motherhood is.

> As president, my father will change the labor laws
> that were put into place at a time when women were not
> a significant portion of the workforce. And he will focus
> on making quality child care affordable and accessible for
> all.

The four kids managed to turn the convention from politics as usual into a family affair. It has long been a tradition that a wife of a candidate would talk about the nominee as a husband and a father, humanizing the event, but with Trump, we heard at least one member of the family every night. Each one talked about Donald from their own personal experience. It showed a different side of a candidate who some thought could be aggressive and insensitive. The kids endeared Trump to voters. People felt they knew Trump's family, and therefore they knew *him*.

And it was obvious how proud he was of his children, tweeting about their speeches. I knew then it didn't matter how much bigger the Democratic National Committee's budget was. No matter what they came up with, it would not sell Hillary to the masses. Nothing could touch the youthful energy and genuine speeches of the Trump kids.

Melania's speech at the RNC would be the first (but not the last) time my name would be all over the news for something I was minimally involved in. But before I talk about her speech, I should talk about the woman herself. Beauty aside, Melania Trump is impressive by any measure. She's classy, warm, and polite, yet there is something elusive about her reserved demeanor. I was taken by her from the first time I met her, and in my proximity to the Trumps, I would learn the truth of their relationship. Contrary to the picture the media has painted, she is Donald's rock. As a couple, they are united and fiercely protective of each other.

My first assignment with Melania involved her speech at the convention, a more delicate matter, since Melania had chosen to remain private for years. She was supportive of her husband's bid, but she also had her own independent ideas. I had searched Melania's speeches and TV appearances, and while I found several interviews with her, such as the one with Larry King, it was clear to me that she did not like doing them. As lovely as she appeared on TV, I could sense her discomfort. I knew she'd rather stay in the shadows, supporting her famous husband and focusing on raising her son. Even so, I was looking forward to working with her on her speech, as I had with the kids, but Melania preferred to do it on her own, with her staff. I guess she felt at home with them, so I respected her decision and turned my attention to other tasks at hand.

It has always been tradition that the spouse of the party's presumptive nominee opens up a convention with a personal speech about the nominee as husband and father. And the presumptive nominee usually sits at home with the children, watching on TV, the speech portraying a warm and loving individual. In other countries, like France, private lives matter less when it comes to politics, but here in America, it's tradition. The American political system has always encouraged the demonstration of family values. The picture-perfect family smiling for the camera. The wives, and sometimes grown-up children, advocating for their patriarch, asking the people's vote.

One thing about Trump is that he likes to surprise, so again, there was another unconventional move at the convention. Unlike other presidential candidates who had showed up at their party's conventions at the last moment, Trump wanted to introduce Melania in person. We had decided to keep this a secret, but of course, when the Trump private jet landed in Cleveland, Ohio, on the first afternoon of the RNC, everybody knew he was in town.

We had discussed how he would surprise the world and introduce his wife. People offered all sorts of suggestions, but Donald chose to get to the point, saying simply: "Melania Trump!"

Melania's speech was genuine and passionate, winning many hearts in the room that night. After the speech, we all felt she had opened the convention on a high note. I thought it was a smart move that she chose to start her speech with kindness toward the other Republican candidates. After months of attacking each other, she wanted to unite all candidates behind her husband. Flattery from a beautiful woman is always helpful. Here is what she said:

> The 2016 Republican primaries were fierce and started with many candidates—seventeen to be exact. And I know that Donald agrees with me when I mention how talented all of them are. They deserve the respect and gratitude from all of us. However, when it comes to my husband, I will say that I'm definitely biased, and for a good reason. I have been with Donald for eighteen years and I have been aware of his love for this country since we first met. He never had a hidden agenda when it comes to his patriotism because, like me, he loves this country very much.

It was clear to us that she was a success, so we were on to the next day, without giving the speech another thought. Meanwhile, Trump flew back to New York with Melania that night. He thought she gave an amazing speech, and it was the first time I witnessed how much he loved her, how caring he could be.

And then came the allegations that Melania had copied Michelle Obama's 2008 speech at the Democratic National Convention. Suddenly Melania was worried she might have ruined the convention. I was with Trump on the phone as he comforted her. "It'll be okay. Don't worry, baby," he said. "You didn't ruin anything. You were great!"

Of course, from then on, we started fact-checking and looking for any possible problem with the speeches ahead. A month before, on June 20, Corey Lewandowski had been fired as campaign manager. He blamed Paul and me for his dismissal, even though it was really the Trump kids who got him removed. So out of spite, he was leaking false information about us, and I found myself becoming the scapegoat for the mistake.

Trump called me the next morning. "Rick, you're not fired," he said. He had Hope Hicks and another aide on the phone. "I know it wasn't your fault." He was joking, and I saw how practical he was. Instead of pointing fingers and prolonging this little scandal, he wanted to move on and win.

People would ask why Melania was the only one who refused to use a speechwriter, and all I could say was that she wanted to do it herself! We met with her on a weekend at Bedminster Country Club and gave her some ideas, but we did not have anything to do with her speech. We just made sure she included one point: acknowledging Bob Dole, who was in the audience, which she did.

Here is what she said:

> I cannot or will not take the freedoms this country offers for granted, but these freedoms have come with a price so many times. The sacrifices made by our veterans are reminders to us of this. I would like to take a moment to recognize an amazing veteran, the great Senator Bob Dole.

She did not even turn in the speech until right before she gave it. I saw the copy an hour before, when we uploaded it on the teleprompter. We found out later that her aide, Meredith McIver, had written the speech. Meredith later made a statement that the alleged plagiarism was the result of a misunderstanding. In a meeting with Trump, he had shown her a passage of Michelle Obama's 2008 speech that expressed sentiments that echoed his own. Meredith, not realizing that this was a direct quote from Michelle's speech, thought Trump himself had drafted the passage and included it in Melania's speech verbatim. Though Meredith had worked with the family for years, she offered to resign over the incident, but the Trump family declined to accept it. One misunderstanding wasn't about to ruin that relationship. Like I said, Trump didn't want to point fingers. He was already focused on the next convention day. The important one.

FIVE

THE CONVENTIONS, THE RUNNING MATE, AND MAKING AMERICA GREAT

Almost every leap year, every four years in the United States, the major political parties hold conventions. Starting in January of a convention year, the parties run primary elections, the goal of which is to elect representatives for each of the party candidates who want to run for president. Those representatives are called delegates, and they are pledged to vote for a particular candidate at the convention. So, while the formal reason for holding a convention is for the delegates to vote for their pledged candidate and to formally elect the candidate and turn him or her into the nominee, in reality, by the time the convention rolls around, the party nominee has already been pre-elected.

In 2016, after more than a year of grueling lobbying and almost six months of voting, seventeen Republican nominees were whittled down. My main concern had always been Ted Cruz. Ever since I joined the Trump team, Ted Cruz had loomed in the distance like a storm cloud. He had the support of the Koch brothers and other major donors. But that Tuesday, April 26, changed it all. There and then, Ted Cruz was forced to put all his cards on Indiana and when he lost there, he had no choice but to drop out of the race altogether. On May 3, 2016, Cruz withdrew, leaving Trump as the presumptive nominee. But there was still another surprise: despite his performance in the primaries, John Kasich was still around. But not for long.

So the convention starts with the presumptive nominee getting the necessary votes. Then he—and in the future, she—accepts the nomination and officially becomes the nominee. That's why conventions seem more like political rallies than anything else, and they have the look and feel of a celebration. It's a legal necessity, but it's also a ritual, and an important one. It's a crucial way for the party faithful to get behind the nominee.

When it comes to the Republican and Democratic national conventions, many just see the festive images with colorful signs and balloons; in reality, organizing and managing a political convention is a long and highly detailed process. The conventions to elect a presidential nominee to each major party take place in the summer leading up to the election—usually in July or August. Yet the process of organizing the convention starts way earlier: at least a year and a half before, when each party decides upon a hosting city and dates, long before the primaries.

It has been tradition that the incumbent party's convention is scheduled last, probably because it gives the party's big event the benefit of a lasting impression. It has also been a tradition that these conventions last four days. That is the length of time needed to build excitement and momentum toward the big night, when the presidential candidate officially accepts his or her nomination. It also allows many speakers to shine, and there is a financial element, of course, to ensure the host city is getting the maximum benefit when it comes to media, tourists, and income.

There have been a few times when the conventions were shortened to three days, such as in 2008 and 2012, and this was simply because of the weather. The Olympic Games, that other big leap-year event that generates media and public interest, have also played a part in scheduling. In 1996, both parties held their conventions in August, following the Atlanta Olympics, which took place in August. In 2016, the RNC and DNC moved earlier to July, before the Rio de Janeiro Olympics in August. Otherwise, the conventions would have had to be held at the very last moment and neither party wanted to take such a risk.

Picking the host city also involves many considerations. First and foremost, it must be a large enough city with airports, so that the full complement of delegates, members of the media, devoted members of the party, and tourists can be accommodated. Sometimes there are additional reasons for picking a city. In 2004, the RNC chose New York as the host city. The party wanted to remind voters, as well as media, how their candidate President George W. Bush was there at Ground Zero, immediately after the horrific attacks on September 11, 2001.

At the last RNC convention, for example, we faced some dancing around. There were 2,472 delegates expected at the RNC in Cleveland in 2016. The large California delegation was put in a nice hotel, which was around an hour's drive from the convention's arena and main events. With traffic, the commute took longer, so, unfortunately, the delegates and alternates had to endure long drives back and forth and couldn't go back to their hotel rooms and change.

On July 4, 2014, the chairman of the RNC, Reince Priebus had officially announced Cleveland as the host city. This was, of course, way before Paul and I joined the Trump campaign. As much as the convention highlights the presidential candidate, it is truly an RNC (or DNC) production. Most things are decided months before it is even clear who the presidential candidates and who the presumptive nominee will be. RNC and DNC conventions have become the most desired platforms, and incredible stepping-stones for young politicians. This has been more the case for the Democrats than the Republicans. Barack Obama, then an unknown new senator from Illinois, took the DNC convention by storm in 2004, when Senator John Kerry was nominated. It took him only two years to announce his own presidential bid and then make history as the first African American president. In 1988, the late John Kennedy Jr. won the hearts of Americans when he spoke at the DNC convention nominating Michael Dukakis. Bill Clinton, too, became famous at another DNC convention before announcing his candidacy.

Traditionally, Republicans had always felt they owed a lot to their senior members and they have shown all due respect. Yet Donald J. Trump was a different kind of candidate. He understood that the surprise factor made headlines and occupied the news cycle. For that reason, he had mastered the news since he announced he was running for president, despite having many fewer paid ads than his rivals.

In 2016, the optics of both parties reversed: the DNC showed respect and obligation to Hillary Clinton, resisting a surprise factor like Bernie Sanders; and the RNC convention welcomed surprise like a breath of fresh air. While this opened the door for a wide range of speakers, there were also one or two inevitable scandals. Some of the speakers at the RNC 2016 found themselves on the transition team after Trump's victory. Some of them didn't.

No one would have predicted that in 2018, just a couple of years after placing second in an aggressive race for the presidential nomination, Republican senator Ted Cruz would be in the fight of his political life, nearly losing his Senate seat to newcomer Democrat Beto O'Rourke. Was it because of the trick Cruz pulled at the RNC convention, taking a prime-time spot and failing to endorse Donald Trump? The Cuban-American senator, who pulled off a victory in the Republican Senate primary that was described by some as "the biggest upset of 2012," almost crushed his promising career as fast as it rose. How did this happen?

Nobody knows this, but we met with Ted Cruz after Trump secured the nomination. I put a meeting together with seven of us—Trump, Jared, Ivanka, Paul, Ted Cruz, his wife, Heidi, their consultant, Jeff Roe, and me—to talk about how Cruz would support Trump. Cruz insisted on talking at the convention and he wanted a prime spot on the main evening, July 19. We reached an agreement that day, assuming Cruz would stay true to his word.

At the convention, we asked to see the speech Cruz had prepared, but he did not make it available to us. We demanded it, and at last, he showed us. I was worried that he might say something unflattering about Trump, but what Cruz had prepared was even worse than that—he wasn't going to mention Trump at all.

Naturally, Trump was upset and didn't want Cruz on the stage, and Jared supported him. We talked to Cruz in an effort to resolve the situation with minimal damage. Cruz made us believe that he would not read the speech word for word; that we should not read too much into it. Paul told him it was not what we agreed upon, and Paul and Ted started arguing the difference between "support" and "endorse." Ultimately, Jared thought, like us, that it was better to let him go ahead and speak. He supported Trump, but he was practical.

I walked Cruz to the stage, and Trump came up to me. "Hey, what's going on?" he asked.

I told him that Cruz was giving his speech and would be followed by others: Newt Gingrich, Ivanka, and then, Trump's big moment. Donald was excited and wanted to go out and watch right away. "Let's go now!"

Melania wasn't in favor of it, but I led them to the VIP box while Cruz was speaking. Trump stood up there and looked down at the stage, and the delegates started to cheer. Then, when Cruz failed to mention Trump's name, the delegates responded with a chorus of boos. Ted lost so much that night. He had been angling himself for a post as a justice on the Supreme Court. Jeff Sessions was all for it, because, he said, all the senators would endorse it, just so they could get rid of Cruz.

Traditionally, after a candidate scores more than 50 percent of the delegates, the search for a running mate begins, and the media is engaged in a game of speculation that lasts for weeks. For example, Mitt Romney managed to surprise many by keeping his running mate a secret. His assistant Kelly Harrison scored a lot of credit by fooling the media and disguising Paul Ryan's identity until Romney announced it. The surprising pick of Alaska governor Sarah Palin in 2008, by then RNC nominee John McCain, is another example.

The question is: How much does a running mate really affect a voter's decision? Some experts feel that although there are two names on the ticket, at the end of the day, the voter considers only the presidential nominee when casting their vote. Fourteen vice presidents in history have gone on to become president in their own right, but in recent history, only one Republican vice president has gone on to be elected president—the late George H. W. Bush. So why is there so much media fascination every four years about the number two spot? Maybe it's because the numbers still say that, historically, whether by death or promotion, more than one-third of vice presidents have made it to the top job.

Most people don't know this, but Melania Trump played an important role in choosing Trump's running mate. It was the second week of July, and five of us met in Bedminster, New Jersey: Trump, Melania, Paul, Reince Priebus, and me. We had just finished an interview with Senator Joni Ernst of Iowa and were discussing the four main candidates. We'd gone back and forth over each name: Joni, House Speaker Newt Gingrich, New Jersey governor Chris Christie, and Indiana governor Mike Pence.

"Melania," Donald finally said. "What's your opinion, baby?"

At that point, all four candidates had been interviewed. We knew that Jared and Ivanka were taken by Newt, and many people thought that Newt was going to get it. Priebus kept telling Paul, "Newt is a done deal."

Yet I knew that Trump had no intention of picking Newt. I had observed him closely by then, and I could tell that Trump only *wanted* people to believe that Newt would be his choice. I also understood how much he relied on Melania's judgment. She didn't know politics, but she cared about her husband. Paul cautioned that Christie and Gingrich, who had run for president before and failed, would position themselves for the next run. He said that if we announced one of them, that moment would become the beginning of their own presidential campaign. I agreed with this observation and told Trump the same thing.

Melania liked Joni Ernst. We all did. But we all concluded that it was too early for her; that her lack of experience might become a pretext for a media field day. Melania listened carefully to our alerts regarding Christie and Gingrich. All she cared about was protecting her husband and making sure we picked a person who would be *loyal*.

And then there was Mike Pence. He and his wife Karen had gone to the Trump National Golf Club in Bedminster to have dinner with Melania and Donald on July Fourth. Mike, by his own admission, is ever the midwesterner—Christian, conservative, and Republican, "in that order." His wife, Karen, is a teacher who met Mike while playing guitar for Mass at St. Thomas Aquinas, the church they both attended at the time.

Such different couples! But the dinner went well.

Back in New York on Monday, I met with Trump at Trump Tower. He filled me in, saying they got along very well.

"But, man, Pence is a real bad golfer," Trump said.

"Well, I told you so!" I laughed.

"What do you think about him being a VP?" he asked.

It looked at that point like he was leaning toward Pence. Among all the candidates, he had spent the most time with him. Melania, he told me, thought the Pences were "wholesome people." That's true. That's what I thought, too. Melania really liked them. Yet Trump was still considering all the options and wanted us to vet generals like Jack Keane. It was already early July, and we explained that we were running out of time. We needed a running mate before the convention, later that month.

We had another meeting—Trump, Melania, Paul, and me—a few days before the convention, at the Trump residence in Trump Tower. At this point, we had interviewed all the candidates, voiced our opinions, and thought about it again and again—and we all favored Pence, so we were trying to coordinate a trip for Pence to come to New York and meet with the kids. Trump still wanted to make a final decision, and he wanted to involve his kids. We decided it worked better for him to go with the kids and meet the Pences at the Governor's Mansion in Indiana. So, on July 13, just three days before the RNC, the Trump jet left very early in the morning, bound for Indianapolis. Since Melania already spent time with Mike and Karen, she stayed in New York. She'd already given us her opinion: Pence would be "loyal to the Trump presidency."

The next day, July 14, I was at Trump Tower, talking with Steve Hilbert, Pence's close ally. We were setting up the time Trump would call Pence from his car. It was delayed, but around midnight the call took place.

The morning of July 15, Trump sent out a tweet announcing Mike Pence as his running mate. Later that day, at 1:00 p.m., we arranged a press conference with both the Trump and Pence families onstage at the ballroom of the Hilton in Manhattan.

––––––––––

We kept telling Trump that we needed to prepare his speech for the RNC. *And no, this time you cannot get away with a spontaneous one!*

This was about tradition, a part of history. So we gathered several speeches for him, such as the ones given by Bob Dole, George W. Bush, and Mitt Romney, and asked him to review them. At the same time, we came up with a suggested first draft, which was a good way to put a speech in his hand and let him get engaged.

Next, we gathered a group of speechwriters, led by Stephen Miller. The goal was to have a good speech that would last thirty to forty minutes. We got a first draft three weeks before the convention. Paul scheduled actual time to sit with Trump and go over his speech as an official part of the convention agenda. Trump provided his initial comments prior to the convention, then the speechwriting team revised the speech accordingly.

A week ahead of the convention we did another round of back-and-forth with Trump. It continued for several days. But only upon Trump's arrival in Cleveland for the convention did Paul, Jared, Stephen Miller, and I sit down with him, and work on the final version and manner of delivery.

The RNC built two identical podiums: one on the stage, and the second at the hotel for practicing. On Wednesday, a day before his acceptance speech, Donald Trump tried the second podium at the hotel. He was given advice by an expert on how to maximize the use of the podium and the teleprompter. He was told not to stare only at the teleprompter and to move his body to the right and connect with the audience, then to the left. Trump liked the speech. And in fact, he applied all he'd learned the next evening with great success.

Here are some extracts from the speech in which Trump "humbly and gratefully" accepted the Republican nomination for the presidency of the United States:

> The American people will come first once again. My plan will begin with safety at home, which means safe neighborhoods, secure borders, and protection from terrorism. There can be no prosperity without law and order. On the economy, I will outline reforms to add millions of new jobs and trillions in new wealth that can be used to rebuild America.
>
> Together, we will lead our party back to the White House, and we will lead our country back to safety, pros-

perity, and peace. We will be a country of generosity and warmth. But we will also be a country of law and order.

That is why Hillary Clinton's message is that things will never change. My message is that things have to change, and they have to change right now. Every day I wake up determined to deliver for the people I have met all across this nation that have been neglected, ignored, and abandoned.

I have visited the laid-off factory workers, and the communities crushed by our horrible and unfair trade deals. These are the forgotten men and women of our country. People who work hard but no longer have a voice. I AM YOUR VOICE.

When innocent people suffer, because our political system lacks the will, or the courage, or the basic decency to enforce our laws, or worse still, has sold out to some corporate lobbyist for cash, I am not able to look the other way.

And when a Secretary of State illegally stores her emails on a private server, deletes 33,000 of them so the authorities can't see her crime, puts our country at risk, lies about it in every different form and faces no consequence, I know that corruption has reached a level like never before.

When the FBI director says that the Secretary of State was "extremely careless" and "negligent" in handling our classified secrets, I also know that these terms are minor compared to what she actually did. They were just used to save her from facing justice for her terrible crimes.

But now, my sole and exclusive mission is to go to work for our country, to go to work for all of you. It's time to deliver a victory for the American people. But to do that, we must break free from the petty politics of the past.

My opponent asks her supporters to recite a three-word loyalty pledge. It reads: "I'm With Her." I choose to recite a different pledge.

My pledge reads: "I'M WITH YOU—THE AMERICAN PEOPLE." So, to every parent who dreams for their child, and every child who dreams for their future, I say these words to you tonight: I'm with you, and I will fight for you, and I will win for you.

To all Americans tonight, in all our cities and towns, I make this promise: we will make America strong again. We will make America proud again. We will make America safe again. And we will make America great again.

The DNC took place after our convention. Usually that would have been a concern, because the thinking is that whoever has the last word will stay in the public's mind. But we knew that they were in disarray because of Bernie Sanders. Many of the DNC delegates felt the superdelegates element was unfair to Bernie and presold the game for Hillary. This issue impacted Bernie's fair chance to win, and therefore their whole convention was in a funk. Frankly, from our point of view, it was about how Bernie was being cheated.

While everyone had felt that our convention would be a contested one, it did not happen. We had taken care of it in advance. We'd picked up enough loyal delegates, and we'd dealt with Ted Cruz, so we were able, for the most part, to present a united front.

As a result, our convention was a big success, and the proof was that we gained 10 percent in the polls as a result.

The DNC, meanwhile, was becoming about, "Did Bernie stand a chance to begin with? Did the establishment favor Hillary?"

To monitor the convention, we sent a "quick reaction" team to Philadelphia. We rented some space at the hotel where Hillary was staying, and we moved about thirty surrogates in so that they would be on hand to comment in real time. Hillary Clinton's campaign had a lot of resources to try to disrupt ours.

From a production and public relations standpoint, the DNC would be over-the-top. Then I came up with a plan. I suggested we could announce members of cabinet while the DNC convention was going on—each night we would announce another member. I raised it with Trump, and he liked the idea. But then Paul was concerned it might backfire. He felt that Bernie Sanders was the main disruptor of the DNC and that we should just let them fight, without adding stuff. And indeed, as much as their convention was well produced, Bernie still dominated it. He portrayed Hillary as someone who was rigging the elections.

Despite our small budget, Trump told me he loved how we turned the stage golden, and how much he enjoyed surprising the crowd and introducing Melania on our first evening. He felt sure our convention went better than the DNC. And then came the Khan fiasco. It was the first of many self-inflicted hurdles the Trump team would have to jump, but thankfully, I was not new at scaling unsurmountable walls. After all, I'd gotten my start in this whole game by learning from Paul.

SIX

THE ROAD TO MANAFORT

By any reasonable means of measuring, Paul Manafort only worked for the Trump campaign for a short time. "Less than four months," Trump said, though the dates show it was closer to five. And yet Paul would impact the Trump presidency, and perhaps the Trump legacy, for months and years to come.

Paul is, indisputably, an accomplished political operator. He knows the ins and outs of politics and how to win elections. In 2016, he mastered the game of dealing with the RNC and led Trump from being a questionable leading candidate, to the RNC presidential nomination, and ultimately, the big winner. The "Never Trumpers" and the many experts who repeatedly said that Trump didn't stand a chance did not consider Paul—the wild card—when setting the odds.

Paul was part of the establishment, and because of that, he knew how they thought, how they acted. In the end, he put the man who ran *against* the establishment at the top of it. I watched the wave of surprise wash over many of them, as one of their own led an outsider like Trump into the heart of the party and all the way to the nomination. Maybe that is one of the reasons that Paul became an interesting target for media reports. Did they want to remove Trump's "secret weapon"?

Even though we were all on a mission and giving it our best, as the campaign progressed, internal tension within the team grew. While Paul did what he was hired to do—guiding the candidate's style and message—I witnessed how Paul's input began to irritate Trump more and more. Even at the best of times, and with the best of intentions, Trump didn't like being told what to do. And unlike Ivanka or Melania, or even me, Paul never learned how to gauge when Trump had had enough.

All this internal heat, during a hectic and tiring campaign, had to explode eventually. The eruption came with media reports regarding Paul's dealings with overseas election campaigns. Paul's activities, communications, and associations would be subject to different investigations and endless media reports. Some of it would be news to me as well. Not only would it put an end to Paul's successful career and lavish lifestyle, but it would drag down others, too—including me.

Trump's presidency would be put under a cloud of investigations regarding his alleged relations with Russia. The constant drip-drip in the media would bring up Paul Manafort's name again and again, regardless of whether his activities were during the short time he worked for Trump or whether Trump had *any* knowledge about it at all.

Through endless hints, innuendoes, and outright accusations, the names Trump-Manafort-Russia would be linked together—justified or not. Which brings me to the two inevitable hypothetical questions:

Would Donald Trump have succeeded in nailing the Republican presidential nomination if Paul Manafort had not come on board—Paul, with all of his sophisticated political acumen and deep knowledge of the field he was playing in?

Would the Russia-associated media reports and investigations have gone full force if Trump had not surprised many by winning the 2016 elections?

I leave it to you to speculate, to float conspiracy theories or more moderate theories, too. Each one of them, I bet, will include one name: Paul Manafort.

My own road to Paul Manafort began in the mid-1990s. After majoring in government at William and Mary, I entered a one-year fellowship program. It included an internship, and I chose politics because I'd always been fascinated by it. I did not know much about the political world at the time, but I thought it would be my path.

My first thought was to work at the Capitol, but I got offered an exciting internship opportunity. My mentor, Charles R. Black, was a partner in the powerful firm Black, Manafort, Stone and Kelly, so I was fortunate to be placed there. That was such a coup! I was quite naive then, and I may have even taken it for granted, but I would eventually realize how lucky I was to have started a politically associated career at the top of a powerhouse.

I worked first at the research group, writing legislation, among other jobs. At this point, we did not have the internet, so I manually searched for articles about different topics and people. Though my main assignments had to do with research, I got to go to the Hill and sit in on client meetings. I also worked with the grass roots of the Republican Party and learned their importance for political victories. It was a great entry into the business.

Ever since high school, I'd been fascinated with the American government, but I had no clue how it really worked. It was then, working with Black, Manafort, Stone and Kelly, that I started to question how efficient it was, and my eyes were opened to many of the dirty tricks involved. I'd always wanted to run for an office—it was my long-term goal—but as I learned more about the reality of politics, this plan faded away, and I chose instead to join the firm as a full-time employee.

Then, during the 1996 elections, a couple of employees left to assist local campaigns, opening up the opportunity for me to do much more. In my first two years with the firm, I'd had maybe two meetings with Paul Manafort. Most of my work was with Charles and Rick Davis. But then, in 1996, Manafort and Davis opened their own company, and I began working in London and for other consulting companies as well. It was invigorating, being overseas again like I had in childhood, and suddenly I felt the world was there for me to conquer.

In 2006, ten years later, Davis asked me to join him and Manafort at their new consulting firm, Davis Manafort. At that point, Senator John McCain was planning to run for president for a second time, and Davis was looking to run McCain's campaign. He had already been running McCain's related political action committee and he had been consulting for him. So I took up the slack, taking on some of Davis's responsibilities and helping Paul some, too.

Going into it, I had heard a lot of stories about the reputed political strategist Paul Manafort. Between 1978 and 1980, he had worked with Ronald Reagan as the southern coordinator for his presidential campaign, but since Reagan's win, he had mostly been operating outside US politics. The only exception was when he ran Senator Bob Dole's presidential bid in 1996. Otherwise, Paul's work was overseas.

Non-US politics was a new field for me, and I welcomed the new challenge. Paul and I started to develop "working relations." Paul might have been different with his friends, but he kept his social life separate from business. At work, he was all about the job. Paul also had a big ego, and like others with a big ego, he thought about himself first, at times sucking all the air from the room. But that, too, was just as well by me. I harked back to the survival skill I'd learned as a kid, moving from playground to playground: "don't shine too much, don't upset the already-crowned leaders, don't create new enemies."

So I took orders. I wanted to learn the political game overseas from the guy who had supposedly mastered it. Paul had a sink-or-swim approach to teaching, and the more I proved myself capable, the more he increased my responsibility. The most exciting field for me was intersection of politics and business, and I developed a growing interest in how the two could go hand in hand. Paul and Rick Davis jointly developed a very effective model of bridging politics and business in foreign countries. For many countries overseas, there isn't just the business risk, but a fair political risk for business investments. For example, after Trump won, Hillary Clinton's assets were not in jeopardy. In certain countries where laws are not that clear, it's different. That's one of the reasons American investors and companies have always been hesitant to invest in certain parts of the world. So if Paul had been working for the winning politician, he could help protect such investments—if this politician *remained* in power, of course.

As I was learning this new field, I was traveling a lot to Europe, sometimes Africa. I loved it! Experiencing different places, cultures, and history. It was so satisfying, watching countries develop into democracies. I didn't just sit in a hotel room: I visited cultural sites, historical venues. I went out and met with the locals. It also helped that the money was flowing. I was traveling and meeting with world rulers and leading business figures, and somewhere along the way, I put aside some of my basic values for a while: not paying attention to rules and regulations, even putting my own precious marriage in jeopardy. Unbeknownst to my foolish younger self, the special counsel would one day track this portion of my past. They would dredge it all up. Every tiny indiscretion. Whether or not it had anything to do with the witch hunt they were on.

And as much as I loved aspects of political life, the more I was involved with it, the stronger I felt about getting out altogether. I was realizing that, for me, my work was just the means to an end. I endured the political stuff, so that afterward, I could do the part I liked more—the business. I needed to navigate the political successfully, in order to get to the business part. It's a dilemma a lot of people can relate to—putting up with something you don't much care for in order to do the thing you really like.

Paul was a different story. He excelled in politics, while I was finding the business side of things more exciting. My relations with Paul developed and over time, and by degrees, I became his right-hand man. But as always, it was just business. Although I was his closest associate toward the end, we were never *personally* that close. I am much younger than Paul, by more than twenty years. I had a wife and four young kids. But even more so, we are very different characters. We would never spend holidays together. I have never even visited his home in the Hamptons. We simply did not have that kind of close friendship. Sure, Paul would send me "holiday greetings," but he did that with other business associates as well.

In 2015, we were coming to the end of our work in the Ukraine. Paul was trying to secure a position with their opposition leader, and we did work that was not related to politics. Then, one day, in late 2015, we had a conversation about the Republican candidates in America. Paul thought that Donald Trump had a good chance to be elected, or, at least, to survive the first cycle of candidates. Paul could feel the pulse of the people and he believed that Trump's message would resonate with many voters. And perhaps Paul believed this because he has a lot in common with Trump. For starters, he is also very confident. Some people simply fear him and perhaps that fear—or awe, or a little of both—was justified. Paul's record was impressive. He won every election while I was working for him. The last time he lost was with Bob Dole in 1996, so, that kind of track record takes more than luck. He understands the political game. He's lived it.

In January 2016, Paul told me, "I need you to pull information about the Republican primaries and the delegates."

It was not his nature to tell me more. "Just do this for me," he would say. So I didn't ask him for more details. Either he would tell me, or he wouldn't. He was always clear about what he wanted. He told me *what* he wanted me to know, but I almost never knew why. Still, I'd worked for him long enough to guess what was going on. I knew he was working on the Trump "case."

After the RNC convention, following an article in the *Los Angeles Times*, a report claimed that the RNC had altered some parts of its platform regarding giving arms to Ukraine for its fight against Russia. The *Los Angeles Times* also suggested that previous criticism against Russia's intervention in Ukraine had been edited into "gentler language."

This claim, of course, was a big deal to Paul, as he was immediately drawn into the issue. He had been working for former

Ukrainian prime minister Viktor Yanukovych, who had tight ties with Russia, so it was a no-brainer that the media would have suspected he was behind such a reported change. However, Paul responded with a strong denial on NBC's *Meet the Press*.

"It absolutely did not come from the Trump campaign," he said, and then went on to insist that he had not been involved in the reported change of the RNC platform when it came to Ukraine.

Donald Trump then told ABC News that he had nothing to do with such a change of policy. But he said that he had heard the original version of the Republican Party platform had been "softened," and it might have been done by surrogates, or people at the campaign office.

I first heard the "Ukraine Connection" allegations after the *Los Angeles Times* article. It was news to me, since my job was to run a convention and make sure everything worked perfectly time-wise and production-wise. My other priority was to talk with delegates and ensure they would not flip and decide not to vote for Trump at the last minute. It was unlikely, because there was no viable alternative to Trump, but it was still possible. So an understanding of the RNC platform was not included in my prior assignments. I had also assumed that the RNC was calling the shots regarding the platform.

I would later discover that Barack Obama had had a similar policy with regards to Ukraine. But this matter, like anything that has to do with Russia in any way at all, would not go away. It would be brought up in relation to Paul whenever he made news. My name would also be attached simply because many people knew of our long business relationship in the past and just assumed that Paul and I were still a duo. The issue would then reportedly reappear in the questions submitted by the special counsel to the president, which was ultimately to be answered in writing with the special counsel's final report, released to Attorney General William Barr on March 22, 2019.

So how exactly did my life become connected to the power struggle in Ukraine, and therefore to Russia, and therefore to the investigation into allegations of Russian interference in the 2016 elections?

Paul had begun working in Ukraine in 2004; I joined his firm in 2006. Our goal was to promote a democratic campaign following the collapse of communism. In 2004, the presidential elections in Ukraine had been overturned. Viktor Yanukovych won the elections but was accused of stealing them. There was unrest, lawsuits, so their Supreme Court overturned the results. Yanukovych's political career would have been gone, but he came up with a brilliant idea—he would bring in the former adviser of Ronald Reagan and Gerald Ford—Paul Manafort. That sent a signal to his rivals: "Watch out! I'll be back soon!"

So Paul's task was to try to rehabilitate Yanukovych. It was an interesting assignment, located in an interesting part of the world. With Paul's guidance, Yanukovych's first step was to create a new political party that would create diversity in Ukraine's political map.

When I joined Paul in October 2006, the party—called the Party of Regions—was already in the works. When we went to Ukraine, we were staying in a hotel for safety reasons. There were still violent elements in Ukraine. Even the very idea of democracy was still so new to them. And it was a very hard new way of life for me. I was away from my family and it was dangerous, but we were operating with that in mind. The hotel was very close to the office, so we could minimize our time on the streets. We were being as careful as possible.

What did we do for Yanukovych? We brought American style to the campaign, using a full arsenal of modern techniques. We employed modern polling, highlighting the differences between pro-West policies and pro-Russian ones. We also established discipline among the campaign's employees, getting them to take things seriously and professionally, making it very clear that you got results from showing up to work on time, not taking three-hour lunches and coming to work drunk. We used American experts to train the new party's representatives on how to craft the messages that would get people to believe in the party and what it hoped to achieve.

All the hard work paid off. In 2006, the Party of Regions, the party we created, won the majority of seats in the Ukraine parliament. Viktor Yanukovych won the first parliamentary election on May 25, 2006, for the People's Deputy of Ukraine and again on November 23, 2007.

Ukraine's elections were nothing like American ones. They were so volatile! Sometimes they were three times a year. On paper, elections are supposed to take place every four years for parliament, and every five years for president. In reality, it took a lot longer to stabilize the transition of governments.

We traveled back and forth between the Ukraine and home. In 2010, during presidential elections, we pretty much lived in Ukraine. We couldn't just leave; it was that intense. The fact that their law allows only ninety days of campaigning made the process even more extreme. Everything we did, every election we had to win, had to be done in less than three months. Yanukovych finally became the fourth president of Ukraine on February 25, 2010.

In the end, our guy stayed in power from 2004 until 2014—first as ninth prime minister, then as people's deputy, then finally as president. He was finally ousted on February 7, 2014, in a sort of coup. He fled the country in a hurry. He was taken totally by surprise. There had been a deal in the making, that he would include more members of the government opposition. But while the negotiations were taking place, demonstrators were starting to attack the palace. That was the end of an era. The end of his era.

Paul would have happily continued working there. He would even try to woo the opposition leader, to become *their* guru, but for me, the show was over. I was tired of living far away from home. My children were growing up and I wanted to be part of their lives again. For me, it was time to move on. I did it without thinking twice or looking back.

And I never did look back, at least not until I joined the Trump campaign, and all the media and investigations would require me to. So the man I worked for, the man who became my mentor, but never my close friend, finally dragged me into an experience before the law that I wish I never had, and that no one else should ever, ever have to go through.

SEVEN

POLITICAL FIASCOES

A political fiasco, perhaps even a scandal, is an integral part of *any* campaign. It comes with the territory. The enormous financial and personal investments of key players. The huge ambition, the stress, the high stakes all contribute to general climate where things may just not go as planned. Where past errors and present miscalculations may get exposed. In recent history, some promising presidential candidates have been eliminated over one "fiasco moment." Just like that.

Well, we, too, had fiasco moments, and each time, we dug into our arsenal to figure out what tools we had to put out the current fire. There was, of course, the Khan incident. Khizr Muazzam Khan and his wife, Ghazala, are Pakistani-American parents who lost their son, US Army captain Humayun Khan, during the war in Iraq, in 2004. We knew that Mr. Khan was going to be one of the speakers (of course we had the DNC convention's public program), but we could never have predicted what was going to happen. Mr. Khan made his speech, while his wife stood next to him on the stage, and attacked Donald Trump over his statements about Muslims, particularly his proposed ban on people from certain Muslim countries entering America.

The next thing we knew, Trump was tweeting, "Mr. Khan, who does not know me, viciously attacked me from the stage of the DNC and is now all over T.V. doing the same—Nice!"

Trump them followed it up with: "This story is not about Mr. Khan, who is all over the place doing interviews, but rather RADICAL ISLAMIC TERRORISM and the U.S. Get smart!"

Trump turned a father who lost his son, fighting for our country, into a symbol of radical Islamic terrorism. And it spread like wildfire. What Trump had meant to say was different, less attacking the father personally. It was more a defense of Trump's policy. When you sat with Trump and discussed the whole issue, it made sense. But it came across different on Twitter. And when Trump feels attacked, he pushes back harder.

The media was all over it. We lost our great convention's momentum overnight and went into damage control. We invited some Gold Star families to meet with Trump privately before a rally and leaked it to the media in advance. Trump was fantastic, as we knew he would be. He met with them in private, explained himself, hugged them, talked with them. He was real and warm. But he didn't change his policy, standing by his opinion that we needed to pull our troops from certain areas. Some of these Gold Star families were moved, deciding on their own to talk with the media and support his message.

But the Khan fiasco did not stand alone. Oh no! Trump would continue to test the political waters. Donald was not a usual candidate, reading from the teleprompter and "staying on message," and even knowing that, we were still caught off guard, catering to Trump's impulse to act on his gut feelings and hit back harder than he got hit.

Some fiascoes raised a media debate: "Can he survive *that* one?"

There was the remark about late Senator John McCain, disputing his status as a hero: "He is a hero, because he was captured?"

Then there was a public dispute with then Fox News host Megyn Kelly about the way Trump mistreated women. Trump attacked Kelly personally, saying, "Blood coming out of her whatever."

I was at the office in New York the day when Trump was at a rally and made a gesture that looked like he was mocking disabled reporter Serge Kovaleski. Ivanka would later explain to us that the gesture was just something her father did. That it was not directed at the man's disability. But it was another disaster for the campaign.

While history would show an almost zero percent chance of surviving such self-inflicted wounds, Trump surprised politicians and experts, walking through each verbal landmine and maintaining his lead in the race. Meryl Streep would remind us of the reporter in an acceptance speech, and Trump would fight back yet again.

Sure these fiascoes had life spans, but like ghosts, they kept rising up to haunt us every now and then.

Judge Gonzalo Curiel had been assigned to a publicized court case involving Donald Trump and the Trump University way before Trump became a GOP presidential candidate. Trump, who doesn't favor legal settlements, knew that such a legal battle could bring questions about his conduct as a businessman and his personal credibility. And he really believed the judge's heritage was playing a role. Judge Curiel argued that Trump's insistence on building a wall to protect Americans from what he described as dangerous Mexicans had made Trump an enemy of many Mexicans. Many would agree that the "Mexico issue" was becoming part of Trump's ID, for better or for worse.

So, while working on the RNC convention, I found myself dealing with the "unfair" Mexican judge narrative. I didn't find Trump to be a racist, although I know some people hold that opinion. What I found was more like a generational issue, or a disregard of political correctness. He said what he saw without using the social filters that have become the vernacular in current American politics.

Trump was holding a rally in San Diego in May 2016, when he suddenly complained to the adoring crowd, "I have a judge who is a hater of Donald Trump, a hater. He is a hater." This fed many in the crowd who believe a judge is supposed to be impartial.

And then, in June 2016, he sat down with Jake Tapper from CNN. Tapper brought up Trump's controversial remarks about Judge Curiel. Trump, as usual, doubled down, saying, "I have been treated very unfairly by this judge. Now, this judge is of Mexican heritage. I am building a wall, okay? I am building a wall."

Trump did not stop there. "I have a case that should have already been dismissed," he added. "I have thousands of people saying Trump University is fantastic, okay?"

Politicians would agree with PR gurus that one should never bring a controversy into the news, let alone repeat it again and again, making it ever bigger news. Lawyers would join them, arguing that it is not a good idea to accuse judges of not being impartial while the case was still being argued in the court system. Trump campaign official Kellyanne Conway, sensing how damaging the situation could become, tried to convince Trump to apologize. But that was not an option for him. Ivanka also understood the severity of the issue, but she knew her father was not going to consider an apology and that he would likely double down again. As for me, I should probably have panicked when Trump did everything against the book, but by that time, I had realized that rules were written for others. They simply did not apply when it came to Donald Trump.

Instead, we employed a new strategy: move the narrative to the next headline. Put him on a rally; even create a *new* controversy. Fight fire by starting another fire: that proved to be the most effective way to get through the latest controversy without looking back.

Later, I would wonder if the reason that none of this stuck to Trump was that by this time, people just felt such an urgent need for a change! Something different. Someone different. Someone who would gladly break all the rules and do so without fear. Someone whose next move you could never predict.

———————

Yoseph Alicia Machado Fajardo became Miss Venezuela in 1995, and was then crowned as Miss Universe 1996. She was the fourth Miss Universe from Venezuela, a country that had invested a lot in winning the world's beauty titles. So, there was nothing extraordinary when she won, until she went into the ring with Donald Trump.

Alicia, like some winners before her, gained weight after she assumed the crown. This is not uncommon, as many beauty pageant contestants starve themselves prior to the big spectacle. But

Donald Trump became the new owner of the beauty pageant, and he had to deal with the media making fun of the larger Miss Universe. Other owners, in an attempt to keep their hands clean, would likely have ignored Alicia's weight gain. Some might have fired her. But Donald Trump saw it as a great opportunity to inject public relations into the somewhat tired organization that was the Miss Universe pageant. So, he hired a trainer for Alicia and made her give media interviews, promising to shed some pounds and get back in shape.

In Trump's mind, he was being generous. Instead of firing her, he was helping her to get back into shape—he was even paying for it! Alicia, however, saw it differently and would continue to carry hard feelings toward Trump for years to come. After Trump became a leading presidential candidate, she reached out to his rival, Hillary Clinton.

On September 27, 2016, during the first presidential debate, Hillary Clinton surprised Donald Trump and pulled the "Alicia card," claiming that, once again, Trump had treated a woman without respect.

Trump's response did not help matters. "This is somebody who likes to eat," he said. "It was her job, as Miss Universe, to stay in shape."

Hillary was having a great moment. She tried to portray Trump as demeaning to women. After the ongoing feuds with Megyn Kelly and others in the press, Hillary was attempting to cement Trump's supposed misogyny in the minds of voters.

Again, as we watched it unfold, we realized it was a situation we could not have controlled or prevented beforehand. The Clinton campaign threw out the bait, and Trump fell for it. To be fair, on this particular occasion, Trump was "less Trump" than usual. Instead of renewing attacks against her, his response was softer:

"Come on! It was twenty years ago!" He merely acknowledged what had happened, explaining his side.

It would have been better to play it down, and not engage in a growing he said, she said. As usual, Ivanka was doing her best to stress how ridiculous this all was. Whenever the media presented Trump as misogynistic or disrespectful to women, Ivanka found herself in the eye of the storm. As an advocate for women's issues and the candidate's trusted adviser, this seemed logical, yet she was sometimes caught by surprise, as were several of us, by her father's remarks. This is normal during such tough political campaigns, but for Ivanka, it was her first campaign, and people aimed at her personally. Melania managed to stay out of the media storms most of the time.

By then, I had stopped trying to avoid the inevitable. Despite all the criticisms about him, the unrehearsed, nonspin aspects of Trump were part of the appeal. The very things that people liked to point out as his weaknesses were also the source of his strength. So I gave in to it all. I understood that I would be better off focusing on damage control, *after* Trump had his shot at hitting back. Only after.

Of all the incidents, the *Access Hollywood* tape was the worst one, both in terms of its content and the timing of its release. I was working between the RNC and the Trump campaign then, and I was told about it by Brad Parscale, Trump's digital media director. The *Washington Post* called the campaign offices and wanted a response to a taped conversation from a decade earlier on the set of the soap opera *Days of Our Lives*. The tape showed Donald Trump and Billy Bush chatting about women in a disrespectful way. They were both wired, since they were about to tape an interview for Billy's show, *Access Hollywood*. I have no idea if Bush knew his conversation was being picked up at the time, but I certainly know Donald was not aware of it.

It was a disaster. Some in the RNC saw it as horrific, beyond repair. They even started to talk about replacing Trump as a candidate, even though it was too late in the game. We knew we were going to be impacted when it came to educated women. But here is the issue—in politics, when something like that happens, it is terrible, but some voters will see it as political game playing. A perfectly damaging story at the eleventh hour, such "perfect timing" can work both ways: it can drop the candidate then and there; or, it can motivate their supporters who may believe it is part of an orchestrated attempt to ruin the candidate. That is why the response of some was "Go, support him, and vote!"

My personal reaction at the time? I thought that most votes were locked in by then. People had already made their decision. Of course, it was damaging, but the real question was, could he overcome it? Hadn't we already asked that many times before? And hadn't we always come out on the other side?

Then, a week and a half later, FBI director James Comey decided to reopen the investigation into Hillary Clinton's emails. As secretary of state, had Hillary allowed traffic of classified documents or classified information to go through her private server? Had her aides, like Huma Abedin, sent and received classified information?

See? Fight fire with more fire. We were already moving forward from the *Access Hollywood* fiasco.

EIGHT

THE REVOLVING CAST OF CHARACTERS

Not all of the headlines were the direct result of Trump's Twitter account. It was August 19, and we were in New York. A few days earlier, on August 14, there were articles published in the *New York Times* claiming that Paul had been receiving illegal cash payments from a pro-Russian political party in Ukraine. Other media reports said that Paul had financial problems with the Russian oligarch Oleg Deripaska, who was suing him for millions of dollars because of a deal that had reportedly gone wrong.

Naturally, the stories made headlines because Paul was chairman of Trump's campaign, and by now, Trump had become Republican nominee. The whole idea was to associate Donald Trump with the Russians, a narrative that had been developing. I could feel that the story was growing by the moment and the atmosphere around Paul was changing. I tried to warn him, but he thought that the story would go away.

Then, on August 18, Paul called. He finally saw the writing on the wall, and he knew the mood had changed against him. He

was scheduled to see Jared the following day. He sensed it would
be a hard conversation, but he was hoping to work out a gradual
and dignified exit.

On August 19, Paul went on TV, appearing on behalf of
Trump. People knew that even if Paul did his best, nobody could
represent Donald Trump as the man himself. That would be Paul's
last appearance as the chairman of the campaign. Shortly after, he
was summoned to meet Jared, who told him it was over. Effective
immediately.

Not so fast. "Gone" in the world of Trump does not mean "cut
off." Not at all. When Paul was let go, he was obviously upset,
especially because the firing became public within seconds. It
was the embarrassment factor. But the same ego that made this so
humiliating for him was the same ego that made him pick his chin
up and keep up appearances. Shortly after, he would embark on a
yacht with his (and Trump's) mutual friend, Tom Barrack, and go
cruising. Some of his friends were told that he was still involved
with the campaign behind the scenes, and in a way, he was.

I would learn that being fired, even abruptly, by Donald, does
not mean the door closes in your face, as many would assume.
Even if one learned about it via tweet, he or she would be invited to
move from employee/adviser/aide to a former employee/adviser/
aide. That meant that you could still maintain access to the circle around Trump. As a "former employee," one would continue
to make suggestions, give opinions, and even talk with Trump.
It's understood that when someone is fired, in the afterlife, they
became sort of associates. Maybe it had to do with what Melania said in her vetting of Pence: loyalty to the family is everything. Even if protocol dictated someone's dismissal, if you were
not deemed disloyal, you could remain in the fold. Trump would
invite their input from time to time, and the "associates" would

check in with him, letting as many people as possible know that they still occupied a place in Trump's world.

I would follow these dynamics with fascination. It would become such a smooth transition: after losing a job, you move to a "post-job" space, where whatever tension existed in the past is replaced by continuing mutual interests and a friendly atmosphere.

There is one important exception to this pattern of smooth transition: if you have attacked Donald Trump personally, you get totally cut off. The few who have done so, have had the Trump door slammed on them forever. Should I mention Omarosa Manigault Newman? Should I mention Michael Cohen?

But none of that applied to Paul. From the earliest days, Paul truly believed in Trump's chances to win the election and was proud to be associated with him. I would find out later on that Paul still had ins and outs, his access privileges, months after he was *officially* gone. He felt he was still part of Trump's world. One way or another.

When Paul Manafort was fired from the Trump campaign, Jared Kushner asked me to stay as the deputy campaign manager. I had worked hard to prove myself and was ready to fly solo. I felt in my bones, it was high time to fly alone, away from the association with Paul. I also realized there were a lot of things about Paul that Trump had not known.

———

Among the outcasts, none were as memorable as Omarosa Manigault Newman. Omarosa became famous, or rather, infamous, when she participated in NBC's reality television series *The Apprentice* in 2004. While she portrayed a villain, hated by other contestants, Donald Trump, the executive producer and the host of the show, loved her. A shrewd businessman, Trump realized her character was great for ratings, so he invited her to participate again in the *All-Star Celebrity Apprentice* in 2013.

And she was a hit. The reality star got such high notoriety that she became a mononymous person, known only as Omarosa. Most didn't know that she'd had her eye on a political career long before she stood next to the RNC candidate Donald Trump. Apparently she had worked at the White House during the Clinton era, and before that, she'd landed a job in the Department of Commerce.

But there would be no comparison between these jobs and the senior position she would get from President Trump. She would not only earn the highest government pay; she would also get the most publicity possible during her year at the Trump White House, and there would be articles speculating what she was actually doing there. There would be colorful stories about her wedding and bringing her bridesmaids to pose in the West Wing. But nothing would prepare the nation for her dramatic departure, when Chief of Staff John Kelly fired her.

Omarosa would document her own experience at the White House, and write a book, *Unhinged*. She would be one of the few Trump aides who would be let go and never invited back. I was following these events with a bit of amusement, and truthfully, I could have seen it coming. It all started the day she joined the Trump campaign. During the hectic RNC convention, Omarosa bumped into Paul while he was running around, handling the wind-down to the convention. The closing of the event is almost as complicated a job as the preparation for it. "Hey!" she called out to him. "I want to take a more formal role. I'm ready."

Paul did not pay much attention. "We'll talk about it later," he said.

She had already bumped into me on the Friday after the big day. "Thank you for everything," she said. "I'm coming on board.

I talked to Eric and Lara. I saw Jared. I'm going to issue a press release."

I was still doing a lot of running around myself, so I didn't give it a second thought. I assumed her appointment, whatever it was, must have been approved by Paul. Later I mentioned it to him. "You gotta be kidding me," he said. "I've never authorized anything!"

Too late. Her press release, which she had written herself, had already gone out, and in it, she announced that she had been named Director of African American Outreach. Amazingly, that is how her work with us all started. It would eventually turn into a job at the White House, and I would learn quickly enough that this was typical of how Omarosa operates. On January 4, 2017, the White House announced Omarosa's official title as Assistant to the President and Director of Communications for the Office of Public Liaison. I still have no clue as to what she actually did, at least officially.

In *Unhinged*, Omarosa describes herself as a key player in the Trump administration, with unusual access to the president's ear. And yet she taped conversations with him and others without their knowledge, accused Trump of sexism, racism, and liberal use of the N-word. The list goes on and on, and it continued to go on until Kelly fired her on December 13, 2017, although it was announced as a "resignation" effective January 20, 2018. Omarosa secretly taped her firing too. And the rest, as we say, belongs to history.

The fact that Trump put his former partner and longtime friend Paul Manafort at the center of the campaign not only birthed new insiders like me; it also raised others from the political dead.

One such person who'd been hovering somewhat in obscurity but was also ready to surge back into the spotlight was Roger

Stone. Stone had been reportedly pushing Donald Trump to run for president for years. He had been involved at the early stages then. Some reports said he quit; others suggested he was let go. I didn't bother to check which was true. But in reality, when Paul joined the Trump campaign, the door also opened for Roger. He, of course, talked with Donald, but additionally, he talked with Paul at least once a week. Roger came up with ideas and suggestions. After all, he was a veteran political operator, too.

He also talked with me, but only in relation to his communication with Paul. If he couldn't get Paul on the phone, he would call and ask me to carry a message. Sometimes Paul asked me to return Roger's calls or follow up on his behalf. Once I even joined Roger and some New York supporters at a dinner on behalf of Paul, who was expected there but could not make it. The subject of the dinner with Roger was about trying to suggest the right delegates for the convention. I did not have any personal relations with him other than that, but there was no doubt in my mind that Roger really wanted Donald Trump to win the election.

At the time, I was so busy, but now, reflecting back, it hits me that what Roger Stone wanted was to be back in the center of the game. The old political trickster wanted to show that he still had what it took. Waiting to prove his value with a piece of advice, a priceless nugget of information?

This need to be an insider with access to crucial facts might explain some of the things that would surface a couple of years later, during the special counsel's investigation. Stone, or his representatives, claimed that they communicated with Julian Assange, the founder of WikiLeaks. Months later, they would say that some of their acts or statements were jokes. I supposed they might be, but why would anybody make jokes like that? That sort of story revision doesn't really sound convincing. Thinking back, in Stone

I saw a person who needed to be needed. Someone longing for the good old days, using any tactic that came to mind, in order to be heard, to stay relevant.

When Paul was fired, Roger's calls to me decreased drastically, and I did not complain. In Steve Bannon, Paul's replacement, Stone had a new master to charm, in order to stay even semi-relevant in Trump's final stage of the campaign. So, Stone's incredible energy and ongoing focus were redirected there. Some of his emails to Bannon would later become public in connection with his indictment, and they would occupy the media. As would the larger-than-life Roger Stone.

NINE

FOREIGN POLICY

Foreign policy was a tricky subject from the first day we joined the campaign. One of Trump's key slogans was "America First"—a comment on the idea that for too long American government and its leaders have been putting themselves before the people. Donald Trump repeated this phrase again and again during rallies and media appearances. So, because of this focus on domestic issues, we could not devote time to global ones as traditional candidates had been doing for years. But we knew any presidential candidate who wanted to be taken seriously needed to present his policies regarding the United States' relations with other parts of the world. No matter how much you wanted to put America first, you needed to have foreign policy and be able to talk about it.

It was back on March 21, shortly before we arrived at Trump Tower, that the Trump campaign had announced a Committee for National Security, which would supposedly touch on foreign policy. It included twelve members, most of whom I had not heard of before, but two of them I did know of—George Papadopoulos and Carter Page.

The only household name of the bunch was then-senator Jeff Sessions. He might not have been an expert on several foreign topics, like most of the others were, but he was a veteran senator, and that brought a much-needed credibility to the table. Since we'd inherited this committee and didn't really know its members or anything about their expertise, we chose not to use it at all. Instead, we employed inside campaign resources in order to develop a campaign platform about foreign issues. In practical terms, Jared and Jeff Sessions were in charge of dealing with Trump's foreign policy. We also knew that aside from presenting Donald Trump as president, we also had to present Donald Trump as a head of state—a statesman—who would be able to meet with world leaders on an even footing.

At that point, some conservatives kept saying, "He's just not presidential." So, we planned for his first big speech to be about foreign policy. It took place on April 27 in Washington, DC. Stephen Miller wrote the speech, and the final draft was a collaborative effort between Jared, Paul, Ivanka, and me. It covered a wide range of issues of foreign policy: Middle East, NATO, the United Nations, Russia.

We sat with Jared Kushner and Jeff Sessions and decided together that all requests and inquiries from ambassadors or other foreign entities would be forwarded to both of them to be handled appropriately. Trump's main message in his speech was somewhat simple: "We *must* improve the US's stature in the world, after Barack Obama damaged it." It was the first time Trump read a written speech, and many who were used to his off-the-cuff speeches at rallies were surprised. Our goal was to show another side of Donald Trump . . . and it worked! At that time, Trump was still facing two rivals: Ted Cruz and John Kasich. They both talked about foreign affairs, so we needed to match them. Later on, we would start to rely on people who were experts in the field, like K. T. McFarland. Jared had built a relationship with Dr. Henry Kissinger, so Trump went to meet with him, which added extra prestige, and naturally, it made the news.

Even focusing on "America First," we still dealt daily with a couple of key foreign issues simply because early on in the campaign, Trump had made statements about them—Mexico and Muslims. Both sets of statements created extreme emotional reactions, at both ends of the spectrum. Trump had expressed his opinions about these sensitive topics from day one, so when we came aboard, they were already planted in everybody's mind, for better or worse. Trump's positions were clear. He had reinforced them over the many months of speeches, so there was not much room to maneuver.

The first executive order Trump would sign after being sworn in was Executive Order 13769, or as it was also called, the Muslim ban. It was pushed by Steve Bannon and Stephen Miller. They were so passionate about it, but had not done enough research, and some of it would be found to be illegal.

Growing anger was driving political movements on both sides of the Atlantic in 2016. While Donald Trump had been surprising many in the United States, there was something similar happening in the United Kingdom. Nigel Farage, who led the United Kingdom Independence Party (UKIP), was busy stirring his own pot, encouraging many bitter British citizens to vote for exiting the European Union. While he didn't come up with it himself, he popularized the term with which we would all too soon become familiar—Brexit.

Amazingly, none of the other presidential candidates in the United States paid much attention to Brexit, but Donald Trump did. He had sensed the British people were growing frustrated with the increasing immigration and declining economy. He understood that many of them had had enough of "politics as usual." They wanted to be heard. Unlike others, who dismissed Brexit as a gimmick or a red herring to distract from more crucial matters, Trump started to follow it closely, and predicted that many British citizens who had never voted before would cast their votes at the referendum regarding Brexit in June 2016.

Earlier that year, in April, President Obama visited the United Kingdom. He played golf with then British prime minister David Cameron and made strong statements against Brexit. Obama backed Cameron, who'd been fighting for his country to stay in the European Union, as well as his own political future and legacy. Obama's statements were so extreme, they might have achieved the opposite result. He said that if the United Kingdom exited the European Union, the United States would send it to the "back of the queue." This sound bite was perceived as everything from a foreigner interfering in the UK's internal business to, frankly, a threat. Boris Johnson, London's mayor, wrote an article ripping into Obama and encouraging more readers to be vocal.

And so, on June 23, many around the world were caught by surprise when the British people voted to leave the European Union. Was it sheer luck, or perhaps a plan based on his gut that caused Trump to open his golf club, Turnberry, in Scotland, just a few hours after the shocking Brexit vote?

Trump owned the big victory, telling the media he had predicted it. He added that the same would happen in the United States: people who had never been involved in politics would go and vote for him out of the same sheer frustration with the status quo. The media's interviews took place at his new club, with his three adult kids around him. It was an amazing double promotion for both the club and the campaign, masterminded by a brilliant promoter who knew how to seize a media opportunity and run with it.

As for me, my reading of the Brexit victory was the same. I noticed the excitement in Trump's rallies, the mounting small donations. Brexit was just another indication that something new and different was awakening. After the Brexit vote, Trump wanted to meet with Nigel Farage. Nigel was described not only as a politician, but as a media personality: "flamboyant," and "someone who knows public relations." Does all this sound a bit familiar?

Trump and Farage met in an unlikely setting: Mississippi. We held a rally there on August 24, and Farage was invited by our campaign. Then, as Trump liked doing, he surprised many and asked Farage to come up onstage. It worked brilliantly. It was just after the big Brexit victory, and Brexit was then associated with his name. He had become a hero.

"We reached those people who have never voted in their lives," Nigel told the crowd, "but believed by going out and voting for Brexit, they could take back control of their country, take back control of their borders, and get back their pride and self-respect."

There was no need to spell out that Trump was aiming for the same kind of shocking victory. The crowd at the rally got it, and their cheers were almost deafening. From then on, Trump kept in touch with Farage and met him from time to time. Farage became a repeated guest at the Trump Hotel in DC. The stories about his charming personality after several drinks made him even more interesting. We caught up with Farage early one morning, around 6:00 a.m., sipping an espresso next to an empty bar at a sleepy hotel. He'd had a late night of partying after a presentation but was already on his phone, charming someone, somewhere.

Time would prove that Brexit was not thought out that well. Theresa May, who succeeded David Cameron as prime minister, would inherit an incredibly messy situation. Most of her term would be clouded by the shadow of Brexit and the setbacks of negotiating a way out of the European Union. She would be described as weak.

It is up to experts to assess Nigel Farage's place in British history. For Trump, Farage was yet another guy who showed him that political change really can come from unlikely candidates. That he was on the right path for a big upset. Another boost on a bumpy path to a historic victory.

———————————

It's the ultimate foreign achievement. The biggest challenge, worth maybe even a Nobel Prize: peace in the Middle East.

What would it mean to attain what all other postwar American presidents had tried, but failed, to achieve? Jared Kushner had been talking about it from the beginning. Of course, as a Jewish American, he cared deeply about this issue. His family donated heavily to Israeli causes, including supporting some Israeli settlements. Jared's grandparents had survived the Holocaust. I was told that his grandmother, Rae, was among some brave Jews, who had drilled a tunnel out of their concentration camp and had managed to escape the horrors of the Nazis. I also saw that Jared—because of his family's close connections to Israel, let alone

Prime Minister Benjamin "Bibi" Netanyahu—felt more in touch with how peace in the Middle East could actually be achieved.

As for the Arab side, Tom Barrack introduced Jared to couple of influential players. After Donald Trump won, Tom, who had been doing business with the Arab world for years, considered himself as an expert in this complicated area. He wanted to be a special envoy or a senior influencer on behalf of President Trump, and since nobody told him otherwise, he was preparing for it passionately.

One day Tom heard a rumor that former British prime minister Tony Blair had met with Jared, reportedly seeking to become a special envoy for negotiating peace in the Middle East. Blair had been a special envoy for a quartet of international powers from 2007 until 2015. He had worked on behalf of the United Nations, the United States, the European Union, and Russia. That raised a big red flag to Tom Barrack. Naturally, Blair had lots of knowledge about the long historical dispute, so Tom felt that Jared might want to benefit from his experience. Tom also presumed that Donald Trump might have been taken by the fact that a former British prime minister wanted to work for him. At this point, he was a new president, who had been elected against the odds, and he was still looking for impressive people to associate with, names who would add credibility to his administration.

So, as in many times in my career, I was asked to do one of the dirtier jobs. I looked at many newspaper articles about Blair and his work with other countries ever since he had left No. 10 Downing Street. I put together a pattern, drawing a picture of "A Politician for Hire." Instead of a statesman who believes in certain enduring principles and policies, Tony Blair has been described by some of the media as a politician-turned-businessman, dedicating himself to pleasing his high-paying masters. I gave this package to Tom.

Jared's position was that he just met with Blair out of respect to a former British prime minister, and though he felt it was wise to listen to him, no position was offered, and no commitment was made. Naturally, people assumed that Blair expected to be considered for a position, after meeting with Trump's influential son-in-law. In the end, Tony Blair was not appointed to be an envoy for peace in the Middle East on behalf of the Trump administration. Blair was upset about media reports concerning his encounter with Jared Kushner. After journalist Michael Wolff wrote about the Blair/Kushner non-event in his book about the Trump administration, *Fire and Fury*, Blair told BBC Radio 4 that Wolff's report about his ambitions had been "fabricated."

Blair continued: "Of course I've met him, and we discussed the Middle East peace process," he said. "I wasn't angling for some job. I did the quartet role. I'm still very active on the Middle East peace process, but I've got absolutely no desire for an official position. I never sought one, it was never offered, don't want one."

Whether this ambition to be player was out there, or just assumed by others, the question remained: was Tom Barrack (and my media analysis) what had killed it?

Or maybe Jared felt that he wanted to develop his own personal relations and strategies for peace in the Middle East? Maybe he wanted to do it his own way, since others, including Blair, had already tried and failed so many times before? Or maybe it was all of the above? Given Jared's commitment to going his own way, Tom would remove himself from involvement in Trump policy in the Middle East as well.

And as for how the Middle East peace process has progressed in these first years of the Trump administration? Well, there would be big statements made that would fade out and come to nothing. I recall that in the beginning, Donald Trump was focusing on immigration, borders, economy, and so on. He did not make the Middle East a priority in the least, so he let Jared pursue it. Trump would only get involved later.

He would become the biggest presidential supporter of Israel in a long while, even moving the American embassy from Tel Aviv to Jerusalem in May 2018, implicitly acknowledging Jerusalem as the capital of Israel. Then he would recognize that the Golan Heights were part of Israel's territory in March 2019. That would cheer American Jewish donors like Sheldon Adelson, at the same time further cementing Trump's connection with evangelist groups that had shown him support. Jared, meanwhile, continued to believe in the importance of this program to benefit many others. He worked hard on it and had high expectations of what the results might be.

But as it turned out, Jared would come to hit one obstacle after another. Trump's favoring Israel and close relations with its Prime Minister Bibi Netanyahu almost inevitably upset the Palestinians. And after Donald Trump moved the American Embassy from Tel Aviv to Jerusalem, the Palestinians walked out from any further negotiations led by the United States. Jared was planning to involve Saudi Arabia, but then the brutal murder of Saudi journalist Jamal Khashoggi at the Saudi Consulate in Turkey shocked the world and put a negative light on the good relations Jared had been developing with Saudi crown prince Mohammed bin Salman.

Jared is still working on achieving peace in the Middle East. Maybe this proves that he really is a true believer? That, for Jared, lasting peace in the Middle East isn't just an opportunity for an ambitious man to write himself into the history books, but that it really is part of a dream for a better world?

TEN

HILLARY

Hillary Clinton had been preparing to be the first woman to run for president ever since she served in the White House as a First Lady. In fact, her ambition was even more specific—to be the first ever *First Lady* to become president.

The master plan was brilliant. Moving her residence from the White House in 2000 to New York State. Doing a "listening tour" there, convincing the residents of New York—particularly the most powerful ones—that the Clintons, previously associated with the Midwest and Arkansas, were really "one of them." It might seem like a long shot, but it worked! Hillary transitioned smoothly from being the wife of President Clinton to a junior senator from New York.

Whether it was luck that Rudy Giuliani had to withdraw from the race because of cancer, or her incredible determination alone, we'll never know. But the same players would meet again as rivals in 2016: Hillary as a DNC nominee and Giuliani as a loyal supporter of the RNC nominee Donald Trump.

Hillary decided not to run in 2004, leaving the DNC nomination to John Kerry. That gave her plenty of time to prepare for a perfect presidential bid for 2008. Even before she announced her candidacy for the 2008 election, Hillary was considered the frontrunner. The Clinton name did the trick when it came to exciting the media, as well as the donors. The fact that there could be a woman on the ticket for the first time added to the excitement. Close friends warned Hillary about announcing too early. There could be a dark horse coming in at the last moment, at the eleventh hour. But Hillary ignored this caution, and sure enough, Barack Obama surprised her and many others, taking the DNC by storm. He nailed the DNC nomination in 2008 and left Hillary with tears in her eyes.

Still, Hillary is nothing if not relentless. She didn't give up her dream to become the first woman president of the United States. After serving as secretary of state during the first Obama administration, she took a break and started to plan her next presidential bid. Again, she relied on the Clinton name, the Clinton machine, Clinton donors, and Clinton celebrity friends. And again, she ignored any warning about dark horses. The speculation of her running started way too early, according to some experts. In the end, she was hit by the email scandal and needed to delay her official announcement. Perhaps this distraction kept her from noticing the two unconventional candidates emerging right in front of her—Bernie Sanders and Donald Trump.

Like many others, we in the Trump camp had assumed all along that Hillary Clinton would *inevitably* be the DNC's presidential candidate.

Many had also expected that the Republican convention would be a hotly contested one; that even if Trump were to lead, the RNC would *actively* prevent him from being the nominee. But then we surprised everyone and got the delegates needed. As I have mentioned before, whatever our prior divisions, at the RNC we presented a united front—well, near-enough anyway.

By contrast, the DNC convention was not so fortunate. They had to deal with outright protests within their own ranks, including Bernie supporters who were angry, who felt cheated.

When we joined the Trump campaign in March, Paul and I had considered Hillary as *our* opponent—at least our only serious opponent. So we included "The Hillary Factor" in every poll we did, and the results were telling. The level of distrust toward her was so high on the Republican side that any other candidate like that would never have had a chance of luring swinging voters.

But our presumptive candidate also had "character issues," according to the polls. So, both candidates polled poorly when it came to character. Therefore, since character was a problem on both sides of the fence, we decided to stay away from anything related to it and keep the focus on policy—national security, economy, and immigration.

In mid-July, after the DNC nominated Hillary to be their presidential nominee, we started to prepare for the general elections. On paper, Hillary looked good, but in reality, Bernie supporters felt she had won the nomination unfairly. She also had an image problem: she was hard to relate to. Voters were not hooked on Hillary. Voters weren't committed to Hillary. African Americans did not support her automatically, even though many assumed they would. There was also the perception that Hillary had already reached the pinnacle of her career when she tried to be nominated in 2008. She had momentum then, but Obama surprised and outmaneuvered her. In 2016, eight years later, she was a weakened candidate. The Clintons had lost a lot of support by then and the Clinton brand no longer meant the same thing it had eight years before.

I personally felt like we were reliving the Bob Dole campaign of 1996. Back then, he was the most senior, the "heir apparent" of the Republican Party. Instead of picking a good candidate who had a genuine chance of winning against the Clintons, the Republicans chose Dole because they felt they *owed* it to him. And it turned out to be a joke. At the age of seventy-six, at the start of what would have been his presidency, maybe he was just too old? He would have been only slightly younger at the beginning of his presidency than Reagan was at the end of his. As it turned out, Dole failed physically, and he failed politically. I felt the same about Hillary: she was past her time.

Yet I was still concerned. Maybe she wasn't quite past her time enough. Hillary's much bigger campaign had been organized for months, and she had much more money in the bank than we did. Paul might have been gone from the campaign but as I had learned from him, budget wasn't everything.

The second debate between presidential nominees took place on October 9. It was tough, because we had just been hit by the *Access Hollywood* tape. Then Steve Bannon came up with the idea of bringing the "Brilliant Foursome"—Paula Jones, Juanita Broaddrick, Kathleen Willey, and Kathy Shelton—to the second debate. The first three women had famously accused Bill Clinton of sexual misconduct. The fourth woman was a rape victim, and Hillary Clinton was the young lawyer who'd defended the rapist and helped him get a conviction on a lesser charge. In the end, Shelton's rapist served only ten months in jail.

Bannon wanted to sit them in the first row, at the family seats, in front of Hillary. The place was set so Hillary faced the Trump family, and Trump faced the Clinton seats. There was some back-and-forth. Members of the Trump family did not want to do it. Ivanka was the most against it, but Jared and Eric agreed with her. Don Jr. was fifty-fifty. He thought it was a good idea, but he was not sure how it could be done. But Bannon was backed by some right-wing people, and he was pushing for it. In the end, Trump thought it was a good idea, so it was a go.

Only we faced a little problem. The deputy chairman of the debate warned us that if we brought these women to the front row, he would shut the debate down. I don't know if he would really have done it, but unable to take that risk, we decided to change course and seat them right after the Trump family so that when Rudy Giuliani walked them in, it still created a distraction.

And it worked! It was the first time I saw Hillary sort of break down. Here she was, trying to portray Donald Trump as someone involved in sexual misconduct with women, and these four women were there, in view, powerful reminders that it was her husband, Bill Clinton, who'd had big scandals with women. And even she herself had a troubling record standing up for women's rights.

Even though later polls showed that a majority of those asked thought that Hillary had won the debate, we knew we had scored a major psychological victory. Hillary had to have realized that, on some level, she lost credibility, and more important, moral authority that night. People in glass houses . . .

So what did we think of Steve Bannon's tactic? It worked brilliantly. And who was there to execute that cruel spectacle? Her old rival, Rudy Giuliani.

Recruiting Rudy to the Trump campaign took effort, though to many New Yorkers, it seemed like an organic development. After all, Giuliani had had his own bitter history with Hillary. In 2000, then-mayor Giuliani was legally unable to run for a third term as New York City mayor. The mayor, who had an image as a "tough guy," was supported by the state's Republican Party to run for the Senate seat that had been recently vacated by Democrat senator Daniel Patrick Moynihan. It all looked promising for Giuliani, until then–First Lady Hillary Clinton announced she was running for the same desired Senate seat. Hillary was leading in the polls, but Giuliani was about to give her a fight. At least he was until spring of 2000, when Giuliani was diagnosed with prostate cancer. At the same time, his extramarital relations with Judith Nathan became headlines, taking his wife, Donna Hanover, by surprise. Donna was still residing in Gracie Mansion, the official residence of the mayor of New York City. It was all too much for many conservatives to digest, so on May 19, 2000, Giuliani announced he was withdrawing from the race to be a New York senator.

When Paul and I joined the Trump campaign, we put an effort into recruiting some big names to support Trump. At that point, there were still several candidates in the Republican race. Even the "names" who told us privately that Donald had a real shot were very careful. Going out there, supporting him publicly, was too risky for them, at that stage. This is a classic problem in politics and in business, too. Power comes from being seen as a prophet. You obviously know things, if you back a winner from the beginning. Paul's successful career was built on reputation for backing winners, perhaps even being a "kingmaker." You definitely don't want to back a loser because nobody wants to be on the losing side. But if you back a winner too late, you look like an "also ran" who's late to the bandwagon. It's all about the timing.

We wanted to have the support of Rudy Giuliani. He had been a presidential candidate himself, so he knew the game. And he was a New Yorker, like Trump. To have the endorsement of "America's mayor," the hero of 9/11, meant a lot. It was a major stamp of approval.

Paul had good relations with Rudy, but at first, like so many others, Rudy was hesitant. There were still a few candidates in the race: Marco Rubio, Ted Cruz, and John Kasich, names that were, on the face of it, easier to endorse for a Republican public figure.

But we kept working on it. We went ahead and set up a meeting with Rudy at the Trump residence. By then, we'd already had some indications that Rudy was becoming receptive to supporting Trump and playing a role in the campaign. The meeting, including Donald, Jared, Paul, and Rudy, went really well. The feedback I got was positive: Rudy told them that Trump wasn't making it as a presidential candidate because he hadn't had the support of the establishment behind him. He suggested bringing more credible names, beside himself, on board. That observation sat well with our line of thinking. It was tricky, because we still needed to face the fact that people simply found it less risky to back Marco Rubio or Ted Cruz. I personally felt that Rudy had been leaning toward backing Marco Rubio prior to us courting him and that meeting with Trump. After the meeting, Rudy became a surrogate for Trump and started appearing on TV, which worked both him and us. Rudy liked the idea of speaking on Trump's behalf and arguing against political correctness. Not only did he do a good job, but we could tell he was enjoying it; it was his cup of tea.

Then Rudy started to appear at rallies, as did Mike Flynn. Our campaign started to have more known names attached to it and was getting the credibility it needed. Rudy became more and more vocal on Trump's behalf, until eventually, he proved himself the ultimate supporter when Trump needed a "talking head," a backer, after the *Access Hollywood* debacle. When the *Washington Post* broke the story about the tape in October, Republicans panicked. Nobody senior was willing to go public and defend Trump. Even his running mate, Mike Pence, a family man and father to daughters, made a statement distancing himself from Trump's actions. Everyone ducked under a rock . . . everyone but Rudy.

Rudy was a New York tough guy. He'd had his own scandals around women. Looking back, there were three people who were known to the public and who remained loyal to Trump: Jeff Sessions, Mike Flynn, and Rudy Giuliani. But Rudy was the most effective on TV.

I don't know who started spreading stories, but people have often asked me if Rudy's reported drinking affected his behavior. Oddly enough, I saw him most of the time at the Havana Club in New York. One of these nights, I needed to talk with him urgently. We needed him to attend a national security address the next morning at 8:30 a.m., and I couldn't find him. It was getting late, so at 10:30 p.m. I went to the Havana Club. Sure enough, he was there with a glass of whiskey and a cigar. Had he been drinking? Had he been drinking too much? I told him we needed him ASAP early in the morning, and Rudy said he would do it.

I was happy that I found him, but I wasn't sure if he would even remember the details the following morning. Would he recall that we met? Would he show up? Then, very late that night, security got a call from Rudy's people to schedule the meeting. He did remember that we talked, and he showed up promptly the next morning. I must add that Rudy was very effective on the campaign trail. He was also very helpful when it came time to prepare for the debates.

Of course, with big names comes big ego, and Rudy later tried to hijack some of our national security meetings. I don't know if he did it knowingly, but he felt he needed to shine. Not so fast with Donald Trump. He sort of let Rudy do it, giving him a longer leash than he would have most other people, but then Trump came to the meetings and added other people on the phone. He asked lots of questions and sought out different opinions. Trump took the control back.

Whatever other people might have said about him, there's no doubt that after the *Access Hollywood* tape, Rudy Giuliani became the number one loyal guy among the "names." And after the victory, came the rewards. Rudy was tapped by the transition team for attorney general. He went to talk with then President-elect Trump and made it known that the only post he was interested in was secretary of state.

Trump knows how to play these situations in a cool manner, and suddenly there were leaks regarding Rudy's deals with Turkey and Qatar and other countries. I have no idea who was behind these sudden publications, if there was anyone at all. Some believed the source was Steve Bannon, but it might have involved others. In the end, as a result of these published reports, both positions were a "no go" for Rudy, and he was viewed by many as having fallen out of favor. Trump then asked him to chair the White House Cyber Terrorism Task Force. It didn't seem to be that important a post at the time, no big deal, but, ironically, because of the later claims of Russian collusion to steal the election, Rudy's position became much more important. And then he would be appointed to his next gig, which again had him front and center and earned him the colorful title, the President's TV Lawyer.

Bernie's voters liked him because he was not part of "the establishment." And guess what? Neither was Trump. So, our voters had things in common: both liked outsiders and were willing to back a dark horse. Bernie voters and Trump voters had the same suspicions about party elites and vested interests. In their own way, each candidate believed that government had lost touch with ordinary Americans. This commonality was most apparent when polls showed that 12 percent of Bernie supporters would rather vote for Trump than Hillary. That was a lot, when you added African Americans, college-educated women, and others. We were careful not to upset Bernie supporters because a substantial number of them had said outright that they would support us. So, we never, ever, touched Bernie. Instead we kept hammering on Hillary. In so many ways, she was a much easier target.

We were traveling to a rally on Trump's plane and Mike Flynn joined us. Trump was working on a speech and the TV was on, as usual. They reported that the FBI had given immunity to several of Hillary's people, regarding the private email investigation. Trump was *furious* and wanted to know why the FBI would enter into so many immunity deals with the key people involved. He just burst out, "Lock her up!" and Flynn loved it!

Of course, in a traditional campaign, a candidate threatening to arrest his or her opponent is a big no-no. But the first thing *any* poll showed us was that people did not like her character— even people who didn't like Trump felt Hillary was just not trustworthy. Trump used to tell us, "I don't need polls to tell me so, I know it! Everyone does."

So, we agreed to let Trump be Trump. Trump and Flynn used the "lock her up" slogan that very same day. It caught on like a fire and became a slogan throughout the campaign, really putting Hillary on the defensive. We were all together at a rally when the "deplorable" bombshell dropped. The Democrats were holding a fund-raising event in New York City on September 9, 2016, just two months ahead of the election, and the audience was predominantly LGBT. Here's what Hillary said, as recorded on Time.com:

> I know there are only 60 days left to make our case—and don't get complacent; don't see the latest outrageous, offensive, inappropriate comment and think, "Well, he's done this time." We are living in a volatile political environment.
>
> You know, to just be grossly generalistic, you could put half of Trump's supporters into what I call the basket of deplorables. (Laughter/applause) Right? (Laughter/applause) They're racist, sexist, homophobic, xenophobic—Islamophobic—you name it. And unfortunately, there are people like that. And he has lifted them up. He has given voice to their websites that used to only have 11,000 people—now have 11 million. He tweets and retweets their offensive hateful mean-spirited rhetoric. Now, some of those folks—they are irredeemable, but thankfully, they are not America. But the "other" basket—the other basket—and I know because I look at this crowd I see friends from all over America here: I see friends from Florida and Georgia and South Carolina and Texas and—as well as, you know, New York and California—but that "other" basket of people are people who feel the government has let them down, the economy has let them down, nobody cares about them, nobody worries about what happens to their lives and their futures; and they're just desperate for change. It doesn't really even matter where it comes from. They don't buy everything

he says, but—he seems to hold out some hope that their lives will be different. They won't wake up and see their jobs disappear, lose a kid to heroin, feel like they're in a dead end. Those are people we have to understand and empathize with as well.

Given that the voting public at the time was almost 50/50 Trump and Clinton, saying that *half* of Trump's supporters were in a "basket of deplorables" was, in effect, saying that a quarter of the voting population—60 million of the roughly 240 million US citizens—was, in her estimation, "deplorable," racist, sexist, etc. By denigrating the voters, rather than her candidate, she was alienating *all* Trump's supporters. It was a huge miscalculation.

To be fair, Republicans have had to deal with this sort of thing too. It reminded me of Mitt Romney's mistake at a fundraising event in Boca Raton, Florida on September 17, 2012. Romney said he would never win over the 47 percent of people who were going to vote for Obama, no matter what, because of their welfare entitlements and because they "pay no income tax."

As far as the "deplorable" comment was concerned, Paul suggested we let the news cycle run it again and again before we hit back. We didn't need a sophisticated strategy. Hillary made a BIG mistake, and we would use it. That simple. To Trump's credit, he saw the power of it immediately, and he turned it around, making voters proud to identify as deplorables. That is his gift. He takes an insult and turns it into a badge of honor. He recognizes opportunities, and he doesn't let them pass him by.

At every step, we had to consider our strategy carefully, since there had never been a presidential campaign against a woman.

Character-wise, it was easy. According to the polls, Hillary was not an attractive candidate, so we worked with that. Then, especially after the *Access Hollywood* tape, we went after her husband's sexual misconduct. But we still had a problem on our hands: we knew Hillary would use her sex to her advantage. So, we countered hard against her, our message: *why would a woman put up, for years, with a husband like that?*

It was a strategy with its own risk; after all, abused women routinely stay with abusive partners. But it was a calculated risk. Toward the end, we also highlighted that she simply was not a good candidate—she could not articulate a good message. We had plenty of anecdotal ammunition to back this up. There were stories about how she treated people with disrespect, particularly her Secret Service people. The stories were out there; all we had to do was use them for our own ends. In many ways, her public persona was her own worst enemy. She didn't come across as personable, and that impression stuck and kept sticking. In hindsight, many people, even many of her supporters, believe that Hillary doesn't have charisma, and that deficiency is a major liability.

But at the time, we had to use everything we could to win. Trump asked me and others repeatedly what we thought about Hillary doing or saying particular things. When it came to issues with women, like bringing the three Clinton accusers to the debate, Trump took special notice of Kellyanne Conway's opinion. She is a professional, so she weighed things as a professional. But she also saw issues as a woman, and in relation to the Clinton accusers, Kellyanne favored Bannon's view, and supported bringing them into the spotlight during the debate. "As a woman, I would like to know if Hillary has been covering up for her husband," she said.

Being a businessman, Trump is comfortable with the cold, hard numbers. They are familiar to him, a language he understands. In politics, it was the same. He fixated on the numbers—how many people attended Hillary's rallies, versus how many showed up for his. It sounded silly, but he had a point. It was something concrete in a world of speculation.

We had a great turnout at the rallies. People came by the thousands, but there were reports of smaller numbers. If one row was empty, the media covered it. But that was not the case with Hillary's campaign. They showed her speaking with twenty people behind her, but no cameras panned the crowd. Trump knew she did not have his big numbers. The portrayal was another way in which the game was rigged, and it would be an ongoing source of frustration for him, the feeling that the media, in general, was out to get him.

Looking back, it's pretty clear to me that we won for two main reasons. The first: Hillary was really a bad candidate! For all her ability, all her political savvy and experience, she didn't come across as a people person. There were just too many question marks about her past, and the mixed legacy of her husband didn't help matters. Something about her made voters think, "I can't trust you," and more basically, "I don't like you." Even George Clooney, a known Democrat who supported her and hosted a fund-raiser for her in his home, said she was a bad candidate.

Second, and I would realize this as the campaign wore on, she simply did not know how to deal with Donald Trump. Nobody did, really. Not even us. He called people names, and if somebody tried the same thing on him, he doubled down, owning the insult and returning fire. Hillary had some advantages—deep pockets of benefactors and throngs of backers—but even with all those resources combined, she still couldn't stop the bizarre offensive of Donald Trump.

ELEVEN

CONTINGENCY PLANS AND TRUMP FORCE ONE

Did *Trump want to win?* I have been asked that question repeatedly. *Did Trump really think he could win?*

After my indictment, I would revisit these questions over and over again, while combing through my own life from the moment I first met Donald Trump. Some claimed publicly that he did not want to win. That he was horrified when he actually did. They portrayed it like a big practical joke that had gotten out of hand and gone horribly wrong. That was not my experience at all.

I think for a long time Donald didn't really believe he could win the elections, but he still thought it was worth a shot. And when Paul asked me to follow him and join the Trump campaign, he told me that Trump had a real shot at winning the Republican primaries. At this point, there were still several good candidates in the race, but some instinct, some feeling acquired from all those years in politics, must have spoken to Paul and he bet on Trump. I trusted Paul's instincts, so I was convinced, too. But as I accompanied Trump for all those months, I was not so sure that he, himself, believed it. I thought he had what it took: charisma in spades, the ability to connect with big crowds personally, and a comfort with playing outside of the box. He would emerge bigger and better out of every fiasco.

But one thing I could not miss was that, first and foremost, it was always about Donald Trump. *His* image. *His* publicity. Yet I also observed how he started to fall in love with some of the political messages that carried his campaign. So, slowly, several different Trumps started colliding into a strong one: Trump the Businessman, Trump the Reality TV Celebrity, Trump the Politician in the Making. A rare combination.

We'd had presidents in the past who had two out of the three. Reagan was a celebrity and a burgeoning politician. The Bush family had both businessmen and politicians, but there had never been all three. Trump was a trifecta, a perfect storm, waiting to happen.

So Trump never told me: "I think I am going to lose." But he did say things like, "If we lose . . ." or, "if we don't win . . ."

Maybe it was his way of protecting himself from a big disappointment? After all, he's not known for taking rejection lightly. Or maybe it was just the businessman in him, forever making contingency plans. But I think he knew, right from the start, that he could never have won within the terms of the traditional political structure. He knew he would not win if he played *their* game by *their* rules. I did not get the impression that Trump did not have a plan B for building Trump TV, in case he lost.

He probably planned to return to real estate and enjoy his much bigger worldwide name recognition and highest-end contacts. His rapidly mushrooming name recognition gave him a wide range of opportunities, in the event he lost. So, in his mind at least, one way or the other, he couldn't lose.

———————

Jared Kushner had another ambition: to push the TV narrative, so he brought in Sinclair Broadcasting. Sinclair, based in Maryland, is owned by a prominent conservative, David Smith, who became a Trump supporter. Sinclair has a blatant conservative slant and a network of stations that cover 40 percent of US households.

Later on, David Sinclair would try to merge with Tribune Broadcasting, based in Chicago, and create another conservative TV channel. Unfortunately for them, the merger would not be approved and would eventually start an ugly legal war between the two companies. I thought that our involvement with Sinclair was way too premature, but we gave their stations some footage exclusively. I think Jared needed to cover more conservative TV bases. His strategy became even more justified in July 2016, when Roger Ailes was forced to resign from his legendary position as the chairman and CEO of Fox News Channel and Fox Business Network. Ailes's resignation followed allegations by former Fox News host Gretchen Carlson, claiming that her contract with Fox News was not renewed due to sexual harassment by Ailes. Carlson's lawsuit, which was questioned by many at the first stages, would become a cornerstone of the "Me Too" movement.

In time, Me Too would topple some of the most powerful men in the film and TV industry. Overnight, they would lose their jobs and reputations, and many would face legal proceedings. When Carlson first filed a suit against the powerful Ailes not many gave her any chance of winning, let alone emerging as one of the crusaders in a major women's movement. Fox owner Rupert Murdoch, his children, and Fox as an organization realized that times were a-changing. And Roger Ailes was gone. Just like that.

Presumptive Republican candidate Donald Trump was one of the only people who would talk nicely about Ailes after his departure. In the film and TV industry, as in politics, when you're ousted, you become toxic. Untouchable. Don't I know it firsthand? But Donald had thought highly about Roger's expertise. After all, he was the guy who had put Fox News on the map.

"It is always difficult to create a flourishing news channel," Rupert Murdoch said when Ailes resigned, "and to build Fox Business, to create a channel or a publication from the ground up and against seemingly entrenched monopolies, Roger has defied the odds. His grasp of policy and his ability to make profoundly important issues accessible to a broader audience stand in stark contrast to the self-serving elitism that characterizes far too much of the media."

Ailes's termination from Fox added yet one more big opportunity for Trump. Ailes, the man who had been praised for building, practically from the ground up, an amazing right-wing media start-up, was so bitter about the reasons he'd been let go, and the manner in which his termination had been carried out. He'd had to read his name in the press, repeatedly linked to the word "disgraced." It was natural that he wanted revenge.

Trump was tuned in to that and would have found some way to make use of it, if he had lost.

Still, I'm still a little hesitant to say that there was ever a *clear* plan B for Donald, but my guess is that he would have had some plan—even a sketch—so that either way, he would come out the ultimate winner. And that is something I'm sure he has always cared about.

———————

Perhaps the best embodiment of Donald's ability to occupy both presidential and business roles is the Boeing 727, affectionately known as "Trump Force One." It was here, at 40,000 feet in the air, that Trump first proved he could exist in both worlds. That something used for business could be molded and utilized to fit the needs of the country.

While Trump was running for president, he still ran his day-to-day business both on the plane and off of it. I was with him in a meeting one day when Ivanka came in and briefed him on the occupancy rates across all their hotels. They went on to talk for a few minutes about a new project in India.

There were several other times when I was in his office, going over our campaign agenda, and he was signing checks related to his business. It may seem strange, but being situated there, at the Trump Tower, it looked natural. This was a guy who was a successful businessman. It was clear, he liked his business. He was on a new path, but he would continue running his businesses even while learning a whole new one—America.

Even before he became president, in many ways Donald Trump already lived like one. Like many high-powered business-men, he owns a private jet. Built in 1968, the first Trump Force One belonged to American Airlines when Trump bought it in 1997 to be repurposed as his private plane. I never saw the first Trump Force One, but if it was anything like the current one, you have to see it to believe it. It was eventually sold and scrapped a couple of years ago. Trump bought the current Trump Force One—a Boeing 757-200—in 2011, when it was already twenty years old. The previous owner was Microsoft's Paul Allen, and Trump apparently paid him $100 million for it. That was *before* the refurbishment, so I can't guess how much that aircraft cost.

Normally this model aircraft is licensed to carry up to 239 people, but Trump Force One is configured to carry around forty. What did he do with all that extra room? Well, it has a few bath-rooms, a shower, a bedroom, a guest room, a dining area, and its own wood-paneled galley. If you enter the plane from the rear door, the galley is the first room you walk through. Ironically, because of Trump's fondness for fast food, the galley is almost never used to prepare food. It looks more like a bar than a kitchen. Moving forward from the galley, you step into the "first-class sleeper area," which has big, plush recliner chairs upholstered in cream-colored leather. They are as comfortable as they look, and each seat has its own audiovisual entertainment hub.

It's no secret that Trump likes gold. (The Oval Office now has gold-colored drapes.) The wall color scheme is the standard boring airplane beige, but it's the detailing that really stands out—all dark polished wood with the Trump family crest in various places. The light fixtures and switches, the bathroom fixtures—even the seat belt buckles—are all covered in 24-karat gold.

Moving forward, you enter a dining area that looks like it's been designed by Martha Stewart. A few more plush recliners sit opposite a checkered couch, and between them, a long table made of the same dark polished timber you see everywhere else. This was Trump's spot. The place where he normally worked. Although the couch was long enough to seat four, the unspoken rule was that in flight, nobody would be sitting next to him, unless we had a particular person who absolutely needed to see him. So the seat next to him would almost always be empty, as well as the three recliners opposite him, and the long table would function as his desk.

Immediately forward of the dining area was the front of the main lounge of Trump Force One, and this is where we mostly worked. There was a fifty-seven-inch screen, and Trump would always immediately put the TV on, and we would flip back and forth between Fox News, CNN, MSNBC, and other news channels. The entertainment system has about 1,000 movies in its library and about 2,500 CDs. Trump even has a "T" button in the entertainment system that lets him access his favorite media. The sound system in the lounge is the same type they use in screening rooms in Hollywood, so needless to say, you can really hear the bass!

Moving forward, there's a short corridor on the left that gives you access to the guest room on the right. The divan in the guest room converts into a bed. The room itself is completely wood paneled and gives the impression of a first-class rail carriage.

Even the toilet seats are fancy—upholstered leather from the Edelman company. An interesting side note: Trump seems to have a weird relationship with toilets. In 2018, he and Melania wanted to borrow a Van Gogh from the Guggenheim in New York to display in the White House. It's no secret that many people in New York hate Trump, which is perhaps why they declined their request, offering an 18-karat gold toilet instead. The piece was the work of an Italian artist, and the toilet is fully functioning. It's still in the Guggenheim, so the Trumps must have said no to the offer.

Farther up front, there's a cabin that is supposed to be a master bedroom, but Trump uses it as a dressing room. A queen-sized bed and a silk comforter, the surrounding walls covered in light gold silk—all of it designed for luxurious comfort, but Trump never went to nap there. In fact, he never slept at all. He always worked. Except one time, on a trip to Scotland, when he was opening the Turnberry Golf Club. During that long flight, Trump slept on the bed in that room while the kids slept on the recliner couches.

In the front bedroom is a small custom theater that is basically a small desk with a wall-mounted TV screen in front of it. Adjoining the front bedroom is the master bathroom with its own shower. Again, all dark wood, gold faucets, gold sink, and green marble bench top. At the very front of the plane is the VIP area, with more of those plush recliners and another couch and forward of that is the cockpit, with its state-of-the-art fittings and navigation system. I've heard that the whole thing costs around $11,000 per hour to run when it's flying, but that's nothing compared to the over $200,000 per hour it costs to run Air Force One.

We, too, were always working in the plane. On every flight, Trump would have two boxes of newspapers, documents, and business memos to go through. Staff would prepare them and his aide, Keith Schiller, would bring them to Trump.

For refreshment, we had drinks like Coke, and Trump's favorite, Diet Coke. The general consensus is that Trump drinks about twelve Diet Cokes a day. I've never bothered to add them all up, but after the countless hours I've spent with him, I don't think that this is too far off the mark. It's probably even more in hot weather. On top of the Coke and other soda pops, the plane would also have plenty of snacks—like Trump's favorite, Lay's Potato Chips. But there was no real food until after the rally or whatever event we were attending was complete. Only then would someone bring in buckets of Kentucky Fried Chicken or burgers from McDonald's. I wonder how many folks know Trump's McDonald's order by heart: two Big Macs, two Filet-O-Fish, and one chocolate shake.

The Secret Service details had privileged status: Chick-fil-A! No expense spared! And with 2,200 locations across the country, a Chick-fil-A wasn't hard to come by. Whenever I could, I would try to exchange my rations for theirs. I like hamburgers, but unlike Trump, I don't have an endless capacity for them. Sometimes, if we were really lucky, we'd get pizza.

So, what was it like on the plane? Usually we were so busy, we didn't have time to appreciate the interior decor. It was just *there*. And truthfully, it's amazing how quickly you acclimate to this sort of thing. But I never really got used to the paradox. There we were, in a $100 million plane, while the future leader of the free world drank Diet Coke, ate McDonald's, and watched CNN, just like any other American.

TWELVE

MITT ROMNEY AND THE NEVER-TRUMPERS

saw the sycophants on both sides. Some wanted Trump to win, and others wanted nothing to do with him. It was March 2, 2016, when former Republican presidential nominee Mitt Romney sent shock waves through his party and made headlines around the world when he called the controversial GOP frontrunner, "phony, a fraud."

"His promises are as worthless as a degree from Trump University," Romney went on to say.

While many conservative leaders could not stomach the thought of Trump as the RNC nominee, they tried to play fair and managed, with some sincerity, to at least say, "Let the best candidate win."

But when Romney said it, he spat it out. If he thought he would further scare Republicans from disruptor Donald Trump, he was mistaken, and in the end, his tactics backfired. That was because the traditional Republicans who disliked Trump did not need Romney's loud reminder. Trump had already been playing as a nightmare in their minds for months.

On the other hand, the more Trump upset traditional Republicans, the more the new Republicans loved him. Here, at last, someone was finally speaking to them, concerned about the same things they were concerned about—addressing their needs! They began to form an identity all their own, and as the media started to consider their importance in the movement, they gave new Trump supporters a name: the Base.

The Romney stuff happened just before Paul and I joined the Trump campaign, so we walked into our new jobs inheriting the situation. Trump hit back at Romney, as expected. He was at a rally in Portland, Maine, complaining to his base, in his usual off-the-cuff style: "You can see how loyal he is. He was begging for my endorsement in 2012. I could have said, 'Mitt, drop to your knees.' He would have dropped on his knees."

It was a somewhat unusual situation, something new. This time around, it seemed to me that Trump was hurt. He took Romney's attitude as a betrayal, cruel and personal—a backstabbing he couldn't have prepared for. "I gave him money. He asked for my endorsement—I gave it to him."

He never imagined in a million years that Romney would turn on him as he did. By now, the public has gotten so used to vicious attacks on candidate Trump that many have forgotten how popular he had once been among political candidates. He'd donated to them; he'd listened to their pleas for endorsements. Suddenly, it seemed, after all he'd done to help them, sharp knives were turned toward him, and it genuinely surprised him. Most of the time Trump rolled with the punches. This was politics after all, but a few times it hurt him deeply, and that was the case with Romney.

In May 2016, after Trump had all the delegates needed, he called me and asked for Romney's cell phone number. Trump had talked about it with Paul and Priebus, and they had convinced him that the fight was over. That now, more than ever, it was important to let bygones be bygones. Unite the RNC around him in order to win. It was very unlike Trump, to put aside such a personal betrayal, but to his credit, he felt it was the right way to proceed.

So, he called me. He was very cagey about it. "Rick," he said, "give me his mobile number."

"Do you have talking points?" I asked.

He thought for a second. "No," he said. "I'm not going to call him." And then he hung up.

A few seconds passed, and Trump called me back. "Give me the mobile."

I felt that Trump really wanted to do it, but every time he reflected on it, he didn't want to put himself in an extra-vulnerable position. Like he was afraid of being rejected while making a graceful, conciliatory gesture. I honestly could not blame him, since there was no way to predict how Romney would react to Trump's olive branch.

In the end, Donald Trump did not call Mitt Romney. "I am not going to call him," he informed us. "I will send him an email."

That email would create a whole "operation" for me. It meant I needed to talk with Romney's people to obtain Romney's direct email, which would alert them that something was up, but it couldn't be helped. That was the least of my worries.

Donald Trump didn't have an email account, so I got Mitt Romney's email and had to send Trump's email from Hope Hicks's email account to Romney's.

Trump kept the message up front and simple: *Just wanted to reach out. To talk about where things are.*

The goal was to get Romney on the phone with Trump, but we needed to make it short and casual, in case it was leaked.

What happened? As far as I know—nothing. I'm not aware of any answer from Romney at all. Trump blew it off, but he was hurt and angry. We'd considered including Romney in the convention, but after that, Trump didn't want to hear about it.

But it wasn't just about Romney. Romney represented a substantial slice of Republican voters. Romney was the face of those voters. He led a movement—the Never-Trumpers—people who would rather not vote at all, or even vote Democrat, than vote for Trump. We'd been dealing with Never-Trumpers right up until the night Trump was nominated at the convention in July. Romney's no-show at the convention actually damaged him. His supporters had no one to rally around.

In November 2016, after Trump won the election, Priebus came up with the idea of interviewing Mitt Romney for secretary of state. Knowing Trump and how he had perceived Romney's treatment of him as betrayal, I was extremely skeptical that the appointment had any real chance. But aides of Romney told me then they really believed he had a shot. They said that Romney wanted it, and Priebus was personally invested in Romney as secretary of state. He wanted it to happen.

One meeting and one public dinner later—it did not happen. Somehow, I felt that Trump and Romney were not yet through. They'd get back in the ring in the near future, either to cement some lost understanding, or to continue their rivalry, round after round.

THIRTEEN

INAUGURATION CEREMONIES—PITFALLS, PROTOCOLS, AND PRETENDERS

During the Trump inauguration, we not only had to juggle the real people involved, we also had to deal with our Pretenders—self-appointed experts on Trump, his business, his family, and politics. Individuals who, for one reason or another, saw the Trump phenomenon as an opportunity to further their own careers, either by pretending to be insiders or by setting themselves up in the chorus of continuing opposition.

Our Pretenders caused some of the biggest headaches. Many of them could not keep their mouths shut. They had to go out and make announcements, pretending to know it all. When it came down to the celebrities and Hollywood, it was a big pie in the face for no reason. They were just lightweights, and Trump knew how to handle Hollywood and the celebs. But other breeds of Pretenders were more concerning, especially those who wielded power and could use any pretext they had to make our lives difficult.

When it came time for the big day, First Lady–elect Melania was our center of attention, but we had to avoid some unprecedented pitfalls. Donald's two former wives—Ivana Trump and Marla Maples—would also be at the ceremonies, and it would be a bit of a trick to accommodate all of them.

Tom Barrack and I talked with Donald about it and followed his wishes. We basically understood that the best way to avoid any possible awkwardness or embarrassment was to keep things as separate as we could. This meant that as much as humanly possible, we would try to ensure the wives did not bump into each other. Since the inauguration was also going to be Melania's big day, Trump wanted her to shine, so we needed to ensure that neither Ivana nor Marla would be caught on camera and steal even a little of the limelight.

It was a delicate operation; there were all sorts of subtle details to consider. We put them in the same row, but on the opposite sides of the Capitol. It was very important to treat them equally, but separately. Then we found out that one of the kids moved Ivana to a different row—the diplomatic section. Still, it worked well.

Ivana's and Marla's invitations were strictly for Inauguration Day, not for any of the prior dinners, and both ladies arrived in DC on Thursday, a day ahead of the inauguration. We put them in different hotels—we were controlling all reservations for hotels, except the Trump Hotel, which was reserved by the Trumps for family and friends. In the end, no one was better at handling that kind of thing than Trump, and he did so with ease.

Originally, the Trump family planned to stay at the Trump Hotel, but we explained that it was a long-standing tradition that the new First Family stay at Blair House, the president's guest house. They didn't want to do it, as their hotel felt like home, but we pushed until Donald and Melania decided to respect the tradition. Ivanka took some sheets from the hotel with her to Blair House, to feel more at home. It made sense. Even the Trumps needed some reassurance on the big day.

There was another area that needed attention: would the First Family get out of the car, and wave to the crowd? Melania was hesitant. She was very concerned about safety issues. Ivanka pushed hard for getting out of the car, because she understood the historical significance of the gesture, and in the end, Melania was convinced. We met in the middle: they *did* get out but walked only a short distance. That was enough for the cameras. In a world where video images are the reality, it was enough to capture that moment forever. We were lucky that everybody was very gracious about everything. Well, almost everyone.

Barack Obama used protocol as an excuse not to accommodate some of the Trumps' requests. So did the then almost-former First Lady Michelle, and most brazenly, the US State Department. Couldn't they have been more diplomatic? Couldn't they have been more gracious, all three of them?

At Blair House, we faced what seemed like an unnecessary challenge. Right up until the end, the outgoing president is still *the president*, and only the president can authorize a stay at Blair House. This meant that in order to follow tradition, we needed then President Barack Obama's permission to accommodate the Trump family. To our surprise, he authorized it only at the actual moment when Donald and Melania checked in. That meant that until Thursday—the day before the inauguration—the kids were not formally invited at Blair House. Don Jr. and Eric arrived earlier that week and had stayed at the Trump Hotel. It was hard not to see this as a subtle snub.

And there were further challenges coming from Obama's end. Again, according to tradition, when a president-elect is coming to DC, the outgoing president offers tea. This usually happens on the morning of the inauguration, before the ceremony. Well, the Trumps did not get an invitation. It created a very difficult situation because we could not really call and ask for it; it had to come from President Obama. But we needed to plan every minute in the schedule, so we made delicate inquiries and were told that Michelle Obama was not sure if she would issue such an invitation.

We told President-elect Trump and Melania about the sensitive situation, and they were initially disappointed, but they encouraged us not to initiate anything, just to wait.

And at the last minute, an invitation came. Melania had prepared for the big day with her team. She wanted to give Michelle a gift and asked us about it. We checked and found that it was not part of the tradition, per se, but it had been done a few times in the past. Melania gave her gift out of kindness, and it was later reported that Michelle could have treated this gesture better.

At the beginning of the week, Tom Barrack wanted to host a dinner and invite all 172 foreign ambassadors in DC. Such a dinner had never been done. Although the ambassadors have always been invited to different official events, nothing of this magnitude had ever been envisioned.

It was planned for a Monday evening. It would be unifying and grand. Everyone seemed to think it was a great idea, but the Obama State Department gave us *such* a difficult time. We wanted to send the invitations from the Inaugural Committee, and the State Department insisted it should go through them.

"Protocol," they said. After that, they even demanded to have their own people—Obama appointees included. That's where we put our foot down and rejected the requirement. After all, they were on their way out and had no business there anymore.

The American presidency is built on traditions every step of the way. These rituals are perhaps to symbolize its power, both domestically and overseas. As with all governments, especially the more established ones, traditions are meant to display and even perpetuate the idea of grandeur.

Instead of displaying armaments like Russia does every May 1, America prefers other gestures of power. American shows of grandeur include ceremonies with presidents who follow inaugural rites of passage. It takes four years to plan for each presidential inauguration, because there are about a dozen main traditions that must be completed by the time the ceremonies come to an end and the president takes the oath of office. That culmination of that tradition is acted out in front of the public and televised live— the president-elect, with one hand on the Bible. It is upon taking that oath that the political transubstantiation of sorts occurs, and the president-elect actually becomes POTUS, the President of the United States of America. And he swears on the Bible—still the sacred book of the United States of America—because, to date, in spite of the huge cultural diversity in the United States, there has never been a non-Christian president. So far!

People don't know how much work goes into each inauguration: at the time I am writing this book, in 2019, there is already a committee working on the 2021 inauguration, without knowing who the president will be. It is a big process, with so many details, celebrating our democracy.

One thing I didn't quite anticipate was all the talk about why we included fewer celebrities at the Trump inauguration. Names were thrown around and rumors flew. President-elect Trump really felt it was the celebration of the American people, and following his instructions, we didn't make the attendance of celebrities the highest priority.

Yet several talks did take place. For decades now, there's been a growing debate between politicians and their campaign teams—how important is it to get the support of celebrities? Traditionally, celebrities from Hollywood, famous musicians, and known sports figures were asked to voice their support for different politicians. Sometimes the celebrities obliged happily. Other times, they were hesitant that the getting tangled in endorsements might cause them to lose some of their fans.

In the past, presidential candidate John F. Kennedy enjoyed the support of Frank Sinatra, who recruited his friends from the Rat Pack, like Dean Martin, Sammy Davis Jr., Peter Lawford, and others. Sinatra even adapted his song "High Hopes" for Kennedy's campaign. And you could argue that those endorsements worked.

When you look at more recent history, the first celebrity endorsement that comes to mind is Oprah Winfrey. When Oprah told Larry King, in an interview, that Obama had her full, active, support, her fans listened. She had a popular daily show, and her interactive fan club bought books and shopped for items following her recommendations. Many people would go on to attribute the amazing victory of an unknown senator from Illinois—the first American black president—to that pivotal moment when

Oprah announced she was backing him. Some estimate that she brought in around one million voters for Obama!

But the relationship between celebrity and a presidential hopeful is not always so straightforward. When Hollywood A-listers like Robert De Niro and Gwyneth Paltrow endorsed Democrat candidate Al Gore in 2000, it did not help him to win. So maybe the Oprah advantage was not her celebrity status so much as it was her giving him access to a massive media platform.

These considerations became even more relevant during the 2016 elections. Hillary Clinton enjoyed the support of Hollywood elite: Steven Spielberg, George Clooney, Katy Perry, Beyoncé, and Jay-Z were only a few names who campaigned, hosted fund-raisers, and threw their full support behind her.

Some Republicans got a bit concerned. Others wondered whether liking an album by Beyoncé or a movie with George Clooney had anything to do with a person's vote. Another argument of the past was that celebrities bring media—period. Well, in 2016, this time it was a celebrity who was running for president. Donald Trump occupied the media cycle from the moment he glided down the escalator at the Trump Tower and announced he was running for president.

Trump would manage to turn a disadvantage into an advantage, a perceived weakness into a strength. I can think of a perfect example of this when, only a few days before the primaries started, Donald stood alone on a stage. "Hillary has Beyoncé, Jay-Z, Katy Perry," he told the big crowd, "and I am here *alone*, asking for your vote."

The crowd exploded with excitement.

———————

Of course, there were celebrities who wanted to be involved. As I said before, in the prepolitical life of Donald Trump, he had always had a long list of rich and famous friends. And for the inauguration, there were early contacts with his old friend Elton John, but we kept all these conversations confidential, sharing them only with members of the financial committee of the inauguration.

It was Thanksgiving Day when I suddenly got a call from Tom Barrack. Trump was on the other line, and he was furious. Apparently, a member of the financial committee, Anthony Scaramucci, appeared on TV and dropped Elton John's name as one of the celebrities who would perform. At that point, nothing was finalized. Even Elton's team did not know if he was available for the dates that we had given. Trump was livid, and rightfully so.

From there, we were put into an awkward position where we needed to make a statement saying that Elton John had not been asked to perform. And we needed to do this *before* his people could say that he refused for whatever reason. It was very unfortunate.

Even though he's not an American citizen, Andrea Bocelli really wanted to perform at this celebration of the American democracy. I spoke with his wife, Veronica, and she was also excited, but when Andrea was in New York, rumors about his potential performance started to surface and he received threats—both physical in nature and regarding his career. We were all sad; still Trump was gracious and said that Bocelli should not put himself in this position.

There were also preliminary talks with Kid Rock, and even Taylor Swift. Kid Rock wanted to come, he wanted to perform, but he wanted big money for it. He was willing to accept a reduced fee, but then we started adding up his entourage and expenses. While we appreciated the support, the price tag helped us reach a decision: the cost and all this drama were just not worth it.

We had been collectively trying to figure out who would sing the national anthem when Jackie Evancho, a young classical singer who rose to fame at age ten, came to our attention. During the campaign, she had stated that she was supportive of Trump, and it was an even bigger deal because she had a transgender sister. She was attacked by the media, but her response was that she wanted to support the nominee who she felt would listen. So Tom Barrack and I suggested her name to Trump.

"Oh, terrific," Trump said immediately. "I really like her."

Then—of course—we had to deal with the demands. She wanted to bring something like eighteen people, and we had to say no because we needed to limit hotel rooms, flights, and so on. In the end, she brought her whole family, and I have to say, watching them there supporting her, I understood. It was a big moment for her.

There are few Hollywood stars who could get away with supporting Trump. Thankfully for us, Jon Voight was one of them. Others—I will not mention names—were scared to voice their support. It's no secret that the Hollywood establishment hates Trump, and many conservative-leaning celebrities—James Woods comes immediately to mind—have stated quite openly that their support of Trump has cost them, has turned them into untouchables. Our campaign's relationship with Voight started when he narrated the video for the convention. Laurie Gay, a friend and former business associate of Paul Manafort, had reached out to Voight about it, and once he agreed, I talked with him several times, comparing notes about the video. Of course, we invited him to the convention, and then later, the inauguration, and we even asked him to be the emcee of a dinner at the Library of Congress on the third night.

Trump made an appearance there and thanked him for "being a patriot" and for his strong support. Later on, President Trump would congratulate Jon Voight for his special award at a party held at Mar-a-Lago. Trump would also appoint Voight to the prestigious Kennedy Center's board of trustees.

The Trump kids were also celebrities in their own right, and as such, they had celebrity friends. Don Jr. had good relations with *Duck Dynasty* star Willie Robertson and asked him to speak at the convention. We flew him over and gave him a prime-time spot. Later on, three weeks before the inauguration, Don wanted to bring Willie to a different kind of an inauguration gala—he wanted Robertson to help him host a "hunting" inaugural ball with the National Rifle Association. Don wanted to do it on Saturday night, after the inauguration night, and said he would bring his father. At that point, his father would already be a sitting president. It all sounded a bit crazy to me.

We also knew that the Women's March was planned for that Sunday, and this kind of event, apart from the bad timing and placement, would just make for terrible media. But Don and his friends had already started to work on it, despite the fact that it was going to create a backlash. Tom had to go tell Trump, who immediately told us *not* to go ahead with it.

FOURTEEN

TRUMP WORLD

Each time we went to DC for congressional meetings, or to campaign, we checked in on how the Trump Hotel was progressing. Trump was so passionate about it. That's when I first witnessed his attention for construction details—making sure a pipe got fixed, or a paint had just the right amount of blue. He was really hands-on when it came to the renovation and the look of the hotel.

The Trump Hotel in DC is inside a historic building, the Old Post Office and Clock Tower. It's listed in the National Register of Historic Places. It's a miracle that the building, completed in 1899, has survived, as over the past century it's been threatened with demolition several times. It was used as the city's main general post office until 1914, at the beginning of World War I. Major renovations happened in 1976, and again in 1983, but the modern look of the building is due to Trump. While Trump owns the hotel and the hotel business, he doesn't own the building itself. On February 6, 2012, the Trump Organization won the bid from the

General Services Administration (GSA) to redevelop the building. Many of the bidders felt they deserved this ambitious project, and one of them, BP–Metropolitan Investors, even filed an official complaint against GSA. The group, which included Hilton worldwide, claimed that GSA ignored Trump's past bankruptcies, and too-optimistic predictions.

So instead, a consortium headed by a Trump holding company holds a sixty-year lease on the building and the building itself is still owned by the US government and is leased through the GSA. But the ownership of the building is a technicality, and for all intents and purposes, it is a Trump hotel.

Trump had been planning the DC hotel opening for months—ever since I came aboard the campaign, the date was there. The hotel would open in September 2016, with then GOP candidate Donald Trump and his family cutting the ribbon and dominating headlines. A regular hotel opening would never have got such prime coverage. Trump wanted to highlight that he finished this project earlier than expected and for less cost.

Two months later, Trump would surprise many and win the election. It would be the first time in history that a US president owned a hotel, just a few blocks from the White House. The hotel would attract guests who wanted to bump into members of the Trump family or senior members of the new administration.

At the beginning, Secretary of the Treasury Steve Mnuchin was staying there, with his then fiancée, Louise, while she was renovating their home. Linda McMahon, administrator of the Small Business Administration, also stayed there. Appointed ambassadors chose to stay there, and other movers and shakers chose the Trump Hotel lobby as the place to be seen. The quick popularity of the hotel would generate lawsuits from rivals, claiming that they could not compete with a hotel that is owned by the president, who sometimes comes to dine there, with cheering guests equipped with cameras. Special counsel Robert Mueller, reportedly, would start looking into it, too, on the basis that Trump owning the hotel was in violation of several laws designed to prevent an incumbent president from profiting from his term in office as president because of his status.

Tom Barrack appointed me to be the inauguration deputy chairman. Since I knew the hotel by then, I reached out to Trump's assistant Rhona Graff. I asked about the Trump Hotel for guests and as a venue for events. It is a beautiful hotel and it is close to the White House, so it was a natural choice. Rhona said the hotel had been reserved for the Trump family and friends for the week of the inauguration.

We intended to plan some inaugural events and some non-inaugural events, since the kids had planned to stay there. Actually, I can reveal now that President-elect Donald Trump had planned to stay there, too, but security concerns changed the plans.

The key team that worked with Tom and me on the inauguration started to spend more and more time in DC. Tom was staying at the hotel and since we worked around the clock, I sort of lived there, too. It was convenient. Although most of the publicity and attention is centered around the suites, even the "ordinary" rooms in the Trump Hotel are stylish and luxurious.

In spite of what you might think, even though we have to do a lot of traveling, accommodation isn't automatically part of our employment packages and a lot of the time we have to pay for our accommodation out of our own pockets. Then Boris Epshteyn, who had worked as a senior advisor to the Donald Trump campaign and whom I appointed to be the spokesperson for the inauguration, got us a special discount deal. He reached out to someone and gave us a family and friends' rate. Funny enough, with the discount, it became cheaper than other hotels.

Though we sometimes gathered in the lobby, we preferred to hold more important meetings in the conference rooms downstairs, or in Tom's room. At night we sometimes had drinks with Steve Mnuchin, Linda McMahon, and others who lived there. Tom was an early riser, and Tom and I and Tom's assistant, Mathew, went to the gym regularly. Then we had a morning meeting. Sarah Armstrong (CEO of the inauguration) held a staff meeting at 8:30 a.m. at the GSA building next door to the hotel. Then we scouted different venues and had many meetings outside. In short, the hotel became a mix of a workplace and a temporary home.

Many of Donald Trump's critics have attacked him for spending so many weekends and holidays at his golf properties. They base it on a criticism Trump made while campaigning, talking about Barack Obama vacations. I don't want to get into that debate. What I witnessed was a businessman, running for president, against the odds and against savvy politicians from his own party and then later against a much-better-funded Democrat candidate, *who had been preparing for this race for years.* Being the underdog, he campaigned tirelessly, being in as many states as he could. His energy and hard work amazed us, and he asked that we kept to his grueling schedule as well. He had to, if we were going to win.

Still, not knowing if he would win, Trump continued to micromanage his businesses. It was a lot of pressure on one man. It is a known fact that he likes golfing, and I quickly noticed that whenever he was at one of his golf properties, he suddenly relaxed. Living with Secret Service monitoring his movements 24/7 would be a tough adjustment for anyone, especially for an outdoors-loving personality like Trump. Not to mention that he likes being spontaneous—which is one thing security details hate.

I saw how much he enjoyed visiting his clubs. He felt at home among the members and liked mingling with them. He could destress by playing golf and enjoy a familiar outdoor scene. Even someone who travels as much as Trump takes some comfort in familiarity. So between long stretches of campaigning aggressively around the country, these golf clubs were "home" for him and Melania. He would continue focusing on the campaign and even at the resorts his days were demanding. Yet I felt that, at the same time, he was recharging. It was clear how much he needed it. And I enjoyed being there as well.

Mar-a-Lago is a historical landmark in Palm Beach, Florida. The by-invitation-only club resort comprises 126 rooms, a spa, and other high-end hotel facilities. It was built in 1924 by Marjorie Merriweather Post, who was a cereal company heiress—Chips Ahoy, Bran Flakes, Grape Nuts—yes, *that* Post. Ms. Post had envisioned it as a "Winter White House" and dreamed about state visits there. Upon her death in 1973, she willed Mar-a-Lago to the United States government for that express purpose, but there were not enough funds to maintain the property and the security needed for such a "presidential" use, so the property was returned to the Post Foundation in 1981.

Donald Trump had originally viewed this amazing property much earlier than some people know. He understood its rare potential and fell in love with it. He made a bid but was turned down. Years later, in 1985, Trump returned and got this fantastic property for a bargain price. He then came up with the idea to turn it into a members' club. He had been making media rounds, talking about an initial $100,000 membership fee to join. He floated big names who were considering joining his new club.

Whatever the truth, it would make waves. And Trump knew how to recruit the right wealthy people, in this seasonal high-end town, to join his club. Some members say that they signed for much less the $100,000 and others for as little as $25,000. They joined, paid annual fees, wined and dined. A club was created from scratch! After Trump won the election, the fee jumped up to $200,000. But, to be fair, this was not a lucrative new venture for the new president, as the club had already been established way before 2016.

Mar-a-Lago is a beautiful place, full of golden decorations. When you walk in, the dining area is outdoors. There is a bigger ballroom, for events like weddings and parties, which opens out to a pool and a garden. Trump likes to dine with Melania at the cozy area. Since he became president, he has a routine of going out with golf pals and enjoying a game and a lunch, but dinner-time is always reserved for him and the First Lady. They enjoy a table for two, looking completely at home. While there is a rope around their table, close friends can stop by, if invited. But more than anything, it is their private time every evening.

As it is such a glamorous venue, I could understand how Paul felt so comfortable when he went to see Trump in March 2016. Paul had been used to this high-end lifestyle, and he joined Trump's campaign shortly after. But I was laughing out loud when I heard former national security advisor H. R. McMaster's account about the place.

A top celebrity interviewer hosted cocktails at the Trump Hotel in order to introduce McMaster and Tom Barrack. I had coordinated the meeting from Tom's end and joined them. The interviewer asked McMaster to tell us how he got that job, and the decorated general told us about being summoned to Mar-a-Lago to meet the president after Michael Flynn had been let go. He was under the impression he was coming for one meeting, so he didn't pack anything. The meeting went well but then he was taken by surprise when he was asked to stay overnight and meet the president again the following day. McMaster found himself in this place of golden luxury, with no spare clothes, looking for a toothbrush. The next morning, Trump told McMaster that he was his pick for the NSA post. Trump insisted on announcing it there and then.

Mar-a-Lago had become a "Winter White House" after all, as the late Ms. Post had always wanted. A feat only possible when the owner was elected as the forty-fifth president of the United States.

Right after Trump's surprise victory, members of Mar-a-Lago came in with political suggestions and bids for prestigious posts. Many of the members applied to be ambassadors—an act that was ill-received by the media—but only one Mar-a-Lago member would become one: Robin Bernstein, US ambassador to the Dominican Republic. And she is not one of the "billionaires" the media had been concerned about. The press has reported that Mar-a-Lago is the secret clubhouse for billionaire ambassadors, and yet there is only one. It's still a nice place to stay, though.

———————

Bedminster is a private golf club on Lamington Road in Bedminster, New Jersey. Donald Trump purchased it in 2002, for $35 million, and the thirty-six-hole club was opened in 2004. The members' fees went up to $300,000.

I first went there on the first weekend of June 2016. By then Melania had been going there for most of the summer, since it was where Barron was attending summer camps. She saw it as the family' summer home, so we came for several weekends realizing that Trump needed to be there to recharge if he was going to make it through the grueling summer.

On the first weekend of July, while we were there, we hit an unexpected problem. A scandal emerged about the Star of David. Trump had tweeted a graphic criticizing Hillary. It showed a red, six-pointed star, a wall of cash in the background, and was titled, "Crooked Hillary—Makes History!" The text inside the star graphic read, "Most corrupt candidate ever." It had meant to reference a sheriff's star, but sheriff's stars have small circles at their points and the graphic didn't have these, so it looked like a Star of David and implied that Hillary was part of some sort of Jewish conspiracy. It also didn't help that the phrase "America First" was also misconstrued as anti-Semitic because of its use in World War II. Like every other misstep in the campaign, it became a huge issue.

So Trump was accused of being anti-Semitic, and the accusation mushroomed quickly. Trump tweeted about "dishonest media," then added the following statement: "These false attacks by Hillary Clinton, trying to link the Star of David with a basic star often used by sheriffs who deal with criminals and criminal behavior, showing an inscription that says: 'Crooked Hillary is the most corrupt candidate ever' with anti-Semitism is ridiculous."

The scandal continued. So, we had Jared pen a letter, defending his father-in-law. As I've said, Jared comes from a religious Jewish American family. Ivanka went so far as to convert to Judaism before marrying him, so that, according to Jewish law, all of their children are Jewish too. Usually, we wouldn't have asked Jared to do something so personal, but we needed to put things into perspective. Having worked with Trump, I can say categorically that this allegation that he was being anti-Semitic is so baseless it would be laughable in other circumstances.

Most other weekends in Bedminster were less eventful. It's a beautiful club, one more beautiful property among many. Trump's cottage is next to the pool, and the clubhouse is at the other end. There were dozens of guests in private cottages. Jared and Ivanka have their own cottage there. We each got a guesthouse: Paul, Stephen Miller, and Hope Hicks.

I am quite a good golf player, but I didn't get to play since we were always working. Trump would constantly be meeting people—members, friends—at the club. He was always asking questions, and "getting the feel of the room." He loves it there. Paul and Reince Priebus came to meetings there and it was there that Mike Pence originally came with his family to be interviewed for the position of Trump's running mate.

I accompanied Trump the weekend he was hosting the Pence family, and when we pulled in, we were told that the Pences had already arrived and that Governor Pence was taking a walk, with his daughter, on the golf course. Trump showed his side as a host. He was worried, since it was dark, and it was Pence's first visit to the club. So, he went to settle in, but he assigned me to stay behind, making sure that Pence and his daughter were safe.

I liked the property, but I was always on call. The only luxury I had was the golf attire—I didn't have to wear a formal outfit. We still had a regular schedule: Trump ate by himself at his cottage. He liked time in the early morning for himself, so we started to meet at 9:00 a.m. Also, around 9:00 a.m. he would take club members or guests out. They played the eighteen holes. Trump is a real good player, and he likes good golfers around him. Then we would go to lunch. It was a pretty consistent menu: cheeseburgers, fries.

In the evenings, we went to dinner and Melania joined us. Sometimes he preferred to dine with Melania alone.

I liked going there. I was away from my family on weekends, which was not easy, but I could see how Trump was relaxed there. It was pleasant and we could get things done. We stayed at Trump National Doral Miami—another one of Trump's golf courses—after the RNC convention, on July 27. The golf course is pretty open, and it includes a beautiful clubhouse with another BLT eatery like the one at the Trump International Hotel in DC. That's where we would have dinner. The rooms are sort of classic Florida style. I didn't get the sense that Trump spent a lot of time there, not like Bedminster or Mar-a-Lago.

We had planned to go to Mar-a-Lago, in Palm Beach, but we had to change to Doral, since we had an event with law enforcement in Miami the next morning and Doral was much closer. The DNC convention was going on, so we did a press conference at the Doral club that day. It was shortly after Trump got into a feud with the Gold Star father, Khan, and we were trying to handle the resulting fallout. Trump met with Gold Star families in private. It was a truly emotional meeting. He then showed a donation check he got from a Gold Star family.

We decided to do a press conference and it went well. He was attacking Hillary Clinton and her missing emails. Suddenly I heard him saying, "Russia, if you are listening, I hope you're able to find the 30,000 emails that are missing."

My phone started to ring immediately. I knew what that meant. Reporters went crazy, telling us, "This is sounding treasonous." The statement is ambiguous. You could interpret it as Trump assuming that Russia already has access to the emails and that Trump knows about that fact already.

In my opinion, that is the morning that the Russia collusion theory was born. He set the fire then and there. From that point on, it would prove impossible to control this narrative. I remember this moment vividly. I knew Trump's body language by then. He was joking, but it was out, and we couldn't stop it anymore.

Right afterward we were bombarded by all kinds of articles, investigations, and theories about the change on the RNC platform with regard to our foreign policy about Ukraine. I bet that Trump has worked over this moment at Doral in his mind again and again. I feel, in retrospect, he would think twice before joking like that. But it was done, and after the press conference, Trump felt it was a great success. "I talked with the press for an hour and a half," he told us. "We are getting a lot of coverage."

We sure did.

FIFTEEN

AMERICA FIRST PAC AND THE PLAYERS

T he institution of political action committees is unique to American politics. PACs are not-for-profit, tax-exempt organizations that are designed to influence the selection, nomination, election, appointment, or defeat of political candidates at all levels of government. PACs pool together funds from campaign contributions and donations to support campaigns both for and against candidates as well as to try to push forward legislation. A PAC is an engine for political change.

The PAC is an American phenomenon, and as a person who believes in the American system of politics, the institution has become part of my DNA. I've been involved with many PACs, but my involvement with the America First PAC had a special meaning for me, because I really believed in the Trump revolution. His victory felt like a personal triumph for me. While in Ukraine, I'd grown tired of politics and only did it because it led me to business. I was, in the beginning, equally tired of American politics, of the same old system. I wanted to take it to another level, but prior to Trump, I only knew one way to do politics. Yet, over the many months I was involved in Trump's campaign, I had also learned from a leader how to be lean and mean. Some saw Trump's base as "a movement" and "a revolution." In a way, it was. I felt, like others, that we wanted the revolution to grow. Without entirely realizing it at first, I had become a revolutionary.

———————

Before the inauguration ended, Trump's media director, Brad Parscale, reached out to me. He and Nick Ayers, who was Vice President Mike Pence's top aide, had started the America First PAC to raise money and push the Trump-Pence agenda. It was the brainchild of Jared, and the PAC had three goals: supporting Supreme Court nominees, abolishing Obamacare, and promoting tax cuts. They asked me to be involved in the day-to-day running of it. This was the time when everyone who had worked for the campaign, or helped, tried to get posts inside the administration. Would this be my next venture? I liked this PAC, and I liked its goals.

So I took the position and we hired five people. I had learned from the campaign that it was best to keep it lean and mean. So we were: Brad, Nick, Marty Obst (a businessman close to Pence), and Katrina Pierson (our spokesperson). Brad dealt more with the data, while Nick and Marty brought in some of the initial donors.

We started meeting on a regular basis at the Trump Hotel. It was sort of our headquarters. We began arranging dinners and fund-raisers with Vice President Pence. We needed to get both him and Trump involved early on so that we would attract the donors. Pence got it. Trump got it, too, but naturally, it's difficult to coordinate with a president's schedule, even though we were all dedicated to achieving the goals.

———————

After Trump won and appointed Pence immediately to take over the transition team, Nick became his right hand there as well. Pence trusted him. It was a very powerful position, but Nick also chose to stay outside the administration. He had a company, C5 Creative Consulting, which was buying media. He made lots of money and wanted to continue making money. Being so close to power would be a big factor. Both he and Marty opted to stay outside the administration, but they served as nonpaid advisers to the vice president. That gave them access to the White House and allowed them to benefit from both worlds. Truthfully, I thought it was a wise decision.

But things didn't go as planned. Josh Pitcock, who had served as Pence's chief of staff, stepped down. Some said he was too nice for the job and could not run the VP operation the way a VP operation needed to be run. Pence needed a tough guy to get the job done, so Nick became chief of staff. He took a leave of absence from his company and started to travel with Pence.

My work with America First was intense, but fulfilling, and then the trouble came. In March 2017, an article in the *New York Times* came out reporting that I was still working actively at the White House. The article associated me with Paul and implied that we were still in business together, and in doing that, it suggested that my presence in the White House might give privileged access to Paul's former clients.

It got me so frustrated. Paul had been gone for months. I'd continued working for the Trump campaign and then for the Trump inauguration, way after Paul was let go. I was trying hard to carve my own identity away from Paul, and the results of my work were good. They all knew how hard I had been working. And now, that article. It created problems.

Brad called me and told me not to worry. But then, there was a meeting at the White House about it.

Brad and Nick came back and they both said, "We know you are loyal, but it is a distraction."

I sat with Brad first, then Nick. Nick ultimately made the call. "Why won't you take leave, until this Russian stuff clears up?" he said.

I have been around politics long enough to know that a decision had already been made. It wasn't really Nick's decision; he was just doing the logical thing to protect the president. There was no sense in fighting it. At this point Robert Mueller had not even been appointed, and we all thought the "Russian stuff" would go away soon enough.

So, Katrina worked with me on a press release that basically said that I had been assigned to set the PAC up, and afterward, to move on. At that point I was already working with Tom Barrack and his company, Colony Capital. I liked working with Tom. I tried to make light of it, but somewhere, deep inside, it was very difficult for me to deal with this. My association with Paul kept haunting me, but I felt determined to keep working hard, proving myself, and to overcome it.

Two years later, when Nick would turn down the offer to serve as President Trump's chief of staff, he would head back to America First and run it as a successful tool to win the Trump-Pence ticket in 2020. Nick continues to be involved, behind the scenes, with the America First PAC. It's no secret that Nick wants to race Pence for president in 2024. It is a well-crafted, long-term plan. Nick is smart and knows how to build relationships and achieve goals. Sometimes people see through it, and it brings him enemies, but the bottom line is that he is a savvy operator and will contribute the most for Trump, and ultimately Pence, by going back to the America First PAC, its original structure and its original goals.

SIXTEEN

TRANSITION TEAMS

While there had been great moments and not-so-great moments during the campaign, the Trump transition was altogether a different story. There we learned how to shoot ourselves in the foot as the team of cohorts started to compete among one another.

During the campaign, we had told Trump that he needed a transition team, but he wasn't really into it. "If I win," he said, dismissively, "I will bring the best people in."

That make a lot of sense. That is how a CEO thinks. But things work differently in politics. Setting up a transition team before an election is a powerful signal that the candidate is confident that he or she can win the election. A well-established transition team also affects the Secret Service. There's a lot of paperwork and things that must be worked on in advance to allow the winning candidate to take over as smoothly as possible.

Trump had really felt that if he won, he would come in and change many things, and quickly. He found out later that civil servants are very protective of their territory. It's difficult to replace them, and he never meant to replace all those many positions anyway. So we kept stressing to him the importance of appointing a transition team, just to make life easier for everybody. Even in his dealings with cutthroat business leaders, I don't think Trump was prepared for the entrenched resistance and the laws protecting those already in office from losing their positions, even if they were clearly not doing their job. Ego abounds, everyone is playing the long game, everyone has an agenda. Because of bureaucracy, everything moves with glacial speed. The game is nothing like setting up a business, so Trump could not have foreseen the need for a transition team even though it was absolutely imperative to get the ball rolling long before he wanted to start.

At last, in May, after he had finally nailed the RNC nomination, Trump appointed Governor of New Jersey Chris Christie to lead his presidential transition team. Jared wasn't a fan of Christie, but he let the appointment happen anyway, and as usual, I watched Jared and admired his tact in letting the situation play out. Instead of fighting Christie's appointment from the beginning, Jared moved aside, letting Christie make enemies, as he knew he would.

While Trump and Christie had never been close, they'd known each other for years. They were never close, but they had a relationship. Christie had been one of Trump's fellow candidates in the race for nominee, but Christie didn't have the numbers and withdrew early on in February 2016. When Christie got out of the race, he came and supported Trump at once. For a time, he'd even been considered for the role of Trump's running mate. So Jared knew what he was up against and did not want to pick that fight there and then. Jared knows when to pick his battles.

This position of leading the transition team is super power-ful, and Christie was pleased to have been appointed. If the candidate wins, the one who heads the transition team has a big say in appointing people to desirable positions. Plus, Christie was still under the impression that he would be the next chief of staff if we won. However, back in 2013, an order to close access lanes onto the George Washington Bridge at Fort Lee, New Jersey, had created a scandal—Bridgegate—that did enormous political damage to Christie. Bridgegate was still hanging over Christie like the sword of Damocles, and the ongoing inquiry into the politically motivated bridge closure threw a wrench in his plans. Two of Christie's aides were indicted and testified that they had been responsible for the bridge lane closures, letting Christie off the hook. Unfortunately, one of them was a single mom, and Trump went ballistic that Christie would let her, a single mom, take the blame for a decision that he should have owned.

As Jared had anticipated, Christie created enemies fast. Two of them were powerful in their own right: Senator Jeff Sessions, the first senator to have supported Trump, and therefore got his ear; and Reince Priebus, the chairman of the RNC. They both wanted their own choice of people in key posts. Paul Manafort understood that game well. Though he had been fired from the campaign, as I said before, he was not out. He was still involved behind the scenes. Then we found out that Christie had been promising posts like ambassadorships and other positions to a whole list of people. This was a problem, too.

And then, after we won, the media reported that the transition team was not ready at all and that no serious preparation or legwork had been done. To be fair to Christie, he'd been instructed by Trump not to do much, so he did as he was told. Should he have known better? It was all really bad media, which led Trump to

make a quick decision, replacing Christie with Vice President–
elect Mike Pence.

———————————

From early on, Jared had been interested in foreign policy. During
the campaign, several ambassadors asked to meet with Trump
and Paul, and I sat with Jeff Sessions and Jared and went over
these initial requests. Paul and Jared decided that from then on,
Jared and Jeff Sessions would handle foreign affairs.

Jared's family had made donations to Jewish settlements and
supported Israel. He was following the violence in the Middle East
closely and was aware that people had come to believe that nobody
could ever solve it. After all, several American presidents had
made efforts with varying degrees of success. So, in Jared-fashion,
he got ambitious. Some may see this as arrogant or even ignorant,
but it was his ambition in the first place that had made him believe
that Donald Trump would win the election against all odds.

Trump, because of Jared and Ivanka, and casino owner and
Republican Party donor Sheldon Adelson, became especially
receptive to Jewish values and to Israel. That led ultimately to
moving the US Embassy in Israel from Tel Aviv to Jerusalem in
May 2018.

Jared was an active member of the presidential transition
team, but he didn't take a specific territory to himself. Instead,
he inserted himself wherever he felt he was needed or could add
value. When a candidate's name came up for an ambassador's
post, that's when the jockeying started, and the divisions and fac-
tionalism would form. There were different factions who tried
to put up more of their own people. For example, Steve Bannon
and Jared against Reince Priebus and the RNC. Oh yes, at the

very beginning, Bannon and Jared were aligned. But then things evolved differently.

I met Nick while Paul and I were running the Trump delegates. We had been given three contacts for Governor Pence, who was being considered for Trump's running mate: Steve Hilbert (a businessman who was also close to Trump), Nick Ayers, and Marty Obst.

At that point, Nick had not worked for Pence for that long but had come to Indiana to work for Pence's reelection campaign as governor. He had been involved in several races then, and when Pence announced he was not running for reelection because he was being designated as Trump's pick for vice president, Nick helped Eric Holcomb, who ran instead of Pence and won.

Nick was smart, a quick learner, and became an important political adviser to Pence in no time. Also, like Mike Pence, Nick is religious. They have more in common than meets the eye. Nick had established his political career and name working with Georgia' s Governor Sonny Perdue for several races. He earned a name as a shrewd political operator. I talked with Nick about scheduling the Pence trip to Bedminster to meet Donald and Melania. I told him Trump wanted to play golf. I asked if Pence was a good golf player, since I knew it might affect the weekend. Nick told me Pence was pretty good. When I repeated it to Marty, he laughed and said point blank, "Nick is lying to you. Pence is a horrible golf player!"

So, I briefed Trump that Pence wasn't a great player. After the Pences came and left, Trump told me, "Pence is a horrible golfer."

I said, "Well, I sort of told you—"

Trump cut me off. "He's really a bad player!"

That was my first significant interaction with Nick, but we got along and worked well after Pence was announced as Trump's running mate. We both wanted the Trump-Pence ticket to win. Once Pence was announced as Trump's running mate, we moved the Pence people—Marty, Nick, John Pence (Mike's nephew), an assistant, and members of security—into a suite at Trump Tower. Marty preferred to stay back and operate from headquarters, since he felt he could do more from there. Like Paul, Marty saw hanging back as a way to connect with the growing campaign team and interact with members in person. And like Paul, he felt it was valuable.

Nick was rarely there. He was next to Pence while campaigning, traveling most of the time. The first time Nick had quality time with Donald was during a fund-raising event in Nantucket. Trump and Pence went in one car in the motorcade, while Nick and I were together in another car, after them.

Nick would become closer to Trump much later, months into his presidency, when Nick was appointed as Vice President Pence's chief of staff in July 2017. He made headlines for months, reportedly being considered to take John Kelly's post as White House chief of staff, when relations between President Trump and Kelly suffered more "downs" than "ups." Then, to the media's surprise, and shortly after Trump announced that Kelly was indeed departing at the end of 2018, Nick declined the offer. Trump-style, Ayers announced it on Twitter, saying that he was ending his role as the vice president's chief of staff and returning with his family to Georgia.

I spent a lot of quality time with Nick Ayers, and his move, which took some political experts by surprise, seemed logical to me, even predictable.

SEVENTEEN

BILLIONAIRES AND THEIR WIVES

When Donald Trump started appointing members of his cabinet, the media, as expected, had a heyday. The nicknames were flying: the "Club of Billionaires," the "gold-plated cabinet," among others. And that was even before many learned about the list of candidates to ambassador posts.

There have been millionaires who served the country before. For example, John Kerry, who is married to Teresa Heinz. But there had not been this volume of multimillionaires, let alone billionaires, serving a single administration. How did it happen?

For the voters, and for Donald, his wealth meant success and independence from the usual political players and donors. Because Trump was independently wealthy, his supporters felt that he couldn't be bought. After he won the election, it made sense to Trump to appoint people he knew for important posts and hope that they would do as much good for the country as they had done for themselves and their businesses.

Then there is another theory that cabinet and other governmental posts should reflect our diverse society. That would guarantee that appointees are connected with the people. Many of the
names Trump appointed were not household names. As billionaires or leading businesspeople, they were known only in their
own industries, their own states, and their own communities,
but few people have Trump's gift, or even desire for self-promo-
tion. But now the game had changed, and their appointments
would bring them national exposure, especially since most posts
required Senate confirmation.

Senate confirmation is a grueling, invasive process, which
caused several of the nominees to withdraw their names. Many
of the ones that stayed faced unpleasant moments in the Senate as
well as in media coverage. It was a new territory for them, but they
were willing to pay the price. I would come to know many of the
mega-wealthy players while working for Trump.

Steve Mnuchin was just one of them. Mnuchin had a background as an investment banker, and he came on board and was
quite helpful to the campaign early on. We recruited him as a
finance chair. Nobody had asked him to do something like that
before, and though he had little experience with raising political money, he did not hesitate to jump in. We didn't have the
big-dollar donations. Most donations were small and orchestrated by Brad Parscale. Mnuchin had no impact on these, but
he had great names and contacts in the financial world, which
added a lot of value to our campaign. His demeanor was friendly,
which often proved helpful during a stressful campaign. It was
no secret that Mnuchin wanted to be secretary of the Treasury.
Jamie Dimon from JPMorgan Chase was being considered and
really wanted the position, but the idea of Dimon in that role
upset many who thought he would implement his own policies.

Many people assume that all these guys are fast friends, that they have their hands in each other's pockets. Trump and Dimon had known each other for years and had a mutual respect, but it was only after Trump was elected that they became closer. Steve Bannon considered Dimon as a "globalist," which was a bad thing, as it implied that he wouldn't necessarily put "America first." So Mnuchin resurfaced as a candidate.

Mnuchin is a Yale graduate who worked for Goldman Sachs for years and became the company's chief information officer in 2002. He then founded several hedge funds and sat on boards like Kmart. He was a positive, stable presence on the campaign, and overall, I'd say he earned the position of seventy-seventh secretary of Treasury by working hard.

Carl Icahn was another one who fell into the category of rich friends who got posts. He is the founder and controlling shareholder of Icahn Enterprises, a diversified conglomerate holding company, and he's known Trump for years. Many assumed that he had been there, as a great supporter, since Trump announced his candidacy in 2015. Immediately after the election, Icahn was announced as Special Adviser on Regulatory Reform, an unofficial, unpaid position that was not part of the administration but gave him great access and influence. Some critics accused Icahn of conflicts of interest resulting from his wide-ranging business endeavors, and he eventually stepped down from his role as adviser in August 2017.

What I noticed about some billionaires was that they wanted the influence, if and when Trump was elected. Some got excited by the idea of the possible access, but then often excitement would dissolve into cautiousness. They wanted their own policies to be heard, even though Trump had been campaigning on his own ideas and policies and planned to deliver all of them if he won.

After elections in each state or super primaries, we had a routine of throwing parties for friends and supporters at the Trump Tower. Trump would come down and make a short speech. It was a fun idea. Trump always invited his New York friends, among them billionaires and CEOs of large corporations. I noticed immediately that most of them didn't show. The message I got was clear: doing business or playing golf with him was one thing, but they didn't want to take the risk of associating themselves with some of Trump's policies.

As we got closer to the election and secured the nomination, the ground started to shift. And after Trump surprised many and won, some of these businessmen said, "I was always there for you."

But Trump wasn't blind. We all knew who was really there, and when. He also used donations as a barometer of support. "How much did Carl give us?" he'd ask. "How much did Tom?" Trump knew, as well as anyone, that when it comes to billionaires, money speaks louder than words.

Tom Barrack was on board before the Trump ship left the harbor, but his company was going into a merger, so he needed to be careful. Still, he spoke with Trump often. Paul asked Tom to speak at the convention, and Trump liked it. Tom was the only one who didn't use the podium, but he spoke off the cuff. Like Trump, he knows how to engage an audience through spontaneity.

Tom and Trump went back for years. Tom is a private equity real estate investor and the founder of Colony Capital. They did business together and developed a friendship. He hosted his first fund-raiser at his home in the Brentwood section of Los Angeles on May 25, 2016, at a time that was particularly challenging for us. We'd gotten into a fight with the RNC. Trump had gotten the 1,237 delegates and declared, "If I am going to the fund-raiser all the way to California, the whole money raised there should go to me."

I agreed with him, but I also understood that the RNC needed funds for structural and running costs, among other things. For example, what if we needed a recount? Who was going to fund that? In the end, we agreed to keep all small donations for Trump and allowed the RNC to use the Trump name for raising RNC small donations, then we split the latter between us.

After Trump's victory, Tom was under the impression that he would be very involved in the Middle East. Trump had indicated that he was interested in being the first American president who would really achieve a peace in the Middle East. He had added that his son-in-law, Jared Kushner, was very committed to this goal. For weeks, Tom thought that as an American businessman from a Lebanese background, and someone who did business successfully with some Arab countries, he would be consulted—especially since he and Donald had been friends for so long. Tom had other assumptions, too: involvement in US foreign policy in South America. He even showed interest in being an ambassador to Argentina. Then to Mexico.

But while going through the long vetting process, Tom decided to quietly withdraw. I don't know if it was because his name was mentioned in the media regarding the investigation into his friend Paul Manafort—as it was Tom who initially suggested Paul as campaign manager—or other reports about financial matters regarding the inauguration.

Disillusioned, Tom Barrack decided to lower his profile. He snuffed out the political career that had flamed up so quickly, and the story he told close friends is "I decided to go back and tend to my company."

Jared and Ivanka had reached out to entities like Palantir and Founders Fund, and the venture capitalist and cofounder of PayPal Peter Thiel. Trump and Peter were not close friends yet, so their relationship was mostly the result of Ivanka's efforts. Peter hoped to raise his mainstream profile, and as a supporter of gay rights, he was keen to influence the GOP's position on gay issues. He saw an opportunity to change the party when it came to LGBT people.

Peter was interesting. He was willing to help us on several things. He sat on the Economic Committee, but he was reluctant to be a surrogate. It wasn't that he cared if it was known that he supported Trump, but he is kind of shy, so his speech at the convention was a big success. I gotta hand it to Ivanka!

As a longtime Republican, Thiel had endorsed Ron Paul in the past. He also gave donations to John McCain during his presidential bid in 2008. In 2016, he supported Carly Fiorina, but after she dropped out of the race, he decided to support Trump. He made his mark at the key night in the convention when he said, "And I am proud to be gay." In October 2016, Thiel gave a donation of $1.25 million to the Trump campaign. Why so late? He said that he didn't know it mattered until he was asked by the campaign, so he did it.

Harold Hamm was another successful businessman turned surrogate for Trump. Trump and Harold had a young friendship. Harold was from oil and gas. He was different from the real estate guys. Harold got involved early on in the campaign, and I worked closely with his team. We had a round table in New York, which we called TLC (The Leadership Council). That morning at the Four Seasons, on June 9, 2016, we did a big RNC fund-raiser, which Harold supported, and then the TLC at the Trump Tower, which was executed very well. I was impressed.

After the victory, there were rumors that Hamm was being considered for secretary of energy, but he took himself out of the running before he was offered anything officially. My impression was that he, like others before him, had been flattered. Then the rumors of his possible appointment faded out. Hamm is known for the development of the big shale oil resources of the Bakken Formation. As of January 2018, Harold Hamm's net worth was estimated to be $14.2 billion, making him the seventy-ninth richest person in the United States. In 2012, presidential candidate Mitt Romney named Hamm as his energy adviser. Hamm then made monetary and advisory contributions to Romney's election campaign.

During inauguration week, Kellyanne Conway stopped Harold at the Trump Hotel in DC. "You!" she said. "It was not only about the money you gave, but the advice, the support."

Though Hamm has not landed a cabinet seat or another position, he was invited to Trump's State of the Union, as well as different parties in the White House.

Wilbur Ross is yet another American investor who got involved with the campaign early on, agreeing to serve on the Economic Committee. Paul Manafort and Steve Mnuchin also knew Wilbur well. He spoke on a few occasions, but more behind the scenes. Ross's background was as a banker and investor. He was raised a Democrat and President Bill Clinton appointed him to the board of the US-Russia Investment Fund. In 1998, he donated $2.25 million to the campaign of his then wife, Betsy McCaughey Ross, who was trying to get the Democratic nomination for governor of New York but ultimately failed to do so. Ross was an important name to have attached to the campaign. Right after Trump was elected, he felt he owed two guys: Wilbur Ross and Jeff Sessions. They had come and given their open support to the campaign when others had hesitated.

Wilbur would have taken secretary of the Treasury if he had been offered it, no doubt about it. But because of his age—late seventies—he was offered secretary of commerce, and he was one of the first to accept his position. Then he would have to face a Senate confirmation process, which would prove to be more complicated for him and others. Ross was eventually confirmed successfully, though a few questions about his testimony would continue to linger and occupy the media from time to time.

And then there was Woody Johnson, the great-grandson of Robert Wood Johnson, the cofounder of Johnson & Johnson. Woody, along with his brother Christopher of the New York Jets, has been an important donor in a long line of Republican presidential candidates. In May 2008, at an event for John McCain, he was responsible for the largest amount raised in one evening—$7 million. Then he helped cover some of the $10 million deficit after the convention took place. In 2011, Johnson threw his support toward Romney's 2012 campaign, and in June 2015, he became the financial chairman of Jeb Bush's 2016 presidential campaign. Then in May 2016, Johnson announced he was endorsing Donald Trump.

Trump and Woody Johnson had known each other in New York. It was no secret that Johnson was interested in becoming the US ambassador to the United Kingdom, and it had actually been in the works for years, since he had supported John McCain. Johnson was close to Rick Davis, McCain's confidant. I had worked for Davis, in several capacities, so I was also in the picture. I was under the impression that Johnson would not be interested in any other post, but Donald kept him waiting. He wasn't sure; he wanted to weigh it up longer. Yet Woody raised tons of money and that impressed Trump, and he ultimately nominated him.

Woody checked into the Trump Hotel in DC before the Senate confirmation. He brought his entire family, including his ninety-plus-year-old mother, Betsy. He was nervous before the hearing, and visibly emotional after the Senate committee confirmed him. A longtime dream came true.

Joe Craft and Kelly Knight Craft are a wealthy, prominent couple from Kentucky. Joe Craft is the CEO of Alliance Resource Partners, a big coal producer, and the Crafts were early supporters of Trump.

One day I got a call from Tom Barrack. "What are you hearing about Canada?" he asked. He was talking about the ambassador to Canada role.

I made a phone call and was told: "We are giving it to Randy Evans, a close pal of Newt."

"This is the same Randy Evans who had said Trump will never get enough delegates!" Tom said. "We must stop it. Push Kelly Knight instead."

So I called Mike Pence and asked him if he was okay about Kelly Knight Craft being nominated for the role. I reminded him that she was a loyalist and business-oriented, and Pence said, "I love her!"

Pence spoke with Trump, Tom Barrack spoke with Trump, and he agreed. Kelly had her first political appointment in 2007, when President George W. Bush appointed her as an alternate delegate to the United Nations. There she focused on the US involvement in Africa. In 2016, Kelly and Joe donated millions to several Republican candidates who bid for the nomination for president. They supported Marco Rubio but then hosted a small sit-down dinner at their home for Donald Trump and donated $2 million to the Trump campaign. Kelly was a Trump delegate at the RNC convention in Cleveland on behalf of the state of Kentucky. One of the reasons the couple supported Trump was his policy on coal.

Kelly took the nomination for ambassador seriously and employed a team to help her prepare. During the several weeks of her diplomatic school she stayed at the Trump Hotel in DC, and was ready every morning, with a cup of coffee to go, ready to start another school day. She shared that being humble had never worked for her, and planned to appear before the Senate committee, discussing her accomplishments and experience. She dressed up for the big day—all in red! The committee process was a smooth one. She was confirmed and became the first woman US ambassador to Canada.

Then there was Lewis Isenberg. Lewis cofounded the private equity firm Granite Capital International Group LP and has been a prominent political fund-raiser for years. Lewis was the chairman of the Port Authority of New York and New Jersey, which operated and administered the World Trade Center, on the horrific day of September 11, 2001. Though Lewis had been a longtime party supporter, he wasn't close to Donald Trump. While he didn't interact much with Trump, he raised tons of money. He also worked well with Steve Mnuchin, which mattered to the campaign. I must note that Lewis worked hard.

After the victory, Lewis wanted to be the US ambassador to Italy. Reince Priebus lobbied heavily for Lewis and Steve Mnuchin supported him as well. Tom Barrack joined the effort. Trump was initially hesitant. Someone asked, "How can we send an ambassador who doesn't speak Italian?"

"Why won't we give him Finland?" Trump half-joked. "It's nice in Finland."

But then he came around. Or maybe not? It is typical Trump: he looks like he is opposing someone, but actually he's asking people about him and finding out if he is legit and has enough supporters. In the end, Trump nominated Lewis Eisenberg to be the US ambassador to Italy in July 2017, and his nomination was confirmed the following month.

We heard from a top media exec that Larry Ellison, CEO of Oracle, had hosted lunch at his home for Marco Rubio. He then talked with this exec, stressing how important it was to get Israeli-American philanthropist Miri Adelson behind Rubio as well. Her husband, Sheldon, is the chairman and CEO of the Las Vegas Sands Corporation, a large casino operator. Sheldon had reportedly favored Rubio, but Miri had been leaning toward Ted Cruz. Ellison told the media exec that if the Adelsons supported Cruz he would have to put more money behind Rubio. It was better for them to unite.

The media exec told him she was not going to get involved, since she was supporting Donald Trump. Shortly after her encounter with Adelson, the same media exec visited Miri Adelson in Vegas, and she shared the conversation at Ellison's home, and explained to Miri why they were supporting Trump. She told Miri about how she had known Trump and his family since she had started her TV career in New York, and they talked about Israel as well. It was enough to turn Miri for Trump.

When Sheldon Adelson got involved, he made it clear that he wanted a Republican majority in the Congress, so his money was going into all kinds of PACs. When he eventually came around to Trump, Jared dealt with him a lot, but Trump got involved as well, and Sheldon pledged $200 million for a PAC for Trump.

Of course, pledging is only the first stage. That's when Tom Barrack and Sheldon Adelson had a disagreement. Corey Lewandowski was trying to start a PAC and Steve Mnuchin was starting a PAC. Trump had been fighting against PACs—he didn't want them initially—and we had to explain that we needed much more money in order to win. So, he reluctantly gave in. At that point, everyone was trying to start a PAC and it became an internal fight.

Adelson pledged $200 million, but only to Trump's PAC. The super PAC was formed by May. We asked for some of the donation in advance, but he was committed not only to the Trump

PAC. Then we started to get it in small portions. Then Adelson clarified that the $200 million was the amount covering *all* his donations to various PACs and other organizations for the entire election cycle.

The RNC was being difficult because they were eyeing the same money, so he gave donations to the super PAC, too, but it was different from what some people had understood or hoped for. Then, after the victory, Adelson stepped up and gave $5 million more. He was the largest single donor in the presidential election, with donations in the order of about $40 million in the end. Not an insubstantial sum.

Steve Wynn was another big player. Casino mogul and art collector, he was known to support both Democrats and the Republican Party. In 2008, he supported Barack Obama, but later on criticized some of his economic policies. From 2012, Wynn gave big donations to the Republican Party, and in 2016, he gave $833,000 to joint funding committees of the party. However, he wasn't completely committed to the Trump campaign until the very end. Steve Wynn and Donald Trump had known each other for years. After all, they both owned casinos and they both operated in Las Vegas.

I was in the car with Trump during some of those calls with Steve. He'd say something like, "I am buying a new plane. Who did your design?" Trump was campaigning around the clock, focusing on winning; that was what he cared about at that time, every candidate knows that. So I found these conversations a bit amusing. Wynn was friendly. He always wished Trump good luck but nothing more.

Around the third debate, which took place in Vegas, Wynn gave an interview. He said he was "neutral" regarding the debate's outcome and his support for Trump. At this point, Trump had learned that some of these guys would not support him publicly, but I could see that it still hurt him. After Trump won, Wynn was publicly "in," so Trump decided to appoint Wynn the financial chair of the inauguration. Trump and Wynn had had ups and downs before, and Tom Barrack even brokered a peace meeting at one point.

With Steve, there is never a dull moment. Boris Epshteyn had just been appointed as the communication director of the inauguration, and Tom and I made a conference call with all the vice chairs of the inauguration. There were fifteen of them, including Woody Johnson and Anthony Scaramucci. Steve Wynn's secretary was holding for him to take the call. We were all waiting.

At last, he came to the phone, so we could start. Boris started to make a speech he had prepared for this call, "Let me introduce myself."

"What the fuck is it?" Wynn screamed after two minutes. "I am not supposed to be on this call."

"Well, you are," Tom said calmly. "You are part of this committee."

"Okay," Wynn said, cutting him off. "I will call you later."

He left us all on the line, just like that. I found out later that he thought he was going to have the president-elect on the line. Instead he got Boris. Knowing many wealthy people by now, I knew how they worked: they don't have time for anyone other than the decision makers.

Later on, Trump would support Wynn's appointment as the financial chair of the RNC. That's what Wynn wanted, and that's what he got. Months later there would be headlines about Steve Wynn's alleged cases of sexual misconduct and consequential financial settlements at his hotels. He would step down from his position at the RNC, as well as his own company.

There was also Betsy DeVos. They say that money meets money. Betsy's father, Edgar, founded the Prince Corporation. Her brother Erik Prince, a former U.S. Navy SEAL, made headlines after he founded the controversial Blackwater USA company. Her husband, Dick DeVos, was the CEO of the marketing company Amway, founded by his billionaire father, Richard DeVos. Betsy was the chair of the Michigan Republican Party. She has been a longtime Republican, and was known for favoring school choice, school voucher programs, and charter schools.

At the beginning of the 2016 race, the DeVoses donated to the campaigns of Jeb Bush and Carly Fiorina. Later on, they supported Marco Rubio. Betsy even said in March 2016, "Donald Trump does not represent the Republican Party."

In the Michigan primaries Trump won big-time, so Betsy came around and, with her husband, supported Trump with a donation. Betsy and her brother Erik are super close, and it was Erik who pushed for her to get a cabinet seat. She wanted to be the secretary of education. After Trump announced that he was nominating her for that post, it created big debate between teachers' unions (who opposed her) and those who favored school choice. Her confirmation hearing at the Senate in January 2017 was very heated. Democrats spoke the whole night before the vote. After thirty hours on the Senate floor, the vote took place. Since it was fifty-fifty, Vice President Mike Pence had to come and break the tie and only then did Betsy DeVos become the eleventh United States secretary of education. Later on, DeVos would face protests and would make further headlines about her costly around-the-clock security.

Linda McMahon was another who ended up in the ranks. A super-successful wrestling executive, Linda had been involved in politics for years. In 2009 she left the WWE (World Wrestling Entertainment) and ran for the Republican Senate seat from Connecticut. She lost to Democrat Richard Blumenthal. Then she tried to run for the other Senate seat in 2012 and lost again to Democrat Chris Murphy.

Linda and Vince McMahon have known Donald Trump for years. In 2007, Trump made an appearance at the WrestleMania 23, and Linda and Vince donated $5 million to the Donald J. Trump Foundation, in addition to his fee. In 2016, they donated $6 million to Rebuilding America Now, a super PAC that backed the election of Trump for US president. And then they donated more than a million dollars to Future45, a PAC that sponsored anti–Bernie Sanders ads.

Linda and Vince had stepped out early. They gave millions and hosted a fund-raiser for Trump, and he appreciated it. I observed that he was well aware of who really supported him from the beginning. In December 2016, Trump nominated Linda for the administrator for the Small Business Administration and the nomination was confirmed in January 2017. The position is a really great fit for Linda; after all, she had developed her own small business into a very successful one. When she was offered this cabinet seat, she was very excited. I got to know her during the preparations for the inauguration. We all stayed at the Trump Hotel in DC, and sometimes, in the evening, we would end a long working day with drinks in the lobby: Tom Barrack, Linda, me, and a few others.

Finally, there was Papa Doug Manchester. The 2016 convention of the California GOP (CAGOP) was supposed to be just another convention, featuring top party politicians. It was held in Burlingame at the Hyatt Regency San Francisco Airport and had announced speakers like presidential final candidates Ted Cruz, John Kasich, and Carly Fiorina, who'd already been picked by Cruz to be his running mate, if he won the nomination.

But then the CAGOP chairman, Jim Brulte, with the help of Eric Trump and the same media exec that flipped Miri Adelson, was able to spice things up and bring in candidate Donald Trump. The eleventh-hour announcement that the convention was about to kick off with a Donald Trump lunch made huge waves. The lunch's tickets were sold in minutes and the media rushed to the area where the convention was taking place. And so did liberal demonstrators who tied themselves to each other and blocked the roads to the convention's venue. The police followed at once. The CAGOP convention became "breaking news" on Friday morning, April 29. Frontrunner Donald Trump could not land and then drive to the convention.

While this drama was going on, some big donors and VIPs were sipping wine and waiting to meet and greet Trump. Doug Manchester, aka Papa Doug, was standing beside his wife, who was dressed to impress. Papa Doug is the chairman of the Manchester Financial Group and former publisher of the *San Diego Union-Tribune.* He is a successful developer who is credited with building hotels and office buildings in San Diego. And he was an early supporter of Trump. He and his wife were placed at the lunch with others who were handpicked by the Trump campaign. They were the extra-large donors, or people that the campaign wanted to treat extra nice. The plan had been to allocate private time for them to get to know Trump.

But the demonstrators had other plans for that Friday, and Trump proved his reputation for thinking out of the box. The image of Trump walking over and under fences to reach the hotel where the convention took place replayed in the news all over the country. When at last Trump arrived at the venue, Papa Doug and the few other donors had to settle for a quick photo op.

But that would not be the end of Papa Doug's journey with

Trump. He donated $454,800 to the Trump campaign in 2016, in addition to a $50,000 donation to a Trump-related PAC in 2015. And then, after Trump won, he gave $1 million to the Inaugural Committee, whose chairman was his friend and business associate Tom Barrack. And Papa Doug was rewarded. He was nominated by Trump to be the US ambassador to the Bahamas.

That started colorful stories—accurate or not—at the White House and in State Department corridors. One fantastic story described how Papa Doug was telling friends he was planning to sell the US embassy building in the Bahamas. That was before he was even confirmed by the Senate! Another tale described how he did not know if the Bahamas was an American territory or not. Naturally, if it were a territory like Puerto Rico, the US would not have an embassy there. Rumors were flying that there may be another nominee for this post. Then it was denied. As of the time I'm writing this book, Papa Doug is still a nominee, awaiting a Senate confirmation.

What I witnessed while working for Trump was that these were the people he associated with, played golf with, did business with. They were the people he knew. As a capitalist, he valued successful businesspeople. This is a man who has been flaunting his wealth since he first got media attention. During his early appearances, after he had announced his presidential race, he said, "I am rich. I am very rich." And the crowd cheered. Donald wasn't intimidated and didn't mind keeping a few people waiting as he weighed his decision. He was committed to having a different type of presidency—a better one—and he assumed that his appointees would share his commitment. This logic makes perfect sense on paper, but as we would all come to find out, these processes are more complicated than that.

EIGHTEEN

THE PLEA

On February 22, 2017, 118 days after my life changed, I secluded myself away from the kids for four or five hours. I was working on a letter for family and friends to be sent late that night. Brooks was helping me, while also checking in with the kids. It was tough. I tried to include all the elements we had been living with for months, since I had been indicted. It also gave me an additional chance to look over the arguments one more time, but I knew my final decision. I would plead guilty.

When Brooks and I felt the letter was complete, we asked my lawyer to go over it, and then we sent it to our close circle of family and friends. We wanted them to read it before my plea would hit the news the following morning. Of course, a couple of sentences from the letter were leaked to the media.

Here is the complete letter:

To our friends and family:

Given the news reports from last week, I wanted to

give everyone an update about some events that will occur today. Since the indictment was handed down last October, there has been great pressure on our family, and these last several months have been excruciating. Last weekend there were several news outlets that wrote false and misleading statements concerning my situation. Despite my initial desire to vigorously defend myself, I have had a change of heart. The reality of the present situation, how long this legal process will likely take, the cost, and the circus-like atmosphere of an anticipated trial has led me to this decision. I will better serve my family moving forward by exiting this process. The consequence is the public humiliation, which at this moment seems like a small price to pay for what our children would have to endure otherwise. I am doing this to protect our family from further anguish and believe that ensuring their well-being is first and foremost. This is one of the most difficult decisions that I have ever had to make. Please continue to pray for us, for strength, for perseverance, and for protection. Your love and support will carry us through this difficult time.

That moment to give up fighting came after weeks and weeks of debate. After the initial shock of being charged, I started to think. It was clear to me that the special counsel wanted me to reach an agreement. It was clear that they had thrown all this stuff at me, like claims that others broke the law. While there had been no big deal about it before, they suddenly made the same old claims into huge criminal cases. They threw it at me because they wanted me to plea.

I was not happy with my lawyers at the time. Shanlon Wu and Annemarie McAvoy had represented me ever since

I needed to let my public defender go. I wish I could have kept him. He was so good. My lawyers kept running up bills, and I saw how my situation was getting worse by the day. We started to dispute strategy. Their bills kept coming.

In January 2018, I engaged lawyer Tom Green to represent me. Green is known as a white-collar defense lawyer who negotiated plea deals with federal prosecutors, so the media interpreted that as though I was ready to cut a plea deal. I was not a lawyer, so I just needed to have a lawyer I could trust, that had my best interests in mind and who knew the game.

I would later find out that agreeing to a plea deal is more than meets the eye. It's not just some legal tactic. It's a decision that will mark the rest of your life. Technically, it is just telling the truth, helping to corroborate true, or not-so-true, facts in return for a lesser sentencing. But my family and I would learn that people would make judgments, without understanding the situation. In reality, we would learn that many people would view it as weak. We would find out that some people feel betrayed and develop animosity towards the plea-dealer, because they have no way of knowing what that person is actually saying to the authorities. By the same token, the person who is cooperating, some would say "collaborating," can only guess how others feel about them. Neither side has access to all the truth.

While a decision to fight the charges might be portrayed as brave, the legal process is very costly and long, often lasting years. It can take over your life: your work, your friends, and most important, your family. I talked about it with Brooks and few close people I trusted. I felt more and more frustrated that I could not debate it with people who had worked with me at the Trump campaign or with the Trump inauguration. After all, cutting a plea deal meant I would have to answer many questions about what was going inside these operations. I had no clue what questions, or how many, I would face, but I assumed it would have to do with certain people: President Trump, Jared Kushner, Tom Barrack, and of course, Paul Manafort. I was terrified that President Trump and others would assume I'd turned against them. Betrayal never crossed my mind, but of course I couldn't tell them that.

While I found myself in this very public legal position, because of my proximity to Trump, Kushner, and others, I could not reach out to them any longer. From the moment I was indicted, all communication lines were gone. I'd never felt lonelier. And as I thought and talked about it more, cutting a plea deal had become a more viable option. And there were people who advised me not to sign a plea deal. Friends of Paul pushed me hard. They tried to convince me that I could wait, I could do it in the future. They said I should first fight for the truth, that there were false accusations against me, and the only way to defend myself and my reputation was to fight in court. I knew that *Paul's* friends didn't have my best interests as a priority. Ironically, as I listened to them, my choice was being made. Their arguments were transparent. They were terrified that if I collaborated, I would give true information about Paul and make the cases against him stronger. The whole game of the special counsel was who would plead *first*? By December, we learned that Mike Flynn had already been quietly cooperating with the authorities and had reached a deal. If I decided to do the same, I would become the second senior Trump associate to do it. The rest, the special counsel assumed, would fall into line and reach their own deals.

He was right.

In January 2018, I felt that the pressure was mounting. Being in court takes a toll. Facing a legal battle is draining. I learned that some decisions would be unfavorable toward me. It left me feeling more frustrated and helpless. By then I had begun to realize that fighting the charges would take huge resources, both financially and mentally. I understood that fighting against the US government could be endless and exhausting. Did I have the right to put my children's future in jeopardy? I kept weighing all the pros and cons. I debated until the very last minute.

On February 22, the special counsel slapped additional charges against Paul and me. It was a thirty-two-count indictment, regarding loans that Paul obtained. Again, I understood that one of the purposes of these additional charges was to increase the pressure on both of us. And it did! It added massive pressure on me and my family. And at that point—after 118 days of this—I had already understood that more pressure would be coming, unless I was willing to collaborate. Then and there it became clear that this was the right way.

There were only two factors I considered in the end: my family, and my belief that this would not be the last chapter of my life. The belief that I would come back, learn my lessons, and have another chance to contribute to society. The moment I decided, I felt a sort of relief. It was temporary, since I would face so much, but the pressure of making the decision was lifted.

Despite some reports in the media, my experience was that as much as the special counsel's team wanted me to reach an agreement, they did not let me do it lightly. Although my decision to plea marked their own victory, they walked me through all the steps, explaining the risks and the consequences. They insisted that I understand how much would be required from me. They said I would face tough moments. For example, would I have ever dreamed that I would need to answer questions in court about my private life? Talk about adultery and put my family in such a position? They wanted me to be well aware of the consequences of my decision and talk with my family, especially my wife, about it.

One of the prosecutors told me, "Sometimes cooperating is the worst option."

But the moment I told them of my decision, the atmosphere changed. They were more relaxed and accommodating. The deal we reached was that I would plead guilty to two charges. That was a huge relief down from thirty-two. I must stress again that the two charges I plead guilty to have *nothing* to do with my role working for Donald Trump.

Charge One:
Conspiracy against the United States, for impeding, impairing, obstructing and defeating the lawful govern-

mental functions of a government agency, namely the Justice Department and the Treasury Department.

Charge Two:
Making false statements to the special counsel and the FBI.

It said that in February 2018, I lied to them regarding a meeting that took place in March 2013, with Paul Manafort and an unnamed congressman and an unnamed lobbyist. It would then be revealed that the member of Congress was California representative Dana Rohrabacher and the lobbyist was former member of Congress Vin Weber. Rohrabacher was the chairman of the relevant European Subcommittee. His spokesman said that the congressman had long acknowledged the meeting, and as part of his role, he listened to point of views about Ukraine during this gathering.

The charge said that I failed to disclose that the meeting included discussion about Ukraine. According to the plea deal, I would be facing between four to six years in jail for these two charges. However, the prosecutors would ask the court, following my cooperation, to be lenient.

I take full responsibility for both charges to which I pled guilty. Yet, at the time, did I understand the full picture of pleading guilty to the second charge? Since George Papadopoulos and Mike Flynn had pleaded guilty for lying to the FBI, it seemed like the usual charge one pled, as part of the plea deal with the special counsel. I *did* make a false statement to them. I regret it and decided to change my life when I took the plea. But, did I understand then that some people would label me "liar" from that point on? Did I comprehend at the time how this image would stick to me, tainting everything I had worked so hard to accomplish for our country and for others? How difficult it would be for me to reverse it?

My other concern was how to convey to my former colleagues in the Trump orbit that my decision was dictated by the enormous pressure I had been put under. But the indictment had dropped an iron curtain. A new reality of total isolation and no power to communicate, to fight rumors, to tell my side of the story to the people I'd grown to care about. To let them know that my intention was to answer all the questions I would be asked, provide facts, and in no way throw dirt on President Trump or his campaign. I still feel so privileged to have served him, but there was no way for me to tell him that. I could just imagine how betrayed he felt when the media reported my collaboration, but I had no means to reach out, to explain, to set the record right. It would haunt me for months to come.

Still, close friends responded well to my decision, and my family gave me the support I needed during such a testing time. They witnessed what Brooks and I were going through—the constant shackles of indecision, the cameras outside the house. The fear that if I didn't just give in and take the plea, the charges would keep surfacing, the lawyer bills would keep piling up, the thought of providing for my family again would be a distant memory. I knew that Paul would not support my decision, and indeed, he made a public statement:

I continue to maintain my innocence. I had hoped and expected that my business colleague would have had the strength to continue the battle to prove our innocence. For reasons yet to surface, he chose to do otherwise. This does not alter my commitment to defend myself against the untrue piled up charges contained in the indictments against me.

It was clear that Paul was trying to insult me and portray me as weak, hoping I would be forced to respond to his claims. Ironically, after being convicted in his first trial, Paul would cut a plea deal as well in order to avoid a second trial and reduce his sentence. The special counsel would then claim that Paul broke the deal, by lying to the prosecutors. There would also be reports that Paul's lawyer was sharing information with Rudy Giuliani, Donald Trump's lawyer.

As for me, from the moment I appeared in front of Judge Amy Berman Jackson and declared that I agreed to the deal, I was committed to comply fully. It was such a tough decision, but after my court appearance, when it was done, I was swept with a strange feeling of peace.

I had not felt that way in months. It was as if an ongoing heavy weight were lifted off my shoulders. Or was it only a brief relief?

NINETEEN

THE PRESIDENT'S MEN WHO PLEA

Daphne Barak Writes:

Rick Gates was the second senior Trump aide and third person who decided to cut a plea deal with the special counsel. The first one was George Papadopoulos, whose deal was exposed the day Gates and Paul Manafort were indicted. The second was former National Security Agency director Mike Flynn. Then there were several more who cut complete or partial deals with the special counsel, in order to try to reduce their sentencing, or for other reasons.

Paul Manafort was among them, but the special counsel walked back on his deal, claiming Manafort lied to his team. And then there was Michael Cohen. Though the special counsel gave him good reviews for his collaboration, the Southern New York District did not. Cohen made headlines regarding his transformation from blind loyalty for Donald Trump to hatred and revenge.

Rick Gates observed the 180-degree change of Michael Cohen with amazement.

"I could never see it coming," he said. "And some of the things he said later would be so difficult to digest because of what he had said to me during the campaign."

Rick was never close to Cohen. "We had cordial relations during the campaign. He was obviously close to Trump. He was sitting at the twenty-fifth floor, next to the Trump's children. He sometimes took calls on Trump's behalf."

Rick recalls that Cohen wanted to be involved in the campaign, but the hints he got from Trump was to let Cohen handle the organization and personal matters only.

"So, I was polite to Cohen," Rick said. "But he had no input in my decisions on how to run the campaign. The only area that Michael had input in was the Diversity Council. That was a committee that Michael founded with Pastor Darrell Scott. Its mission was to represent different voices of the communities and support Donald Trump. Michael was very involved in it. It was a good idea. It was in relation to the Diversity Council that were the only times he was on the campaign trail."

During the campaign, Michael Cohen told Rick that he wanted to be the chief of staff if Trump was elected.

"In a way, it made sense to him," Rick said, "because he was sort of a chief of staff of Donald Trump at his headquarters in New York. Of course, he had no clue what the roles of a White House chief of staff were, among them to have good contacts in Washington DC."

"Cohen told me about his ambition few times," Rick remembers. "At the same time, Cory Lewandowski also wanted to be the chief of staff."

So, it was strange for Rick to hear Cohen testifying that he had never wanted any White House position. "Especially, since he was devastated at the Trump Hotel, when he understood at last that it was not going to happen."

Still, Rick says, Tom Barrack put Michael Cohen on the Finance Committee of the inauguration, among several others. Newly elected President Trump still maintained that Cohen was his "personal lawyer." Trump then appointed Cohen to be the deputy finance chair of the RNC, which was a great position. Trump's friend Steve Wynn was appointed to be the finance chair.

Rick is still bewildered about the extreme change of Michael Cohen from the guy who would take a bullet for Trump, into the guy who fires bullets. "I was never friends with him," Rick said. "I did not know him well. It is still a shocking development."

As for the first one who cut the deal—George Papadopoulos— Rick Gates has never met him. "I know that my name was mentioned regarding some emails he sent," Rick said. "But I don't know him. I have never met him. Our paths did not cross. When Paul and I arrived, we added more credible names to the Foreign Committee. So yes, he sent us emails, regarding his ambition to set up a meeting between Trump and Vladimir Putin. I just answered that a very low-level letter could go forward. Nothing more! I remember that Paul was against it as well."

Later, Rick Dearborn, a former White House aide and member of Trump's transition team, told Papadopoulos and others that they were no longer associated with the campaign.

On the other hand, Rick Gates did develop a friendship with Mike Flynn. "I was his point person for the National Security Committee of the Trump campaign. I worked closely with him, Jeff Sessions, General Keith Kellogg. We spent time on the campaign trail. We shared meals. We also spent long hours putting strategy together. I liked his input. Flynn was excited about a Trump presidency! Some said that it was also because Barack Obama had fired him. I saw his chemistry with Trump in real time, and how he believed that Trump would be the president America needed."

Was Rick shocked that Flynn cut a plea deal then? He might have been, except that Rick was facing the same growing pressure and mounting legal bills as Flynn. He also knew firsthand that cutting a plea deal was about telling the truth, answering many questions, which would aid investigations. But it did not mean, as many assumed, turning against Donald Trump. Rick Gates was asked by the special counsel team if he had any valuable information about "Russian collusion" of the Trump campaign, he answered, "There was no Russian collusion."

TWENTY

THE 119TH DAY AND BEYOND

For Rick Gates, deciding to collaborate with the special counsel provided a temporary relief after months of anxiety. A closure after daily debates and questions.

Not so fast.

Rick Gates signed a deal that was supposed to protect him from a long, or hopefully short, jail sentence. Meanwhile, he continued to wear the electronic bracelet on his leg. "Since we protected our children from the whole thing," he told me, "I could not wear shorts for a year until it was taken off at last." And this small freedom would come only after he finished testifying against Paul Manafort. Even so, his passport has remained with the authorities. He could only travel around his home in Richmond, Virginia, and Washington, DC. Any trip outside this area would have to be submitted to the judge's decision.

Judge Amy Berman Jackson let him go with the children to Florida in 2018. Then again in 2019, just before the Mueller report was released. However, she has questioned other requests he has made, so he has learned to ask for less, in order not to be rejected. For instance, when he was flown to New York to collaborate with the investigators there, he wanted to spend a bit more time in the city where he'd lived and where he'd spent so many exciting hours, working for Trump, but he was instructed to return home immediately after he finished answering the questions of the Southern District of New York. It was his first trip to the Big Apple since he had been indicted. Rick was exchanging notes with me about a superb French restaurant he used to dine at. It was not far away from Trump Tower, where he had camped. Michael Cohen was seen at this eatery, after his hotel suite, home, and offices were raided. Rick was probably hoping to visit it again, but that was not granted. This New York visit was just another reality check about how his life has changed ever since October 29, 2017.

And even if the judge had allowed him to stay another night in New York, I doubt that he would dare to make reservations there, under what is now his infamous name. And even more, walk in those glass doors and risk bumping into people—people who would have smiled and waved, maybe tried to buy him coffee, but now might have turned and walked the other way as though Rick were a societal leper. As if somehow by physical proximity they too might be drawn into one of the greatest scandals in American history.

Even in DC, Rick's nature to be in the shadows proved to be an asset in this tough new reality. One day, in between filming our documentary, Rick and I bumped into one of Trump's former campaign aides. This person had tried to reach Rick in the good old days so he could support him for a role in the administration. Rick slipped into the background while the aide and I hugged. I glanced back at Rick, worried the aide would notice, but Rick just blended among the guests at the hotel lobby.

The same thing happened to us again with a former major Trump donor, who had to step down from his RNC post after embarrassing facts emerged in the news. The donor and I exchanged pleasantries, and Rick was a few steps away, unnoticed and invisible again.

———

Rick needed to be available to Mueller's team on short notice. He spent days and days with them, and then with other teams from the Southern District of New York, regarding several ongoing investigations. He was required to be available wherever they wanted, whenever they wanted, and for however many days they needed him. These long hours required him to be on his toes. The barrage of questions, circling him over and over again, meant he had to be careful that, in his exhaustion, he did not to slip. He could not even give one, small, inaccurate detail. After pleading guilty to lying to the FBI, he had to be very careful.

Pleading guilty for lying under oath had seemed like a technical detail, a formality of the plea deal. And Rick only did it after two other witnesses, General Mike Flynn and George Papadopoulos had already pleaded guilty for lying under oath. So, at the time, it looked to him simply as the way the special counsel was dealing with plea deals. The first time the "liar" label hit him hard was during his testimony. He had not given enough thought to the consequences. The many ripples that would follow once the cold stone of admission—"I am a liar"—had been dropped.

At his trial, Manafort's lawyers did their job, portraying Rick—their client's former partner and the prosecutors' top witness—as a fraud. They attacked his credibility, claiming that he was not only a liar by his own admission as part of his plea deal, and with their line of questioning, they tried to show that Rick Gates had been lying for years. Besides accusing him of embezzling money from several of Manafort's bank accounts, they went into his private life and revealed a bombshell: Rick Gates had been leading a double life. While he had a wife and children in Richmond, he also had up to four mistresses in London.

Nobody knew that this devastating information did not come from the lawyers' own extensive research. Manafort's lawyers might have made headlines outside the court, but they did not surprise Rick. This private and deeply personal information was handed to them by the government, and it had come straight from Rick's own mouth. As part of his plea deal, Rick had had to sit for days with the special counsel's people and bare his soul. He had to tell them anything he had done against the law. If he had missed something that they knew, he would forfeit the deal. That is how he was caught lying about late-night contacts with Russian operator Konstantin Kilimnik. He was then forced to plea for lying under oath, and he learned a hard lesson. Rick needed also to share embarrassing information about his private life, anything the defendant's lawyers might have been able to find out about on their own and use it to tear down his testimony. So, he voluntarily shared the information about his past adultery with the prosecutors. He had not realized that his most private admissions would be repeated by his former patron's lawyers again and again. Naturally, they were fighting for their client, Paul. And Paul felt betrayed by his former partner. It was fair game. Everybody there was in a fight for their lives.

"I had already come clean to Brooks," Rick told me later, "about my extramarital relations in 2009. We dealt with it. I decided then to change my life. Brooks and my children are the most important thing in my life . . . so Brooks had already known about it. But just imagine how she felt, when it became so public, and Paul's lawyers kept repeating it over and over."

As they did that, Rick's anger grew. The trial was, of course, the first time Paul and Rick had met face-to-face since Rick had cut the plea deal, and the court became like a stage in ancient Rome: two gladiators fighting for their lives, bleeding for the audience's entertainment. While some would focus on the hatred on all sides, I choose to focus on one word: "humility." For someone like Rick Gates, who had been interacting with movers and shakers in the United States and overseas, being cut off was a big shock. Suddenly, for the first time in decades, his phone was silent.

Pleading guilty would get rid of millions of dollars in legal bills. However, agreeing to the dance—taking orders and subjecting himself to inquisition with no end in sight—has taken its toll. Finding a job has proven impossible. While it had been easy to get work before the indictment, due to his international and US contacts, Rick could no longer call on anyone. His coveted Rolodex—filled with the private contact information of some of the most influential people in the United States—had suddenly became meaningless. There were also financial insecurities created by the plea: Would he ever be able to get a job again? To provide for his family?

The 2018 midterm elections was a big day in America. For Rick Gates, it was more personal than ever. Contrary to any opinions that he was now against Trump because he had taken the plea, Rick's attitude was completely the opposite. He was still rooting for Donald. Many had predicted that the Republicans would lose their majority in Congress. For Donald Trump, it was a critical time. He knew that if the Democrats won Congress, they would open up several investigations into the Russian interference in the elections, the Trump Organization, the

Trump inauguration, and even his tax returns. We were filming with Rick that day in DC. I felt it was a key day to film. I sensed that the following day, after the midterm elections, might include drastic changes. And while the Republicans won the Senate, the Democrats did indeed win the Congress.

The next morning, while politicians and different commentators were digesting the news, we continued to film with Rick. Suddenly he got a disturbing phone call from his wife, Brooks. She sounded scared. A female FBI agent had knocked on the door and walked into his house. She presented her ID and asked to check the home. The woman said she was checking to see if Rick was complying with the terms of his plea deal. She also added that she knew that Rick was in DC.

After the surprise visit ended, Brooks rushed to call her husband. That was the first time something like that had happened since Rick reached his plea deal. Brooks was alone that morning, which made her feel vulnerable. On the other hand, she was relieved that her children were not home. The three younger ones were successfully kept out of their father's public ordeal. How on earth could she have explained a stranger going through things at their home?

Later that day, in a memorable press conference, President Trump acknowledged that the Congress was now in the control of the Democrats. We would also learn later in the day that Attorney General Jeff Sessions had been fired that morning.

The Rick Gates I have witnessed during these crucial months has moved between two extremes. The first was a cloud of denial. Stories broke with his name and photo splashed all over it; he simply turned away, not watching or reading it. Instead he threw himself into his family life, drove the kids to their activities, helped with their homework, coached them in sports. Then at other times, he would follow the other legal court cases closely, trying to understand what his sentencing day would look like. He was slowly becoming more and more nervous. Though he was spending days with the special counsel's team and the team from the Southern District of New York and doing his best to comply with all of their demands, he started to realize that there were no guarantees in the deal. Taking responsibility for his past crimes, coming clean about his sins, and helping the different investigations could get him a positive review from the special counsel. In the best scenario possible, Robert Mueller's team would ask for no jail time.

Rick would learn that every trial the prosecutors asked him to testify in brought him more credit. He had already been the star witness against Paul Manafort. Then came the big sentencing day for Mike Flynn on December 18, 2018. Everyone—from the media to politicians and influencers—was tuned in. But for Rick, it was personal. It could be an indication of what would happen to him on his sentencing day. Rick had been the second significant Trump top aide to get a plea deal with the special counsel. Both men collaborated with investigators and met all requests. Like many, Rick expected the retired general to walk into the court, take responsibility, show remorse, and get a light sentencing without actual jail time as a reward to him for meeting all his obligations according to the plea deal. Rick was so sure about that outcome that he was not even glued to the news like others.

Mike Flynn arrived at court accompanied by members of his family. Even the president was watching. "Good luck today in court to General Michael Flynn," Trump tweeted. "Will be interesting to see what he has to say, despite tremendous pressure being put on him, about Russian Collusion in our great and, obviously, highly successful political campaign." The president added: "There was no Collusion!"

US district judge Emmet Sullivan was expected to sentence the retired army lieutenant general who had pleaded guilty to lying about his contact with former Russian ambassador to the US Sergey Kislyak. The special counsel's office praised Flynn's collaboration. They also added that since he was the first senior aide to make the plea deal, it made it easier to get others to follow him. What better reviews can one ask for?

But Judge Sullivan had a different agenda. Just before the hearing, Flynn's lawyers did something that irritated the judge. In their filing, they claimed that the FBI had set the general up when they came to question him at the White House and when he was the national security adviser to the president. According to the lawyers, their client was encouraged not to have a lawyer present during the questioning. They added that the FBI agents did not alert their client that lying to them is a federal crime. In addition, the agents failed to inform Flynn that his answers were not consistent with the information they already had and that had prevented Flynn from correcting his answers there and then.

The special counsel countered Flynn's lawyers. Judge Sullivan interpreted it that Flynn was trying to have it both ways. On the one hand, Flynn was avoiding jail in return for pleading guilty, and on the other, Flynn was trying to say that even though he had pleaded guilty to lying, he had not lied. He had been set up.

Judge Sullivan made Flynn go back on the claims made by his lawyers. He made him stand there and say humbly that he had no complaints against the FBI and how he was treated. The judge insisted that Flynn accept full responsibility for pleading guilty. He made Flynn say that he was not a victim. He made him say it loud and clear several times. He then scolded Flynn, telling him he was disgusted by his behavior, shocking the general by adding: "You arguably sold your country out." Judge Sullivan managed to surprise the prosecutors by asking them if Flynn had committed treason. They rushed to Flynn's defense.

The result: the judge told the visibly shaken general that if he insisted on getting a sentence that very day, he could not guarantee that he would not get jail time, despite the special counsel's recommendation! He told Flynn to continue helping the several investigations. Flynn agreed, and the judge postponed his sentencing to March 2019.

Rick was as surprised as Flynn. "You mean Flynn—a decorated general who collaborated and did everything Mueller's team asked for—would get more time in jail than the twelve days George Papadopoulos got?" It was a true moment of revelation for Rick, the realization that whatever he did to comply fully with his plea deal and to get good reviews from the special counsel, there was still no guarantee that he would not serve jail time. His fate was in the hands of one person: Judge Amy Berman Jackson. The same judge who was presiding over the cases of Paul Manafort and Roger Stone.

He started to question himself. Is it better to postpone the sentencing and be available for all kinds of extra investigations and trials, while living with so much restriction? "Good behavior" provides more credits, but then again, how long can that credit last? And what if—after living inside a metaphorical jail for years—he could still face time in a federal prison? Or, is it better to face the music sooner, hoping for a light sentence, and get back his freedom (and society) thereafter? Rick would find himself once again torn in opposite directions: to ask for immediate sentencing, or, to postpone it? The same process that had been tormenting him for the 118 days before the plea deal was still going on.

Rick closely followed the sentencing of Michael Cohen, Paul
Manafort, and of course, the colorful court appearances of Roger
Stone. Roger Stone has always liked making headlines. Even
after his much-anticipated indictment, he challenged the judge's
patience by giving interviews outside her court, imitating the
famous Richard Nixon V-sign with his stretched arms. The media
played along. After all, how often do they have such a colorful
player facing serious charges?

The judge did not easily fall for Stone's provocations. Only
after Stone had been testing her for a while did she issue a partial
gag order. It told him not to make comments about his case outside the court. It was not that difficult to follow, but it seemed difficult for Stone. He shocked legal minds by posting a picture on
Instagram with Judge Amy Berman Jackson and what seemed to
be crosshairs next to her head.

Though his lawyer filed a notice apologizing about the
"improper" posting and Stone took it down, the judge scheduled a
special hearing. Many debated if she would put him in jail, while
waiting for his trial. Rick Gates was following it closely. He naturally disagreed with Stone's behavior, and he wanted to learn
everything he could about the judge who would sentence him.
Judge Amy Berman Jackson had been appointed by President
Obama to the post of the Judge of the US District Court for the
District of Columbia in 2011. So, Rick felt—as did Manafort and
Stone, I'm sure—that she would not side with them, because of the
roles they played in the victory of Donald Trump. Jackson scolded
Stone for his conduct. No, she did not buy his explanation that a
volunteer had posted her photo without Stone's permission.

"I have serious doubts about whether you learned anything at all," Jackson said. "From this moment on, the defendant may not speak publicly about this case—period. No statements about the case on TV, radio, print reporters, or internet. No posts on social media. [You] may not comment on the case through surrogates. You may send out emails about donating to the Roger Stone defense fund."

But she did not put him in jail. Then Roger would put her patience through another test. Though his gag order had become much more restrictive, she was as surprised as others to learn that Stone was promoting his new book. It was a rerelease of his old book, which described special counsel Robert Mueller as "crooked."

Right after her more limiting gag order, she found out that a publisher started selling copies of Stone's book with a new introduction, which attacked Mueller. Still, as much as she might have wanted to rip into Stone, she did not send him to jail. Instead, she gave him a stern warning, that all his actions were being closely watched by her.

Rick Gates had to admit that the judge was practicing extraordinary restraint when it came to Roger Stone. Then came the Paul Manafort sentencing by Judge Jackson. It followed a relatively light sentencing given by Judge T. S. Ellis III, in Virginia. Ellis gave Manafort only forty-seven months in jail, surprising many people by stating that other than these charges, Paul Manafort had led "blameless life." He then added that Manafort failed to show true remorse for his wrongdoing.

Rick was focused on Manafort's next sentencing by Judge Amy Berman Jackson. Many expected her sentencing to be much harsher than Ellis's. Judge Jackson acknowledged the different expectations people had, but she said that her sentencing would not be influenced by the other one, days earlier, in a different court. She then sentenced Paul Manafort. The two sentences together would become ninety months in jail. However, she decided that some of her sentence would be served concurrently with Ellis's sentence. Altogether, it added up to seven and a half years in jail. Since Paul Manafort had reached a plea deal with the special counsel after his first trial in Virginia, part of his plea deal was that he could not appeal his sentences. Later, the special counsel canceled the plea deal, accusing Manafort of lying to his team.

To the casual observer, it might seem that these kinds of deals are one-sided. The prosecutors can take them back any time, if they have reasons to believe the other side did not comply, while the other side is committed to the deal, and has no option of changing their mind. Rick was watching it so closely—Judge Jackson's every word about Manafort was meaningful to him, indicative of what his own fate.

On Friday, March 22, 2019, all US news organizations were on a standby. Special counsel Robert Mueller was about to submit his much-anticipated report.

Rick had sensed, for a while, that the ordeal was coming to an end. On Friday afternoon, the media learned that the report was indeed submitted to Attorney General William Barr. The media continued to be on standby for a glimpse of the lengthy and long-anticipated report provided by Barr. And Barr would decide what to release after reading it. The details of the methods of the report's release would create big battles in a Congress ruled by Democrats who had been demanding that the whole report become public immediately. President Trump and some Republicans also stated that they would like it to have been made public immediately and in full.

After one year, ten months, and six days, the report was delivered. After almost two hundred charges against more than thirty people, it was finished. In short, special counsel Robert Mueller's investigation into Russian interference in the 2016 United States elections stated: "The special counsel's investigation did not find that the Trump campaign or anyone associated with it conspired or coordinated with Russia in its efforts to influence the 2016 U.S. presidential election."

End of the road? Not really. Some investigations in other state courts would continue, being originated by the Mueller report. Lives would be interrupted for years to come

———————

Saturday, March 23, the day after the report was released to Barr, Rick Gates got a telephone call that shocked him. Since Mueller had completed his assignment, Rick was transferred to the authority of the US attorney for the District of Columbia.

He was speechless. He did not know what it meant legally. The deal he had cut was with the special counsel and his team. He had developed working relations with some of the team. Suddenly there was a new team. Would they respect his deal? Who would give positive reviews about him to Judge Jackson when his sentencing day came? It felt like the Mueller team had just skipped town, leaving some people, like Rick, on the street.

Where do we go from here?

Since I have been interviewing Rick and writing this book, I have encountered a new reality: ever since these plea deals were signed, no one connected to these matters—whether you are a president, a former associate, or a friend—can talk, listen, or do anything without thinking it through at least seven times in advance. If one wants to send a goodwill message to a friend, who opted to collaborate to protect his or her family, it could be perceived as an obstruction of justice. Then, if you don't, the "other side" might believe the rumors that a wall of hatred has been built between them. If Rick, or anyone in his position, wanted to do what would seem natural in other circumstances and reach out to, let's say, the president or one of his trusted people to convey that his plea is not about taking sides, he couldn't. Such minimal human contact is not allowed, let alone sharing any details, resulting in a sort of emotional exile.

History might yet reveal an increasingly lonely and isolated president, who has been betrayed by former campaign aides and work associates. Trump has since learned that he's been taped without his knowledge, surrounded by endless leaks. Aside from the many books written by associates about him, President Trump has also faced a mounting number of collaborators with the Mueller investigation and other related inquiries. One can only imagine how he feels each time he learns about someone new, someone who was once close to him is now collaborating. Without the ability to know what the circumstances were that led these people to reach this decision, it could result in anything from disappointment up to an increasing reluctance to trust people ever again.

For many of the players involved, what is most frustrating is the lack of a clear timeline. An unending purgatory of questions and all must be answered. Most programs we engage in life have defined schedules, so we can plan ahead. It is part of our human nature to want to see the end while we are in the middle of a journey, especially when the journey is not so pleasant. Yet here, for Rick's journey, it has seemed as though there's no timeline whatsoever. No end in sight.

And then again.

On Monday, April 15, 2019, the Department of Justice announced that Mueller's report would be released on Thursday, April 18, just in time for an Easter reading. As reported by AP News on April 15, 2019: "The president isn't waiting. As Washington counts down the final hours until publication of the redacted special counsel report—now expected Thursday—Donald Trump stepped up his attacks in an effort to undermine potential disclosures on Russia, his 2016 campaign and the aftermath.

"He unleashed a series of tweets Monday focusing on the previously released summary of special counsel Robert Mueller's conclusions—including a crucial one on obstruction of justice that Trump again misrepresented—produced by Attorney General William Barr.

"Mueller, and the A.G. based on Mueller findings (and great intelligence), have already ruled No Collusion, No Obstruction," Trump tweeted. "These were crimes committed by Crooked Hillary, the DNC, Dirty Cops and others! INVESTIGATE THE INVESTIGATORS!"

Press Secretary Sarah Sanders repeatedly tried to make the same case on TV talk shows. Democrats called for Mueller himself to testify. The House Judiciary Committee, led by Representative Jerry Nadler of New York, has been poised to try to compel Barr to turn over an unredacted copy as well as the report's underlying investigative files.

Mueller officially concluded his investigation in late March and submitted the confidential report to Barr. Two days later, on March 24, the attorney general sent Congress a four-page letter that detailed Mueller's "principal conclusions." In his letter, Barr said the special counsel did not find a criminal conspiracy between Russia and Trump associates during the campaign.

However, Mueller did not reach a conclusion on whether Trump obstructed justice. Instead, Mueller presented evidence on both sides of that question. Barr said he did not believe the evidence was sufficient to prove that Trump had obstructed justice, but he noted that Mueller's team did not exonerate the president.

Portions of the report being released by the Justice Department will be redacted to protect grand jury material, sensitive intelligence, matters that could affect ongoing investigations, and damage to the privacy rights of third parties, the attorney general has said. The scores of outstanding questions about the investigation have not stopped the president and his allies from declaring victory.

The president's surrogates have claimed the House Democrat investigations as partisan overreach and have targeted news outlets and individual reporters they say have promoted the collusion story. The president himself seethed at a political rally that the whole thing was an attempt "to tear up the fabric of our great democracy." He has told confidants in recent days that he was certain the full report would back up his claims of vindication but was also convinced the media would manipulate the findings in an effort to damage him, according to two Republicans close to the White House not authorized to speak publicly about private conversations. In the waiting of the final days, both sides were competing to shape the narrative.

"There was no obstruction, which I don't how you can interpret that any other way than total exoneration," Press Secretary Sanders said on *Fox News Sunday*. While the president unleashed his personal grievances, his team seized on any exculpatory information in Barr's letter, hoping to define the conversation in advance, according to White House officials and outside advisers who spoke on condition of anonymity because they were not authorized to publicly discuss private deliberations.

The victory lap was deliberately premature, they said. But Trump's inner circle knew there will likely be further releases of embarrassing or politically damaging information. Barr's letter, for instance, hinted that there would be at least one unknown action by the president that Mueller examined as a possible act of obstruction. A number of White House aides have privately said they are eager for all Russia stories, good or bad, to fade from the headlines. And there are fears among some presidential confidants that the rush to spike the football in celebration could backfire if bombshell new information emerges.

Trump and his allies also continued to attack the origins of the Russia investigation, portraying it as an effort by Democrats and career officials in the Justice Department to bring him down.

"The Mueller Report, which was written by 18 Angry Democrats who also happen to be Trump Haters (and Clinton Supporters), should have focused on the people who SPIED on my 2016 Campaign, and others who fabricated the whole Russia Hoax. That is, never forget, the crime," Trump tweeted.

His long-asserted accusation—though not supported by evidence—that his campaign was spied upon was given new life when, in April, Barr said in his testimony before Congress that he thought "spying did occur" in 2016. Barr may have been referring to a surveillance warrant the FBI obtained in the fall of 2016 to monitor the communications of former Trump campaign aide Carter Page, who has not been charged with any wrongdoing. The warrant was obtained after Page had left the campaign and was renewed several times. Critics of the Russia investigation have emphasized the fact that the warrant application cited Democraticfunded opposition research, done by a former British spy, into the Trump campaign's ties to Russia.

Barr later softened his tone. "I am not saying improper surveillance occurred," he said. "I am saying I am concerned about it and I am looking into it."

The attorney general's comments have frustrated Democrats, already anxious for the release of the full, uncensored report and concerned that Barr may withhold pertinent information. The report could provide new information that could prompt further investigations or even consideration of impeachment proceedings, a tricky political calculation since Mueller did not conclude there was collusion or obstruction.

TWENTY-ONE

INSIDE THE MUELLER INVESTIGATIONS

When Rick first reported to the special counsel's office, he did not know what to expect. It was an office space next to the river in DC, which featured a semi-dirty-looking carpet and a bunch of old furniture. Everything screamed temporary, but Rick had no idea how temporary. How long would his new chapter last? Would the degree of his collaboration have any input in the timeline?

As he wandered into the office, he bumped into Robert Mueller. Here, in front of him, the name who had cast such a shadow over his life, that scary name behind his indictment, his mounting charges was here, incarnate. The person Rick and his loved ones had been terrified of around the clock. Rick expected to feel angry, finally meeting the man who'd turned his life upside down, but instead he felt empty and unprepared.

"I found him to be older than I thought," Rick said. "Not as tall as I had imagined. And a bit . . . frail."

The dramatic tension ended and the internal dialogue in Rick's head ceased when Robert Mueller glanced at Rick quickly and murmured, "Good morning."

The word "jail" is frightening. Yet Rick would learn that sleeping in his own bed, spending precious time with his wife and children, would be only a part of his new reality. The best part, as he would come to find out that he was owned by the Mueller team and the other investigations they were initiating. He was a ward in their custody, at their disposal 24/7. Being notified the evening before, he would have to drive two hours from his home to their offices and be available to them for hours and hours.

How many hours?

"At one point, we counted four hundred and fifty hours," Rick said. "Then we stopped counting. It is much more by now."

And it's not just the time. It's the intense questions and answers where Rick could not slip. Not make a slight error. There is irony in this narrative: while Mueller charged several of his key witnesses of "lying to the FBI," he was then relying on the accounts of the same "convicted liars" to put his conclusions together. He stigmatized their characters, but then went on to base his much-anticipated report on their testimonies.

It was brutally cruel for Rick to testify against his former mentor, boss, and partner, but that was the key part of the deal he cut. Rick was cast into the role of "the nail in the Paul's coffin." If he had emotional moments, he would be reminded that he was in a tough game of "reward or punishment." Despite his expectations, his electronic bracelet was not removed, after he signed the plea deal. The prosecutors insisted that he would have to wear it through his testimony in court, facing Manafort. It was the carrot of freedom dangled before him, to be removed only after he "successfully" completed his testimony against Manafort.

Even after the long months, Rick and his wife, Brooks, had still not shared what he was going through with their youngest children. So he would have to wear long trousers in the sweaty heat of Richmond, to disguise his bracelet from his kids. The pressure on him to testify "successfully" against Manafort was a daily horror, and the bracelet was a humiliating reminder of what was to come.

Then later, more relaxed investigators came in and posed a trap. Rick kept reminding himself that this new coziness was not about developing new friendships, but it was a tactic, a means of getting him to do what they wanted. From day one—before, during, and after he reached a plea deal—his answer was the same: "There was no Russia collusion. No, I am not aware of any Russian collusion."

The question was repeated again and again in different ways, by different people, but Rick stuck to his answer: "It was the truth, and after I agreed to the plea deal, I could not lie. I needed to tell the truth. Of course, I knew that they were hoping I would point a finger to some Russian collusion. The closer to Trump, the better. But I told the truth: There was not. Even if they had broken me down, and I spouted lies, I would need to prove them. There was no way to prove Russian collusion, because there was none I witnessed."

It went on for a while, but then, around the beginning of summer 2018, it stopped. All of the sudden, they stopped asking Rick about Russian collusion and began to drift to different topics. It was clear to Rick: they knew! They had concluded there was no Russian collusion that early on. Rick kept watching commentators arguing possibilities of "Russian collusion" with conviction on the different TV shows. He wanted to scream: "They already know! There was NO RUSSIAN COLLUSION!" But obviously, he couldn't call anyone or say that to anyone other than Mueller's people.

He wondered when people would find out and demand, "Why weren't we told?"

Knowing that the investigation had moved from its original key mandate, "collusion," into additional areas was even more upsetting to Rick, as though the questions could continue to spiral into infinity. He continued to support Donald Trump. "They are looking for anything they can find. No collusion? So, they are looking for anything else, even if it has nothing to do with Trump. Just to press people in his orbit."

Rick became increasingly frustrated, since he could not share the questions and the names of the people they were asking about. The investigation was expanding from Russian collusion to something more. Some people thought that had nothing to do with what he believed Robert Mueller had been appointed to do. But what could he do besides continue answering questions about wider topics, more and more names, and try to score "credits" so Mueller and his team would recommend a reduced sentence, and, hopefully, no jail time?

Yet there is a light in the midst of this dark cloud: by collaborating, Rick feels strongly that instead of the negative connotation of "flipping," he has actually helped some of the people he has been questioned about. How?

"By telling the truth and ruling out some theories."

For example, the investigators were looking at wrongdoing regarding the "Victory Fund." They suggested some narratives.

But Rick said, "No, it did not happen."

They tried again, and he repeated the truth: "no." Some names who are close to President Trump's former campaign and the 2020 campaign were mentioned. Senior names. Rick insisted that he could not corroborate the different theories about these "targets."

"People don't know, but by collaborating and telling the truth, I helped certain people to avoid charges. Because there was no basis to charge them."

The ongoing questioning by investigators' teams included exchanges like:

Investigators: Trump of course knew about so-and-so.

Rick: No, I did not witness such a thing.

He needed to repeat it again and again, since there were different teams as part of Mueller's special interviews. One was more focused on Jared Kushner, another on Don Jr., another on Paul Manafort. Rick understood the idea behind it: this was how details did not leak to the press, and therefore, could not affect the different investigations. Each team reported their findings to Robert Mueller. So there was only a handful of people who were seeing the full picture.

The need to be totally transparent was another tough adjustment. Rick and the others in his position lost any right to privacy. After signing the plea deal, he needed to give his computer to the investigators. Paul Manafort's computers supplied so much information, going years back. Rick was shocked to be confronted by old emails he had forgotten all about.

"From the moment, you sign the deal, you are required to share EVERYTHING."

That would explain later why Mike Flynn had to share certain voice mails left on his lawyer's phone. Choice was taken away from Rick Gates, Mike Flynn, and others the moment they signed their plea deals. It explains why Flynn had to testify—even if he didn't want to—about several topics like WikiLeaks.

While there were other "big fish" like Flynn testifying regarding communication with Russians or WikiLeaks, Rick was the "big catch" when it came to investigating the inauguration. He was, after all, the deputy of Trump's close friend Tom Barrack, the chairman of the inauguration.

So he faced many questions regarding certain donors. The Mueller team was looking for foreign donations, even if disguised well, through domestic channels. Foreign donations are legally prohibited to be given in any form to political campaigns. That includes the inauguration.

Rick was asked about several names. One of them I can reveal, since a subpoena served on the inaugural committee in February 2019 was reported in the media. It demanded the committee would turn over any records or documents that had to do with donations, VIP invitations, photo ops, and other potential rewards. The only name mentioned in this subpoena was Imaad Zuberi and his California-based company Avenue Ventures. Zuberi had previously given substantial donations to the Clintons and Barack Obama. After Trump won in 2016, Zuberi started to donate to committees associated with Trump and the Republican Party. The donation that got the attention of the investigators was given by Zuberi's company to the Inaugural Committee, in the amount of $900,000. The Southern District of New York was investigating this and other financial matters around the inauguration, and Rick observed, that they behaved as if they had gotten a big lead. He had no clue. As a political veteran operator, he was used to donors jumping on board after a newly crowned leader. This is part of the game. And of course, invitations to VIP inaugural events or photo ops with the new president and members of cabinet are part of the traditional political scene.

Moreover, Zuberi is an American citizen, so Rick had no reason to question him.

"It was not up to us, to vet the donors," Rick said. "We had no means to do that. We simply got them from the RNC. We assumed they had vetted them."

The situation became even more odd. Rick, who could not share what he was testifying about, was with me in DC when he got a panicked call from a White House aide. When an item or a name like Zuberi or others leaked to the press, there was nobody around to comment. The current aides at the White House had no part in or knowledge of the inauguration. The committee spokesperson, Boris Epshteyn, had left the White House long ago and now worked in the private sector. The committee chairman, Tom Barrack, went back to focus on his private business.

So, I was witnessing this bizarre telephone conversation between Rick and a White House aide, thinking again and again, who is left to answer the press inquiries on behalf of the Trump inauguration?

By now we know about one case, the investigation pointed out as "a foreign donation." Sam Patton reached a plea deal with the special counsel and pleaded guilty for soliciting an American citizen to receive money from a foreigner and purchase four tickets for the inauguration for the foreigner.

Yet we don't know about many questions regarding other prominent foreign players. The investigations tried to establish if there was a "give-and-take" between people connected to the Trump inauguration and foreign prominent players. One of them is a very wealthy Saudi who owns hotels, real estate, and oil refineries in other countries in Africa, Europe, and the Middle East. The investigators found out that the wealthy Saudi was invited to the candlelight dinner event where then President-elect Trump, Vice President–elect Pence, and their wives took part. It was a desirable VIP invitation, but the Saudi billionaire did not attend the event! In fact, he would be one of the many billionaires who were held by the Saudi crown prince Mohammad bin Salman at the Ritz-Carlton under claims of corruption after President Trump's visit there in summer 2017. The Saudi was released from his captivity at the Ritz hotel, and has been negotiating his "exit deal" from this situation with the Saudi authorities. One of his wives resides in the United States and he is hoping to be able to visit her, after his situation is cleared.

Still, his name was brought up by the investigators. One would wonder, what kind of give-and-take could occur if the Saudi never showed up to the inaugural events in 2017?

Here comes an answer: intent. The investigators were working hard to find out if there might be any hidden—direct or indirect—intent, behind an invitation, even if the guest simply declined it.

Yes, in addition to foreign accounts, questions were asked about domestic donors as well: was there any kind of rewarding for heavy donors, such as appointing them as ambassadors, or other prestige posts?

Rick needed to answer all questions to the best of his knowledge, focusing on mere facts. However, wasn't it one of the basic rules of politics that supporters and donors got enviable positions? Exclusive invitations? Why would the "deep pockets" give so much to a candidate, let alone an elected official, unless it was to advance their financial interests, and yes, their vanities included? This is how it's been done since the dawn of George Washington. Were the investigation teams trying to reinvent the wheel of politics?

Rick did not even bother to point out that he was just using the donations received to produce the best inauguration events he could. He was definitely in no powerful position to reward any donor with an administration post. In fact, though he put his curriculum vitae into the transition team's system, he never made it himself into the administration.

Rick admits that during the days working on the inauguration, people were drunk with sudden power. He was asked to deliver invitations, to push people into posts. Until he had to use his own somber judgment. Sounds like basic instinct today. Yet, not back then, right after the surprising victory of Donald Trump.

In May 2019, we learned that Stephen Calk, a former CEO of Federal Savings Bank, had been indicted on charges that he authorized millions of dollars in loans to Paul Manafort, and in return, Manafort promised to secure him a high-level government job. Manafort received around $16 million in loans, in three different installments between 2016 and 2017.

Part of the original charges against Rick Gates had specified how he was submitting fraudulent papers to help his boss receive these big loans after the millions from the Ukraine had dried up. The loans were so big for such a small bank. It was almost impossible to explain how Manafort's requests had gone through, unless the bank, or someone with authority there, had a good reason to do it. These charges against Rick were dropped as part of his plea deal.

Rick recalls helping at the beginning, but when Paul asked him to talk with Jared and help Calk get the secretary of the army, Rick thought it went too far. "Ridiculous," he said.

Persistent, Manafort sent his friend's papers directly to Jared on November 30, 2016. The subject of his email: "3 Recommendations for Major Appointments."

But Calk did not get the post.

Why was this extra effort made by the Mueller investigation to dig into the inauguration? Rick associates it with two people who had been close to Donald and Melania, but then had a falling-out. Two separate two friendships that soured, both unrelated to each other.

One was Michael Cohen, Trump's one-time fixer. A self-appointed Ray Donovan who used threats with f- and s-words to protect his boss from just about anybody. The other one was Stephanie Winston Wolkoff.

Only a few days after the Trump inauguration, the new First Lady, Melania Trump, announced her first hire. That is when the name Stephanie Winston Wolkoff became known to American people outside the narrow elite fashion circles. She was appointed as an unpaid adviser to Melania Trump. Her role sounded nice, patriotic even . . . until her previous payments would come to light a year later.

Stephanie seemed to embrace her powerful position and started to plan agendas for Melania. She also made statements to the press on behalf of the very private boss who was still coping with a very public new reality. To be fair, Stephanie did try to position Melania Trump as a serious advocate for some important issues. She even vouched on her behalf to keep Michelle Obama's vegetable garden at the White House.

"Don't underestimate her just because she is quiet and reserved," she told *DuJour* magazine. She continued to say that Melania Trump was not about "Hear me, see me, but she's very confident in her viewpoint."

Melania and Stephanie were the same age. Both fashionable women. It looked like a friendship made in heaven. Stephanie had come across like a savvy woman whom the new First Lady could rely on. Until she was not.

In February 2018, the *New York Times* exposed that Wolkoff's company, WIS Media Partners, was paid $25.8 million by Trump's Inaugural Committee, and Stephanie Winston Wolkoff's company was the biggest single vendor.

With the Trump Inaugural Committee raising $106.8 million—twice as much as Barack Obama's—and Tom Barrack's well-intended early statements to make donations out of this huge amount, Stephanie Winston Wolkoff's incredible compensation was becoming a story. Her friendship with Melania Trump pushed it to the front pages, and shortly after, she was terminated from her nonpaid yet highly visible position at the White House.

On May 2019, she reflected back to the *New York Times*: "Did I personally receive $26 million or $1.6 million? No. Was I thrown under the bus? Yes."

Yet until this "coming out" in the media, Stephanie was lying low, becoming more and more bitter. As these nonscripted events often happen, she started to talk with another Trump close confidant who had same hurt feelings, Michael Cohen. The former lawyer was taping many calls, Stephanie's included. That is how their bitter exchanges were shared with the FBI, after the famous raid on Michael Cohen's New York office, home, and suite at the Regency hotel.

The next step was easily predicted. The US attorney for the Southern District signed off on a grand jury subpoena demanding documents from Wolkoff, as well as a personal appearance. It was all related to her work for the inaugural committee. Stephanie did cooperate fully. If she was upset about this development, she hid it perfectly. Some people inside the Trump orbit perceived it as "sweet revenge."

The Wolkoff-Cohen alliance seemed like a twisted match made in heaven. At no point did the two confidants of the first couple bother to acknowledge how much they benefited from their former friendship: lucrative financial deals, high-end invitations, rare access. Rick felt that some investigators were convinced they had the perfect "duo Deep Throats."

Not so fast. And all of the sudden, there were emails surfing in the media about how Stephanie had alerted Ivanka Trump, Rick Gates, and others that the Trump International Hotel in DC was overcharging for space and events during the inauguration. These emails, from 2016, were suddenly displayed elsewhere. Rick recalls that there were legitimate questions about Stephanie's huge fees and conduct, but nobody dared to ask them out loud, since it was known that Stephanie was close to Melania. Or maybe he was thinking loudly: *Stephanie made sure people knew?*

Rick was also upset that only partial emails leaked, the parts that made Stephanie look good, concerned about how to cut costs and handle public funds. Rick's full replies were not disclosed. Rick had also already realized that a couple of the leaks were out there to embarrass the First Lady. And she was embarrassed, even though there was no reason for her to be. But she felt so deeply betrayed.

And then there was nothing more in the media about it. It came and went.

One day Rick was asked to take a trip to New York and meet a Southern District team there. He had already collaborated with them in DC, but this time they wanted him to come to their offices. Since he was not allowed to leave his jurisdiction without the Mueller team and a judge signing for it, he agreed. The idea of seeing New York, where he used to live, work, dine, and hang out, was inviting. It would give him a taste of the not-so-long-ago good old days.

The evening Rick arrived in New York was a cold, icy reminder about how his life had changed in such a short period. He was booked in a cheap hotel. Though he was longing to visit one of the upscale eateries he had frequented, he could not. The risk of being recognized would have brought questions he could not answer, and conversations he was not allowed to have. He also needed to be focused for the long investigation the following day. And if he had planned to relax after hours of questioning, his request was denied. He was booked on the next flight back, after he finished delivering the goods. On board the plane, as he was lifted up from the city, Rick started to question himself. How much strength was left in him and for how much longer would he need it?

And then came the biggest test of all. Brooks, who had been his rock through all this ordeal, was not feeling well. A series of medical tests confirmed the worst: she was diagnosed with breast cancer. While it was caught relatively early, Rick had to calm his three youngest children, and shield them from more bad news. Their eldest daughter was becoming more and more of an adult, so they shared heavy emotional stuff with her.

Meanwhile, Rick and Brooks were meeting with different doctors, seeking the best options offered to them. They were desperate to get the latest opinions from the best experts before deciding on a course of action. Rick was connected to a world-renowned oncologist through a friend. The specialist was based in California and suggested introducing Rick to specialist expert from a different hospital. Rick was encouraged. He and Brooks needed this hope. So, he asked permission to fly to California to meet the doctor.

His request was denied. While it would have gotten other people angry beyond words, Rick was sort of passive. "At the beginning of all this," he explained, "I asked simple things which had to do with continuing being there for our four children . . . normal activities like camping . . . when I was first told no, I was shocked, angry, upset. Then I learnt not to ask, even if it was important for my family."

He was allowed to take the children for a couple of vacations in Florida. Yes, after hundreds and hundreds of hours of answering questions, testifying viciously against his ex-boss and mentor, and agreeing to testify in at least another trial.

While trying to reach the right decision regarding Brooks, he continued to deal daily with the Mueller team and the other investigations it had triggered. The news about Mueller writing his report and concluding his long investigation came right as Rick and Brooks were preparing for her surgery. A tough physical and emotional process for a mother of four who is hoping she chose the right treatment to beat cancer.

Mueller submitted his much-anticipated report to Attorney General William Barr on Friday, March 22. While the attorney general was going over the 448 pages, Rick and Brooks were preparing for her surgery, which was scheduled for the following week. Both of their anxious families were focusing on Brooks's well-being and praying for a successful operation.

Suddenly Rick was shaken. Rick learned that since Mueller had just finished his report, he was transferred to the district attorney of the Columbia District. While the news occupied just one sentence in the full cycle news that weekend, for Rick, it was almost a breaking point. After building some relations with the Mueller team for months, his fate was, all of the sudden, put in the hands of people he didn't know.

Rick was filled with new scary questions.

Were they obliged to respect Robert Mueller's recommendation regarding crediting him for his full collaboration?

And what if, as Brooks had warned him, he wanted to argue about the content of Mueller's letter about him? Who would have the authority to consider any change?

Rick said, "Brooks told me, 'Mueller is gone. If we need to argue, there is nobody left.'"

Rick put all fears aside for the day of his wife's operation. "Family members are with me at the hospital," he told himself. "It is all about Brooks."

After a successful operation, the focus went back to the ongoing cloud hovering above this family. The pressure was on Rick to testify in as many trials where he could possibly be helpful. That promised him more credits, but it also meant he continued to be in the custody of the authorities: a district attorney instead of Robert Mueller. And it also meant he would continue to be without a passport, restricted to a limited area around his home, with no possibility to get a job or resume his life. And there was no guarantee that the judge would spare him jail time, even if he continued to score more and more and more credits.

Rick was getting into another crucial junction in his life: to take a risk and face sentencing now? Or to continue collaborating until . . . ?

He had already agreed to testify at the trial of Greg Craig, a former Barack Obama associate who was charged with failing to register as a foreign lobbyist while defending Ukraine president Viktor Yanukovych's jailing of a political opponent in 2012.

The trial, scheduled for August 12, 2019, was being held in the court of Judge Amy Berman Jackson. Yes, the same judge who was presiding over the cases of Rick Gates, Paul Manafort, and Roger Stone.

As Rick told close friends, "The message is clear. I should testify." Yet he wasn't quite sure about testifying at the upcoming

Roger Stone trial. "Roger's trial may go on and on," he said. "Then he may appeal."

The Robert Mueller report discusses Stone's conduct and mentions other names like Jerome Corsi, a birther conspiracy theorist. Corsi had announced to everybody who cared to listen that he was refusing a plea deal from the special counsel. "They can put me in prison for the rest of my life," he had said. "I am not going to sign a lie."

Some parts in the Mueller report that refer to Stone have been redacted due to his upcoming trial. Rick had questions about some remarks, and overall, he felt uncomfortable about it. Especially about Corsi: How had he provoked the special counsel publicly and yet seemed to do just fine? Was there anything else going there?

It was not an avenue Rick wanted to take. It just felt bad. And his family had gone through a lot. They were nearing the finish line.

There was still one important document missing in the puzzle: Robert Mueller's letter. Every plea deal is based on collaboration and rewards. The person who signs a plea deal is frankly trying to please his master, the district attorney, or in this case the special counsel, by providing as many as truthful facts as possible.

During this process, Rick felt he'd helped other former colleagues and friends avoid the same nightmare he was going through by telling the truth on their behalf. However, brutal as it may sound, the people who sign plea deals took the best (or only) option they could, in order to get the reward at the end of this painful ordeal. They usually learn whether they are rewarded or not when the master submits his or her letter to the judge. In this case, it was Robert Mueller.

Rick and his family were anxious to know what Mueller had written about him to the judge. After all, the letter was already written. Mueller finished his investigation and returned to the private sector, but the government is still asking Rick to continue collaborating in another trial, then another.

The special counsel or a district attorney do not have to show such a letter to the person whose fate is depending on it. However, since they were pressuring Rick to go on living inside this suffocating cloud, he asked to see it, or at least to know its content. That would enable him and his loved ones to make a decision: to go to sentencing now? Or continue to collaborate until indefinitely.

Rick's request was never denied. He was never told no.

So, did he see it? As of August 2019—no.

They showed good intentions that it would happen. It just didn't. He was kept under the impression that it was coming.

"As frustrated as I am," he said, "I have learned to be so humble, so patient, during this experience."

Yet he was about to decide. Another of Hamlet's crucial decisions.

Meanwhile, the political campaigns for 2020 started to heat up. Rick, a savvy political operator, would have probably found himself back in the ranks of President Trump or one of the other Republican candidates for Senate or Congress. Yet as bad as black humor can get, he found himself being hit by more legal actions and headlines.

In June 2019, Congressman Adam Schiff, chairman of the House Intelligence Committee, made headlines when he decided to subpoena the two key witnesses of the Mueller team: Mike Flynn and Rick Gates. Schiff has been interested in Rick for a while. He had mentioned his name early on, before his indictment. He has noted that though Paul Manafort was fired by the Trump campaign in August 2016, Rick Gates continued to be a part of it, later to become the second person running the inauguration committee. Schiff made a strong public statement about it: "As part of our oversight work, the House Intelligence Committee is continuing to examine the deep counterintelligence concerns raised in special counsel Mueller's report, and that requires speaking directly with the fact witnesses. Both Michael Flynn and Rick Gates were critical witnesses for special counsel Mueller's investigation, but so far have refused to cooperate fully with Congress.

"That's simply unacceptable. The American people, and the Congress, deserve to hear directly from these two critical witnesses. We hope these witnesses come to recognize their cooperation as being with the United States, not merely the Department of Justice."

Adam Schiff also sent a personal letter to both Flynn and Gates. In the letter accompanying the subpoena to Gates, he says:

> Because you have declined to comply voluntarily with the Committee's requests for documents and testimony, the Committee has no choice but to compel the production of the specified documents and your testimony through the attached subpoena. In light of your ongoing cooperation with the U.S. Department of Justice and the fact that you have already testified publicly under oath concerning your own criminal conduct, it is unfortunate that you are unwilling to cooperate with the Committee. While the Committee understands that your cooperation agreement with the Department of Justice only requires you to testify for the Department, the Committee is disappointed that you do not view your cooperation more broadly as an obligation to assist the United States of America, and not merely the Department of Justice.

Now Rick was facing yet another legal decision. "I am discussing it with my lawyers," he said.

Naturally, he did not want to play into Democrat Adam Schiff's hands. He was supporting Donald Trump for 2020, and he understood how testimonies by him and Flynn could be played by the Democrats in such an upcoming presidential race. Also each time, one testifies in front of Congress, the other side would try hard to find "perjury under oath."

Yet he did not want to be held by Congress in contempt! Still, facing a judge who would sentence him played a card. A judge may find that ignoring a subpoena goes against the credits he had worked so hard to earn.

By now the feeling was all too familiar. The premonition, the red flags. Though Schiff's committee was officially investigating intelligence matters, Rick was quick to notice that their interest went way behind Russian interference or other intelligence-related topics. "They are asking about a wide range of topics and names," Rick said.

He was bothered to see his former patron and friend, Tom Barrack mentioned there.

Once again, Rick needed to sharpen his best instincts in order to reach the right conclusion. "Maybe I should take the Fifth?" he asked close friends. But he knew that was a short-term solution with unknown consequences longer term. So, he decided to take it in steps. Start negotiating with Congress about giving them documents they had asked for.

And while this drama was unfolding, there came another surprise. "This one, I did not see coming," said Rick, visibly shaken. Any strong words used by his friends were too weak to describe his feeling of deep shock in assessing how the latest turn of events affected him.

On June 21, 2019, the *New York Times* broke startling news: Andrew Weissmann, a leading prosecutor on special counsel Robert Mueller's team, signed a book deal with Random House to write about his work. The media reports that followed the *New York Times* raised the fact that though Weissmann was not a household name, he was among the most senior people who served under Mueller, investigating possible criminal conduct by President Donald Trump, Paul Manafort, and others.

Rick, like other people who'd been collaborating with Mueller, was told not to reveal anything while the investigation was ongoing, and even after it was concluded, not to reveal things that might interfere with other ongoing investigations. Mueller and his team demanded their silence. In fact, Paul Manafort reached a plea deal with the special counsel (which was then walked back by the counsel), where among many properties and bank accounts he surrendered, he also agreed not to write a book. Mueller and his team were paid by taxpayers. It is beyond unusual that a senior member of the team would benefit and write a "tell all" from inside the job that the American people entrusted him to do, without prejudice, self-interest, and benefit.

So Rick had new concerns to worry about. What would the new author reveal when it comes to him? How much would he reveal? It was clear to him, as to his family and friends, that the publishing house was probably promised some juicy stuff. Who does it involve? Is it even allowed? Why has nobody seen it coming? Did Mueller know of Weissmann's literary ambitions while they were investigating?

He felt so violated. His team tried to get some answers. The one they got from Weissmann's side was as calming as an Ambien: *The book is not from inside the investigation. It's about Andrew Weissmann's career and life.*

Rick did not have the energy to laugh, or fight. He had other issues and needed to choose his battles wisely. The most important was Brooks's recovery, supporting her through the chemo, taking the children to her parents' farm, so they would be distracted. And, of course, engaging in a delicate dance with the district attorney about reading "that Mueller letter." That piece of paper filed sometime in the recent past and would very likely determine his future.

EPILOGUE

So, how will the ongoing assault on the Trump presidency continue to affect the lives of the people entangled in it all?

Should their lives continue to be restricted indefinitely? Does the punishment fit their crimes? Will they have to wait until *all* investigations and related court cases are done? And what if there are appeals? Should these collaborators remain silent about what they know and what they don't? Should they be forced to continue avoiding contact with ex-friends and associates? Their only sounding boards being members of family and daily check-ins with their lawyers? For months? Years?

Since Democrats now hold the House, there is a good chance that more investigations into Donald Trump's campaign, inauguration, business deals, family, and all aspects of his life will be questioned. Who will be the ultimate authority to tell them that it's over? These are all reasonable questions, but does anybody have clear-cut answers to them?

Rick and others associated with Trump whose lives were interrupted so cruelly will have to put the pieces of their lives back together slowly, gently, carefully, and painfully.

APPENDIX

EXTRACTS FROM THE MUELLER REPORT

t was Thursday, March 21. Rumors were circulating that Robert Mueller was to submit his much-anticipated report to Attorney General William Barr at any minute. Journalists and media executives were put on standby. The public, likewise, sat in front of their TVs and waited.

But for Rick Gates, it was just another day. He went about his various household chores; he drove his children to their activities and helped with homework. As in other times throughout his ordeal, he made a choice: he would put his emotions on hold while the drama played out in real time. Not that he didn't care. Of course he did. He and his loved ones wanted this saga to be over. The submission of the report meant an end to his active collaboration as part of his plea deal with Mueller. Mueller would finish his job and return to the private sector, and Rick, having met his obligations to Mueller and the team, would be sentenced and resume his life, right?

Wrong!

The Mueller report was submitted on Friday, March 22, 2019. Another day passed before William Barr produced his own summary to the public. Members of the media positioned themselves toward the release of the 448-page report, salivating, until the redacted version came several weeks after that. All the while, Democrats and Republicans feuded: Republicans claimed the report exonerated Donald Trump, while Democrats argued the opposite. Clearly some Democrats had put all of their hopes into this one basket, envisioning that even apathetic voters would be swept up in the juicy tales of espionage, Russian spies, international manipulations. And yet, when the report finally came, it was like an afternoon shower when everyone had predicted a Category 5 hurricane. Perhaps hopes for the report were so high because of the reputation of the man charged with crafting it. Taking a brief look at the bio of the man who signed the report might explain why he was doomed to fail in the midst of such great expectations.

Robert Swan Mueller III is a decorated Marine Corps officer who earned the Bronze Star and Purple Heart for his service during the Vietnam War. He was famously the director of the Federal Bureau of Investigation (FBI) during the 9/11 terror attack. Though appointed by President George W. Bush in 2001, he continued to serve under President Obama until 2013. A known conservative Republican, Mueller is a dry speaker who uses minimal words when possible. In past public appearances, he's proven himself to be a no-nonsense rule follower. His steady demeanor has been consistent throughout his decades of service to the country, so any expectations by Democrats for a thriller report and an ensuing emotional response belong more to Hollywood than the special counsel.

In fact, Mueller himself would become frustrated that his report would not be read by as many as he had hoped. In a rare press conference, he read a statement that basically sent the media back to his report. He felt it was all there! All the answers were perfectly laid out, awaiting the public's hungry eye. We would also learn that Mueller sent a letter to his boss, William Barr, complaining that Barr's summary takes away from his almost two years of work.

The Department of Justice reported recently that there have been 800 million downloads of the report and copies have been released from three major publishers, making it a literary work in its own right. Still, the report's contents are still largely unknown to many. As this is the historical result of *To Plea or Not to Plea*, I'm including some of it here. These selected portions quote Rick Gates and focus on the Mueller team's attempt to establish if there was any direct correlation between the Trump campaign and WikiLeaks during 2016. The blacked-out redacted passages of the report provide another sort of narrative, and its underlying message is that this bit of history is still unfolding.

b. WikiLeaks First Contact with Guccifer 2.0 and DCLeaks

Shortly after the GRU's first release of stolen documents through dcleaks.com in June 2016, GRU officers also used the DCLeaks persona to contact WikiLeaks about possible coordination in the future release of stolen emails. On June 14, 2016, @dcleaks_ sent a direct message to @WikiLeaks, noting, "You announced your organization was preparing to publish more Hillary's emails. We are ready to support you. We have some sensitive information too, in particular, her financial documents. Let's do it together. What do you think about publishing our info at the same moment? Thank you."[159] ▐ Investigative Technique (IT) ▐

Around the same time, WikiLeaks initiated communications with the GRU persona Guccifer 2.0 shortly after it was used to release documents stolen from the DNC. On June 22, 2016, seven days after Guccifer 2.0's first releases of stolen DNC documents, WikiLeaks used Twitter's direct message function to contact the Guccifer 2.0 Twitter account and suggest that Guccifer 2.0 "[s]end any new material [stolen from the DNC] here for us to review and it will have a much higher impact than what you are doing."[160]

On July 6, 2016, WikiLeaks again contacted Guccifer 2.0 through Twitter's private messaging function, writing, "if you have anything hillary related we want it in the next tweo [sic] days prefable [sic] because the DNC is approaching and she will solidify bernie supporters behind her after." The Guccifer 2.0 persona responded, "ok . . . i see." WikiLeaks also explained, "we think trump has only a 25% chance of winning against hillary so conflict between bernie and hillary is interesting."[161]

c. The GRU's Transfer of Stolen Materials to WikiLeaks

Both the GRU and WikiLeaks sought to hide their communications, which has limited the Office's ability to collect all of the communications between them. Thus, although it is clear that the stolen DNC and Podesta documents were transferred from the GRU to WikiLeaks, ▐ Investigative Technique ▐

The Office was able to identify when the GRU (operating

---

[159] 6/14/16 Twitter OM, @dcleaks_ to @WikiLeaks.
[160] *Netyksho* Indictment ¶ 47(a).
[161] 7/6/16 Twitter DM, @WikiLeaks & @guccifer_2.

through its personas Guccifer 2.0 and DCLeaks) transferred some of the stolen documents to WikiLeaks through online archives set up by GRU. Assange had access to the internet from the Ecuadorian Embassy in London, England. Investigative Technique [162]

On July 14, 2016, GRU officers used a Gruccifer 2.0 email account to send WikiLeaks an email bearing the subject "big archive" and the message "a new attempt."[163] The email contained an encrypted attachment with the same name "wk dnc link1.txt. gpg."[164] Using the Guccifer 2.0 Twitter account, GRU officers sent WikiLeaks an encrypted file and instructions on how to open it.[165] On July 18, 2016, WikiLeaks confirmed in a direct message to the Guccifer 2.0 account that it had "the 1Gb or so archive" and would make a release of the stolen documents "this week."[166] On July 22, 2016, WikiLeaks released over 20,000 emails and other documents from the DNC computer networks.[167] The Democratic National Convention began three days later.

Similar communications occurred between WikiLeaks and GRU-operated persona DCLeaks. On September 15, 2016, @dcleaks wrote to @WikiLeaks, "hi, there! I'm from DC Leaks. How could we discuss some submission-related issues? Am trying to reach out to you via your secured chat but getting no response.

---

[162] Investigative Technique
[163] This was not GRU's first attempt at transferring data to WikiLeaks. On June 29, 2016, the GRU used a Guccifer 2.0 email account to send a large encrypted file to a WikiLeaks email account. 6/29/16 Email, guccifer2@mail.com IT (The email appears to have been undelivered.)
[164] See SM-2589105-DCLEAKS, serial 28 (analysis).
[165] 6/27/16 TwitterDM, @Guccifer_2 to @WikiLeaks.
[166] 7/18/16 TwitterDM, @Guccifer_2 to @WikiLeaks.
[167] DNC Email Archive," WikiLeaks (Jul.22,2016), *available at* https://wikileaks.org/dnc-emails.

I've got something that might interest you. You won't be disappointed, I promise."[168] The WikiLeaks account responded," Hi there," without further elaboration. The @dcleaks_account did not reply immediately.

The same day, the Twitter account @guccifer_2 sent @dcleaks_ a direct message, which is the first known contact between the personas.[169] During subsequent communications, the Guccifer 2.0 persona informed DCLeaks that WikiLeaks was trying to contact DCLeaks and arrange for a way to speak through encrypted emails.[170]

An analysis of the metadata collected from the WikiLeaks site revealed that the stolen Podesta emails show a creation date of September 19, 2016.[171] Based on information about Assange's computer and its possible operating system, this date may be when the GRU staged the stolen Podesta emails for transfer to WikiLeaks (as the GRU had previously done in July 2016 for the DNC emails).[172] The WikiLeaks site also released PDFs and other documents taken from Podesta that were attachments to emails in his account; these documents had a creation date of October 2, 2016, which appears to be the date the attachments were sepa-

---

[168] 9/15/16 Twitter DM, @dcleaks_ to WikiLeaks.

[169] 9/15/16 Twitter DM, @guccifer_2 to @dcleaks_.

[170] *See* SM-2589105-DCLEAKS, serial 28; 9/15/16 Twitter DM, @Guccifer_2& @WikiLeaks

[171] *See* SM-2284941, serials 63 & 6464 ▮▮▮▮▮▮▮▮

[172] ▮▮▮▮▮▮▮▮▮▮▮▮▮▮▮▮▮▮▮▮▮▮ At the time, certain Apple operating systems used a setting that left a downloaded file's creation date the same as the creation date shown on the host computer. This would explain why the creation date on WikiLeaks's version of the files was still September 19, 2016. *See* SM- 2284941, serial ▮▮▮▮▮▮▮

rately staged by WikiLeaks on its site.[173]

Beginning on September 20, 2016, WikiLeaks and DCLeaks resumed communications in a brief exchange. On September 22, 2016, a DCLeaks email account dcleaksproject@gmail.com sent an email to a WikiLeaks account with the subject "Submission" and the message "Hi from DCLeaks." The email contained a PGP-encrypted message with the filename "wiki_mail. txt.gpg."[174] ▆▆▆Investigative Technique▆▆▆ The email, however, bears a number of similarities to the July 14, 2016 email in which GRU officers used the Guccifer 2.0 persona to give WikiLeaks access to the archive of DNC files. On September 22, 2016 (the same day of DCLeaks' email to WikiLeaks), the Twitter account dcleaks sent a single message to WikiLeaks with the string of characters ▆▆Investigative Technique▆▆ ▆▆▆▆▆▆▆▆▆▆

The Office cannot rule out that stolen documents were transferred to WikiLeaks through intermediaries who visited during the summer of 2016. For example, public reporting identified Andrew Müller-Maguhn as a WikiLeaks associate who may have assisted with the transfer of these stolen documents to WikiLeaks.[175] ▆▆Investigative Technique▆▆

▆▆▆▆▆▆▆▆▆▆▆▆▆▆

▆▆▆▆▆▆▆▆▆▆▆▆▆▆ [176]

---

[173] When WikiLeaks saved attachments separately from the stolen emails, its computer system appears to have treated each attachment as a new file and given it a new creation date. *See* SM-228494,1 serials 63 & 64.

[174] *See* 9/22/16 Email, dcleaksproject@gmail.com ▆▆Investigative Technique▆▆

[175] Ellen Nakashima et al., *A German Haçker Offers a Rare Look Inside the Secretive World of Julian Assange and WikiLeaks,* Washington Post (Jan. 17, 2018).

[176] ▆▆Investigative Technique▆▆

On October 7, 2016, WikiLeaks released the first emails stolen from the Podesta email account. In total, WikiLeaks released 33 tranches of stolen emails between October 7, 2016, and November 7, 2016. The releases included private speeches given by Clinton;[177] internal communications between Podesta and other high-ranking members of the Clinton Campaign;[178] and correspondence related to the Clinton Foundation.[179] In total, WikiLeaks released over 50,000 documents stolen from Podesta's personal email account. The last-in-time email released from Podesta's account was dated March 21, 2016, two days after Podesta received a spearphishing email sent by the GRU.

d. WikiLeaks Statements Dissembling About the Source of Stolen Materials

As reports attributing the DNC and DCCC hacks to the Russian government emerged, WikiLeaks and Assange made several public statements apparently designed to obscure the source of the materials that WikiLeaks was releasing. The file-transfer evidence described above and other information uncovered during the investigation discredit WikiLeak's claims about the source of the material that it posted.

Beginning in the summer of 2016, Assange and WikiLeaks made a number of statements about Seth Rich, a former DNC staff member who was killed in July 2016. The statements about Rich implied falsely that he had been the source of the sto-

---

[177] Personal Property
[178] Personal Property
[179] *Netyksho* Indictment, ¶43.

len DNC emails. On August 9, 2016, the @WikiLeaks Twitter account posted: "ANNOUNCE: WikiLeaks has decided to issue a US$20k reward for information leading to conviction for the murder of DNC staffer Seth Rich."[180] Likewise, on August 25, 2016, Assange was asked in an interview, "Why are you so interested in Seth Rich's killer?" and responded, "We're very interested in anything that might be a threat to alleged Wikileaks sources." The interviewer responded to Assange's statements by commenting, "I know you don't want to reveal your source, but it certainly sounds like you are suggesting a man who leaked information to WikiLeaks was then murdered." Assange replied, "If there is someone who's potentially connected to our publication, and that person has been murdered in suspicious circumstances, it doesn't necessarily mean that the two are connected. But it is a very serious matter . . . that type of allegation is very serious, as it's taken very seriously by us."[181]

After the U.S. intelligence community publicly announced its assessment that Russia was behind the hacking operation, Assange continued to deny that the Clinton materials released by WikiLeaks had come from Russian hacking. According to media reports, Assange told a U.S. congressman that the DNC hack was an "inside job," and purported to have "physical proof" that Russians did not give materials to Assange.[182]

---

[180] @WikiLeakes 8/9/16.

[181] *See Assange: "Murdered DNC Staffer Was 'Potential' WikiLeaks Source,"* Fox News (Aug. 25, 2016) (containing video of Assange interview by Megyn Kelly).

[182] Raju & Z. Cohen, *A GOP Congressman's Lonely Quest Defending Julian Assange,* CNN (May 23, 2018).

C. Additional GRU Cyber Operations

While releasing the stolen emails and documents through DCLeaks, Guccifer 2.0, and WikiLeaks, GRU officers continued to target and hack victims linked to the Democratic campaign and, eventually, to target entities responsible for election administration in several states.

1. Summer and Fall 2016 Operations Targeting Democrat-Linked Victims

On July 27 2016, Unit 26165 targeted email accounts connected to candidate Clinton's personal office ██ PP ██ . Earlier that day, candidate Trump made public statements that included the following: "Russia, if you're listening, I hope you're able to find the 30,000 emails that are missing. I think you will probably be rewarded mightily by our press."[183] The "30,000 emails" were apparently a reference to emails described in media accounts as having been stored on a personal server that candidate Clinton had used while serving as Secretary of State.

Within approximately five hours of Trump's statement, GRU officers targeted for the first time Clinton's personal office. After candidate Trump's remarks, Unit 26165 created and sent malicious links targeting 15 email accounts at the domain ██ PP ██ including an email account belonging to Clinton aide ██ PP ██ The investigation did not find evidence of earlier GRU attempts to compromise accounts hosted on this domain. It is unclear how the GRU was able to identify these email accounts, which were not public.[184]

---

[183] "Donald Trump on Russian & Missing Hillary Clinton Emails," YouTube Channel C-SPAN, Posted 7/27/16, *available at* https://www.youtube.com/watch?v=3kxG8uJUsWU (starting at 0:41)

[184] Investigative Technique

Unit 26165 officers also hacked into a DNC account hosted on a cloud-computing service ▮Personal Privacy▮ On September 20, 2016, the GRU began to generate copies of the DNC data using ▮PP▮ function designed to allow users to produce backups of databases (referred to ▮PP▮ as "snapshots"). The GRU then stole those snapshots by moving them to ▮PP▮ account that they controlled; from there, the copies were moved to GRU controlled computers. The GRU stole approximately 300 gigabytes of data from the DNC cloud-based account.[185]

2. Intrusions Targeting the Administration of U.S. Elections

In addition to targeting individuals involved in the Clinton Campaign, GRU officers also targeted individuals and entities involved in the administration of the elections. Victims included U.S. state and local entities, such as state boards of elections (SBOEs), secretaries of state, and county governments, as well as individuals who worked for those entities.[186] The GRU also targeted private technology firms responsible for manufacturing and administering election-related software and hardware, such as voter registration software and electronic polling stations.[187] The GRU continued to target these victims through the elections in November 2016. While the investigation identified evidence that the GRU targeted these individuals and entities, the Office did not investigate further. The Office did not, for instance, obtain

---

▮▮▮

[185] *Netyksho* Indictment, ¶34; *see also* SM-2589105-HACK, serial 29 ▮Investigative Technique▮

[186] *Netyksho* Indictment, ¶69.

[187] *Netyksho* Indictment, ¶69; ▮Investigative Technique▮

or examine servers or other relevant items belonging to these victims. The Office understands that the FBI, the U.S. Department
of Homeland Security, and the states have separately investigated
that activity.

By at least the summer of 2016, GRU officers sought access to
state and local computer networks by exploiting known software
vulnerabilities on websites of state and local governmental entities. GRU officers, for example, targeted state and local databases
of registered voters using a technique known as "SQL injection,"
by which malicious code was sent to the state or local website in
order to run commands (such as exfiltrating the database contents).[188] In one instance in approximately June 2016, the GRU
compromised the computer network of the Illinois State Board
of Elections by exploiting a vulnerability in the SBOE's website.
The GRU then gained access to a database containing information on millions of registered Illinois voters,[189] and extracted data
related to thousands of U.S. voters before the malicious activity
was identified.[190]

GRU officers ▌Investigative Technique▐ scanned state
and local websites for vulnerabilities. For example, over a two-
day period in July 2016, GRU officers ▌Investigative Technique▐
for vulnerabilities on websites of more than two dozen states.
▌Investigative Technique▐ Similar ▌Investigative Technique▐
for vulnerabilities continued through the election.

---

[188] ▌Investigative Technique▐

[189] ▌Investigative Technique▐

[190] ▌Investigative Technique▐

Unit 74455 also sent spearphishing emails to public officials involved in election administration and personnel involved in voting technology. In August 2016, GRU officers targeted employees of ██PP██ , voting technology company that developed software used by numerous U.S. counties to manage voter rolls, and installed malware on the company network. Similarly, in November 2016, the GRU sent spearphishing emails to over 120 email accounts used by Florida county officials responsible for administering the 2016 U.S. election.[191] The spearphishing emails contained an attached Word document coded with malicious software (commonly referred to as a Trojan) that permitted the GRU to access the infected computer.[192] The FBI was separately responsible for this investigation. We understand the FBI believes that this operation enabled the GRU to gain access to the network of at least one Florida county government. The Office did not independently verify that belief and, as explained above, did not undertake the investigative steps that would have been necessary to do so.

D. Trump Campaign and the Dissemination of Hacked Materials

The Trump Campaign showed interest in WikiLeaks's releases throughout the summer and fall of 2016. ████████

Harm to Ongoing Matter

████████████████████████

████████████████████████

████████████████████████

---

[191] *Netyksho* Indictment, ¶76; Investigative Technique ████

[192] Investigative Technique ████

1. ███ Harm to Ongoing Matter ███

a. Background

███ Harm to Ongoing Matter ███
████████████████████████████
████████████████████████████
████████████████████████████
████████████████████████

b. Contacts with the Campaign about WikiLeaks

███ Harm to Ongoing Matter ███
████████████████████████████
███ [193]

███ Harm to Ongoing Matter ███
████████████████████████████

███ Harm to Ongoing Matter ███
████████████████████████████
████████████████████████████

███████████ On June 12, 2016, Assange claimed in a televised interview to have "emails relating to Hillary Clinton which are pending publication,"[194] but provided no additional context.

In debriefings with the Office, former deputy campaign chairman Rick Gates said that, ███ Harm to Ongoing Matter ███
████████████████████████████
████████████████████████████

---

[193] ███ Harm to Ongoing Matter ███
████████████████████████████

[194] *See* Mahita Gajanan, *Julian Assange Timed DNC Email Release for Democratic Convention,* Time (July 27, 2016) (quoting the June 12, 2016 television interview).

[REDACTED] 195 [REDACTED]

[REDACTED] Gates recalled candidate Trump being generally frustrated that the Clinton emails had not been found.[196]

Paul Manafort, who would later become campaign chairman,

Harm to Ongoing Matter

197 Harm to Ongoing Matter

[REDACTED]

[REDACTED]

[REDACTED] 198

Michael Cohen, former executive vice president of the Trump Organization and special counsel to Donald J. Trump,[199] told the

---

[195] In February 2018, Gates pleaded guilty, pursuant to a plea agreement, to a superseding criminal information charging him with conspiring to defraud and commit multiple offenses (i.e., tax fraud, failure to report foreign bank accounts, and acting as an unregistered agent of a foreign principal) against the United States, as well as making false statements to our Office. Superseding Criminal Information, *United States v. Richard W Gates III,* l: l 7-cr-201 (D.D.C. Feb. 23, 2018), Doc. 195 *("Gates* Superseding Criminal Information"); Plea Agreement, *United States v. Richard W Gates III,* l: 17-cr-201 (D.D.C. Feb. 23, 2018), Doc. 205 *("Gates* Plea Agreement"). Gates has provided information and in-comt testimony that the Office has deemed to be reliable.

[196] Gates 10/25/18 302, at 1-2.

[197] As explained further in Volume I, Section IV.A.8, *irifra,* Manafort entered into a plea agreement with our Office. We determined that he breached the agreement by being untruthful in proffer sessions and before the grand jury. We have generally recounted his version of events in this report only when his statements are sufficiently corroborated to be trustworthy; to identify issues on which Manafort's untruthful responses may themselves be of evidentiary value; or to provide Manafort's explanations for certain events, even when we were unable to determine whether that explanation was credible. His account appears here principally because it aligns with those of other witnesses.

[198] Grand Jury [REDACTED]

[199] In November 2018, Cohen pleaded guilty pursuant to a plea agreement to a single-count information charging him with making false statements

Office that he recalled an incident in which he was in candidate Trump's office in Trump Tower [Harm to Ongoing Matter]

[Harm to Ongoing Matter]

[200]

[201] Cohen further told the Office that, after WikiLeaks's subsequent release of stolen DNC emails in July 2016, candidate Trump said to Cohen something to the effect of, [Harm to Ongoing Matter] [202]
[Harm to Ongoing Matter]

According to Gates, Manafort expressed excitement about the release [Harm to Ongoing Matter] [203] Manafort, for his part told the office that, shortly after WikiLeaks's July 22 release, Manafort also spoke with candidate Trump [Harm to Ongoing Matter]

---

to Congress, in violation of 18 U.S.C. § 100 l(a) & (c). He had previously pleaded guilty to several other criminal charges brought by the U.S. Attorney's Office in the Southern District of New York, after a referral from this Office. In the months leading up to his false-statements guilty plea, Cohen met with our Office on multiple occasions for interviews and provided information that the Office has generally assessed to be reliable and that is included in this report.

[200] HOM

[201] Harm to Ongoing Matter

[202] Cohen 9/18/18 302, at 10. Harm to Ongoing Matter

[203] Gates 10/25/18 302 (serial 241), at 4.

[REDACTED] [204] Harm to Ongoing Matter

[205] Manafort also [Harm Harm to Ongoing Matter] wanted to be kept appraised of any developments with WikiLeaks and separately told Gates to keep in touch [Harm to Ongoing Matter] about future WikiLeaks releases.[206]

According to Gates, by the late summer of 2016, the Trump Campaign was planning a press strategy, a communications campaign and messaging based on the possible release of Clinton emails by WikiLeaks.[207] [Harm to Ongoing Matter]

[REDACTED] [208] Harm to Ongoing Matter

[REDACTED] while Trump and Gates were driving to LaGuardia Airport. [Harm to Ongoing Matter]

[REDACTED], shortly after the call candidate Trump told Gates that more releases of damaging information would be coming.[209]

[Harm to Ongoing Matter]

[REDACTED] [210]

c. [Harm to Ongoing Matter]

[Harm to Ongoing Matter]

[REDACTED]

[REDACTED] [211] Corsi is an author who holds a doctor-

---

[204] Grand Jury
[205] Grand Jury
[206] Grand Jury
[207] Gates 4/10/18 302, at 3; Gates 4/1l/18 302, at 1-2 (SM-2180998); Gates 10/25/18 302, at 2.
[208] HOM
[209] Gates 10/25/18 302 (serial 241), at 4.
[210] HOM
[211] HOM

ate in political science.[212] In 2016, Corsi also worked for the media outlet World Net Daily (WND). ▇Harm to Ongoing Matter▇

▇▇▇▇▇▇▇▇▇▇▇▇▇▇▇▇▇▇▇▇▇▇▇▇▇[213]

▇Harm to Ongoing Matter▇

▇▇▇▇▇▇▇▇[214] Corsi told the office during interviews that he "must have" previously discussed Assange with Malloch.[215] ▇Harm to Ongoing Matter▇

▇▇▇▇▇▇▇▇▇▇▇▇▇▇▇▇▇▇▇▇▇▇

▇▇▇▇[216] ▇Harm to Ongoing Matter▇

▇▇▇▇▇▇▇▇▇▇▇▇▇▇[217]

▇Grand Jury▇

▇▇▇▇▇▇▇▇▇▇▇▇▇ According to Malloch, Corsi asked him to put Corsi in touch with Assange, whom Corsi wished to interview. Malloch recalled that Corsi also suggested

---

[212] Corsi first rose to public prominence in August 2004 when he published his book *Unfit for Command: Swift Boat Veterans Speak Out Against John Kerry*. In the 2008 election cycle, Corsi gained prominence for being a leading proponent of the allegation that Barack Obama was not born in the United States. Corsi told the Office that Donald Trump expressed interest in his writings, and that he spoke with Trump on the phone on at least six occasions. Corsi 9/6/18 302, at 3.

[213] Corsi 10/31/18 302, at 2; ▇Grand Jury▇ Corsi was first interviewed on September 6, 2018 at the Special Counsel's offices in Washington, D.C. He was accompanied by counsel throughout the interview. Corsi was subsequently interviewed on September 17, 2018; September 21, 2018; October 31, 2018; November 1, 2018; and November 2, 2018. Counsel was present for all interviews, and the interviews beginning on September 21, 2018 were conducted pursuant to a proffer agreement that precluded affirmative use of his statements against him in limited circumstances.

[214] ▇HOM▇

[215] Corsi 10/31/18 302, at 4.

[216] ▇HOM▇

[217] ▇HOM▇

that individuals in the "orbit" of U.K. politician Nigel Farage might be able to contact Assange and asked if Malloch knew them. Malloch told Corsi that he would think about the request but made no actual attempt to connect Corsi with Assange.[218]

> Harm to Ongoing Matter

[219] Harm to Ongoing Matter [220]

d. WikiLeaks's October 7, 2016 Release of Stolen Podesta Emails

On October 7, 2016, four days after the Assange press conference HOM , the *Washington Post* published an *Access Hollywood* video that captured comments by candidate Trump some years earlier and that was expected to adversely affect the Campaign.[239] Less than an hour after the video's publication, WikiLeaks released the first set of emails stolen by the GRU from the account of Clinton Campaign chairman John Podesta.

> Harm to Ongoing Matter

---

[218] Malloch denied ever communicating with Assange or WikiLeakes, stating that he did not pursue the request to contact Assange because he believed he had no connections to Assange. Grand Jury

[219] HOM

[239] Harm to Ongoing Matter

[239] Candidate Trump can be heard off camera making graphic statements about women.

████████████████████████████████████

[240] Harm to Ongoing Matter

████████████████████████████████████

[241] Harm to Ongoing Matter

[242]

Harm to Ongoing Matter

████████████████████████████████████

[243] Harm to Ongoing Matter

████████████████████████████████████

Corsi said that, because he had no direct means of communicating with WikiLeaks, he told members of the news site WND—who were participating on a conference call with him that day—to reach Assange immediately.[244] Corsi claimed that the pressure was enormous and recalled telling the conference call the *Access Hollywood* tape was coming.[245] Corsi stated that he was convinced that his efforts had caused WikiLeaks to release the emails when they did.[246] In a later November 2018 interview, Corsi

---

[240] HOM

[241] HOM

[242] HOM

[243] HOM

[244] In a later November 2018 interview, Corsi stated Harm to Ongoing Matter ████████████████████ that he believed Malloch was on the call but then focused on other individuals who were on the call-invitation, which Malloch was not. (Separate travel records show that at the time of the call, Malloch was aboard a transatlantic flight). Corsi at one point stated that after WikiLeaks's release of stolen emails on October 7, 2016, he concluded Malloch had gotten in contact with Assange. Corsi 11/1/18 302, at 6.

[245] During the same interview, Corsi also suggested that he may have sent out public tweets because he knew Assange was reading his tweets. Our Office was unable to find any evidence of such tweets.

[246] Corsi 9/21/18 302, at 6–7.

stated that he thought that he had told people on a WND conference call about the forthcoming tape and had sent out a tweet asking whether anyone could contact Assange, but then said that maybe he had done nothing.[247]

The Office investigated Corsi's allegations about the events of October 7, 2016 but found little corroboration for his allegations about the day.[248] Harm To Ongoing Matter

███

███████████████████████████████████████ [249] HOM

███

████████████████ [250] However, the phone records themselves do not indicate that the conversation was with any of the reporters who broke the *Access Hollywood* story, and the Office has not otherwise been able to identify the substance of the conversation. Harm To Ongoing Matter

███

███

████████ [251] However, the Office has not identified any conference call participant, or anyone who spoke to Corsi that day, who says that they received non-public information about the tape from Corsi or acknowledged having contacted a member of WikiLeaks on October 7, 2016 after a conversation with Corsi.

---

[247] Corsi 11/1/18 302, at 6.
[248] Harm to Ongoing Matter
[249] Harm to Ongoing Matter
[250] HOM   Grand Jury   Harm to Ongoing Matter
[251] HOM   Grand Jury   Harm to Ongoing Matter

a. Henry Oknyansky (a/k/a Henry Greenberg)

In the spring of 2016, Trump Campaign advisor Michael Caputo learned through a Florida-based Russian business partner that another Florida-based Russian, Henry Oknyansky (who also went by the name Henry Greenberg), claimed to have information pertaining to Hillary Clinton. Caputo notified Roger Stone and brokered communication between Stone and Oknyansky. Oknyansky and Stone set up a May 2016 in-person meeting.[260]

Oknyansky was accompanied to the meeting by Alexei Rasin, a Ukrainian associate involved in Florida real estate. At the meeting, Rasin offered to sell Stone derogatory information on Clinton that Rasin claimed to have obtained while working for Clinton. Rasin claimed to possess financial statements demonstrating Clinton's involvement in money laundering with Rasin's companies. According to Oknyansky, Stone asked if the amounts in question totaled millions of dollars but was told it was closer to hundreds of thousands. Stone refused the offer, stating that Trump would not pay for opposition research.[261]

Oknyansky claimed to the Office that Rasin's motivation was financial. According to Oknyansky, Rasin had tried unsuccessfully to shop the Clinton information around to other interested parties, and Oknyansky would receive a cut if the information was sold.[262] Rasin is noted in public source documents as the director and/or registered agent for a number of Florida companies, none of which appears to be connected to Clinton. The Office found

---

[260] Caputo 5/2/18 302, at 4; Oknyansky 7/13/18 302, at I.

[261] Oknyansky 7/13/18 302, at 1-2.

[262] 10/12/16 Twitter DM, @WikiLeaks to @DonaldJTrumpJr.

no other evidence that Rasin worked for Clinton or any Clinton-related entities.

In their statements to investigators, Oknyansky and Caputo had contradictory recollections about the meeting. Oknyansky claimed that Caputo accompanied Stone to the meeting and provided an introduction, whereas Caputo did not tell us that he had attended and claimed that he was never told what information Oknyansky offered. Caputo also stated that he was unaware Oknyansky sought to be paid for the information until Stone informed him after the fact.[263]

The Office did not locate Rasin in the United States, although the Office confirmed Rasin had been issued a Florida driver's license. The Office otherwise was unable to determine the content and origin of the information he purportedly offered to Stone. Finally, the investigation did not identify evidence of a connection between the outreach or the meeting and Russian interference efforts.

b. Campaign Efforts to Obtain Deleted Clinton Emails

After candidate Trump stated on July 27, 2016, that he hoped Russia would "find the 30,000 emails that are missing," Trump asked individuals affiliated with his Campaign to find the deleted Clinton emails.[264] Michael Flynn—who would later serve as National Security Advisor in the Trump Administration—recalled that Trump made this request repeatedly, and Flynn subsequently contacted multiple people in an effort to obtain the emails.[265]

---

[263] Caputo 5/2/18 302, at 4; Oknyansky 7/13/18 302, at 1.

[264] Flynn 4/25/18 302, at 5-6; Flynn 5/1/18 302, at 1-3.

[265] Flynn 5/1/18 302, at 1-3.

Barbara Ledeen and Peter Smith were among the people contacted by Flynn. Ledeen, a long-time Senate staffer who had previously sought the Clinton emails, provided updates to Flynn
about her efforts throughout the summer of 2016.[266] Smith, an
investment advisor who was active in Republican politics, also
attempted to locate and obtain the deleted Clinton emails.[267]

Ledeen began her efforts to obtain the Clinton emails before
Flynn's request, as early as December 2015.[268] On December 3,
2015, she emailed Smith a proposal to obtain the emails, stating,
"Here is the proposal I briefly mentioned to you. The person I
described to you would be happy to talk with you either in person
or over the phone. The person can get the emails which 1. Were
classified and 2. Were purloined by our enemies. That would
demonstrate what needs to be demonstrated."[269]

Attached to the email was a 25-page proposal stating that the
"Clinton email server was, in all likelihood, breached long ago,"
and that the Chinese, Russian, and Iranian intelligence services
could "re-assemble the server's email content."[270] The proposal
called for a three-phase approach. The first two phases consisted
of open-source analysis. The third phase consisted of checking
with certain intelligence sources "that have access through liaison
work with various foreign services" to determine if any of those
services had gotten to the server. The proposal noted, "Even if a
single email was recovered and the providence [sic] of that email
was a foreign service, it would be catastrophic to the Clinton cam-

---

[266] Flynn 4/25/18 302, at 7; Flynn 5/4/18 302, at 1-2; Flynn 11/29/17 302, at 7-8.
[267] Flynn 11/29/17 302, at 7.
[268] Szobocsan 3/29/17 302, at 1.
[269] 12/3/15 Email, Ledeen to Smith.
[270] 12/3/15 Email, Ledeen to Smith (attachment).

paign[.]" Smith forwarded the email to two colleagues and wrote, "we can discuss to whom it should be referred."[271] On December 16, 2015, Smith informed Ledeen that he declined to participate in her "initiative." According to one of Smith's business associates, Smith believed Ledeen's initiative was not viable at that time.[272]

Just weeks after Trump's July 2016 request to find the Clinton emails, however, Smith tried to locate and obtain emails himself. He created a company, raised tens of thousands of dollars, and recruited security experts and business associates. Smith made claims to others involved in the effort (and those from whom he sought funding) that he was in contact with hackers with "ties and affiliations to Russia" who had access to emails, and that his efforts were coordinated with the Trump Campaign. [273]

On August 28, 2016, Smith sent an email from an encrypted account with the subject, "Sec. Clinton's unsecured private email server" to an undisclosed list of recipients, including Campaign co-chairman Sam Clovis. The email stated that Smith was "[j]ust finishing two days of sensitive meetings here in DC with involved groups to poke and probe on the above. It is clear that the Clinton's home-based, unprotected server was hacked with ease by both State-related players, and private mercenaries. Parties with varying interests, are circling to release ahead of the election."[274]

September 2, 2016, Smith directed a business associate to establish KLS Research LLC in furtherance of his search for the deleted emails.[275] One of the purposes of KLS Research was to

---

[271] 12/3/15 Email, Smith to Szobocsan & Safron.

[272] Szobocsan 3/29/18 302, at 1.

[273] 8/31/16 Email, Smith to Smith.

[274] 8/28/16 Email, Smith to Smith.

[275] Incorporation papers ofKLS Research LLC, 7/26/17 Grand Jury

manage the funds Smith raised in support of the iniative.[276] KLS
Research received over $30,000 during the presidential campaign,
although Smith represented that he raised even more money.[277]

Smith recruited multiple people for his initiative, including
security experts to search for and authenticate the emails.[278] In
early September 2016, as part of his recruitment and fundraising effort, Smith circulated a document stating that his initiative
was "in coordination" with the Trump Campaign, "to the extent
permitted as an independent expenditure organization."[279] The
document listed multiple individuals affiliated with the Trump
Campaign, including Flynn, Clovis, Bannon, and Kellyanne Conway.[280] The investigation established that Smith communicated
with at least Flynn and Clovis about his search for the deleted
Clinton emails,[281] but the Office did not identify evidence that any
of the listed individuals initiated or directed Smith's efforts.

In September 2016, Smith and Ledeen got back in touch with
each other about their respective efforts. Ledeen wrote to Smith,
"wondering if you had some more detailed reports or memos or
other data you could share because we have come a long way in
our efforts since we last visited. . . . We would need as much tech-

---

Szobocsan 3/29/18 302, at 2.

[276] Szobocsan 3/29/18 302, at 3.

[277] Financial Institution Record of Peter Smith and KLS Research LLC, 10/31/17
Grand Jury   -10/11/16 Email, Smith to Personal Privacy

[278] Tait 8/22/17 302, at 3; York 7 /12/17 302, at 1-2; York 11/22/17 302, at 1.

[279] 279 York 7 /13/17 302 (attachment KLS Research, LLC, "Clinton Email
Reconnaissance Initiative,"Sept. 9, 2016).

[280] The same recruitment document listed Jerome Corsi under "Independent
Groups/Organizations/Individuals," and described him as an "established
author and writer from the right on President Obama and Sec. Clinton."

[281] Flynn 11/29/17 302, at 7-8; 10/15/16 Email, Smith to Flynn et al.; 8/28/16
Email, Smith to Smith (bee: Clovis et al.).

nical discussion as possible so we could marry it against the new data we have found and then could share it back to you 'your eyes only.'"[282]

Ledeen claimed to have obtained a trove of emails (from what she described as the "dark web") that purported to be the deleted Clinton emails. Ledeen wanted to authenticate the emails and solicited contributions to fund that effort. Erik Prince provided funding to hire a tech advisor to ascertain the authenticity of the emails. According to Prince, the tech advisor determined that the emails were not authentic.[283]

A backup of Smith's computer contained two files that had been downloaded from WikiLeaks and that were originally attached to emails received by John Podesta. The files on Smith's computer had creation dates of October 2, 2016, which was prior to the date of their release by WikiLeaks. Forensic examination, however, established that the creation date did not reflect when the files were downloaded to Smith 's computer. (It appears the creation date was when WikiLeaks staged the document for release, as discussed in Volume I, Section III.B.3.c, supra.)[284] The investigation did not otherwise identify evidence that Smith obtained the files before their release by WikiLeaks.

---

[282] 9/16/16 Email , Ledeen to Smith.

[283] Prince 4/4/18 302, at 4-5.

[284] The forensic analysis of Smith's computer devices found that Smith used an older Apple operating system that would have preserved that October 2, 2016 creation date when it was downloaded (no matter what day it was in fact downloaded by Smith). See Volume I, Section 111.B.3.c, supra. The Office tested this theory in March 2019 by downloading the two files found on Smith's computer from WikiLeaks's site using the same Apple operating system on Smith's computer; both files were successfully downloaded and retained the October 2, 2016 creation date. See SM-2284941, serial 62.

Smith continued to send emails to an undisclosed recipient list about Clinton's deleted emails until shortly before the election. For example, on October 28, 2016, Smith wrote that there was a "tug-of-war going on within WikiLeaks over its planned releases in the next few days," and that WikiLeaks "has maintained that it will save its best revelations for last, under the theory this allows little time for response prior to the U.S. election November 8."[285] An attachment to the email claimed that WikiLeaks would release "All 33k deleted Emails" by "November 1st." No mails obtained from Clinton's server were subsequently released.

Smith drafted multiple emails stating or intimating that he was in contact with Russian hackers. For example, in one such email, Smith claimed that, in August 2016, KLS Research had organized meetings with parties who had access to the deleted Clinton emails, including parties with "ties and affiliations to Russia."[286] The investigation did not identify evidence that any such meetings occurred. Associates and security experts who worked with Smith on the initiative did not believe that Smith was in contact with Russian hackers and were aware of no such connection.[287] The investigation did not establish that Smith was in contact with Russian hackers or that Smith, Ledeen, or other individuals in touch with the Trump Campaign ultimately obtained the deleted Clinton emails.

—————————

In sum, the investigation established that the GRU hacked into email accounts of persons affiliated with the Clinton Cam-

—————————

[285] 10/28/16 Email, Smith to Smith.

[286] 8/31/16 Email, Smith to Smith.

[287] Safron 3/20/18 302, at 3; Szobocsan 3/29/18 302, at 6.

paign, as well as the computers of the DNC and DCCC. The GRU then exfiltrated data related to the 2016 election from these accounts and computers, and disseminated that data through fictitious online personas (DCLeaks and Guccifer 2.0) and later through WikiLeaks. The investigation also established that the Trump Campaign displaced interest in the WikiLeaks releases, and that ██ Harm to Ongoing Matter ████████████████

██

██

████████████████████████████████

8. <u>Paul Manafort</u>

Paul Manafort served on the Trump Campaign, including a period as campaign chairman, from March to August 2016.[838] Manafort had connections to Russia through his prior work for Russian oligarch Oleg Deripaska and later through his work for a pro-Russian regime in Ukraine. Manafort stayed in touch with

---

[838] On August 21, 2018, Manafort was convicted in the Eastern District of Virginia on eight tax, Foreign Bank Account Registration (FBAR), and bank fraud charges. On September 14, 2018, Manafort pleaded guilty in the District of Columbia to (1) conspiracy to defraud the United States and conspiracy to commit offenses against the United States (money laundering, tax fraud, FBAR, Foreign Agents Registration Act (FARA), and FARA false statements), and (2) conspiracy to obstruct justice (witness tampering). Manafort also admitted criminal conduct with which he had been charged in the Eastern District of Virginia, but as to which the jury hung. The conduct at issue in both cases involved Manafort's work in Ukraine and the money he earned for that work, as well as crimes after the Ukraine work ended. On March 7, 2019, Manafort was sentenced to 47 months of imprisonment in the Virginia prosecution. On March 13, the district court in D.C. sentenced Manafm1 to a total term of 73 months: 60 months on the Count 1 conspiracy (with 30 of those months to run concurrent to the Virginia sentence), and 13 months on the Count 1 conspiracy, to be served consecutive to the other two sentences. The two sentences resulted in a total term of 90 months.

these contacts during the campaign period through Konstantin Kilimnik, a longtime Manafort employee who previously ran Manafort's office in Kiev and who the FBI assesses to have ties to Russian intelligence.

Manafort instructed Rick Gates, his deputy on the Campaign and a longtime employee,[839] to provide Kilimnik with updates on the Trump Campaign—including internal polling data, although Manafort claims not to recall that specific instruction. Manafort expected Kilimnik to share that information with others in Ukraine and with Deripaska. Gates periodically sent such polling data to Kilimnik during the campaign.

Manafort also twice met Kilimnik in the United States during the campaign period and conveyed campaign information. The second meeting took place on August 2, 2016, in New York City. Kilimnik requested the meeting to deliver in person a message from former Ukrainian President Viktor Yanukovych, who was then living in Russia. The message was about a peace plan for Ukraine that Manafort has since acknowledged was a "backdoor" means for Russia to control eastern Ukraine. Several months later, after the presidential election, Kilimnik wrote an email to Manafort expressing the view—which Manafort later said he shared—that the plan's success would require U.S. support to succeed: "all that is required to start the process is a very minor

---

[839] As noted in Volume I, Section III.D.1.b, *supra*, Gates pleaded guilty to two criminal charges in the District of Columbia, including making a false statement to the FBI, pursuant to a plea agreement. He has provided information and in-court testimony that the Office has deemed to be reliable. *See also* Transcript at 16, *United States v. Paul J Manafort, Jr.*, 1:17-cr-201 (D.D.C. Feb. 13, 2019), Doc. 514 *("Manafort 2/13/19 Transcript")* (court's explanation of reasons to credit Gates's statements in one instance).

'wink' (or slight push) from [Donald Trump]."[840] The email also stated that if Manafort were designated as the U.S. representative and started the process, Yanukovych would ensure his reception in Russia "at the very top level."

Manafort communicated with Kilimnik about peace plans for Ukraine on at least four occasions after their first discussion of the topic on August 2: December 2016 (the Kilimnik email described above); January 2017; February 2017; and again in the spring of 2018. The Office reviewed numerous Manafort email and text communications, and asked President Trump about the plan in written questions.[841] The investigation did not uncover evidence of Manafort's passing along information about Ukrainian peace plans to the candidate or anyone else in the Campaign or the Administration. The Office was not, however, able to gain access to all of Manafort's electronic communications (in some instances, messages were sent using encryption applications). And while Manafort denied that he spoke to members of the Trump Campaign or the new Administration about the peace plan, he lied to the Office and the grand jury about the peace plan and his meetings with Kilimnik, and his unreliability on this subject was among the reasons that the district judge found that he breached his cooperation agreement.[842]

---

[840] The email was drafted in Kilimnik's DMP email account (in English) Investigative Technique

[841] According to the President's written answers, he does not remember Manafort communicating to him any particular positions that Ukraine or Russia would want the United States to support. Written Responses of Donald J. Trump (Nov. 20, 2018), at 16-17 (Response to Question IV, Part (d)).

[842] Manafort made several false statements during debriefings. Based on that conduct, the Office determined that Manafort had breached his plea agreement and could not be a cooperating witness. The judge presiding in

The Office could not reliably determine Manafort's purpose in sharing with Kilimnik during the campaign period. Manafort ▉Grand Jury▉ did not see a downside to sharing campaign information, and told Gates that his role in the Campaign would be "good for business" and potentially a way to be made whole for work he previously completed in the Ukraine. As to Deripaska, Manafort claimed that by sharing campaign information with him, Deripaska might see value in their relationship and resolve a "disagreement"—a reference to one or more outstanding lawsuits. Because of questions about Manafort's credibility and our limited ability to gather evidence on what happened to the polling data after it was sent to Kilimnik, the Office could not assess what Kilimnik (or others he may have given it to) did with it. The Office did not identify evidence of a connection between Manafort's sharing polling data and Russia's interference in the election, which had already been reported by U.S. media outlets at the time of the August 2 meeting. The investigation did not establish that Manafort otherwise coordinated with the Russian government on its election-interference efforts.

a. Paul Manafort's Ties to Russia and Ukraine

Manafort's Russian contacts during the campaign and tran-

Manafort's D.C. criminal case found by a preponderance of the evidence that Manafort intentionally made multiple false statements to the FBI, the Office, and the grand jury concerning his interactions and communications with Kilimnik (and concerning two other issues). Although the report refers at times to Manafort's statements, it does so only when those statements are sufficiently corroborated to be trustworthy, to identify issues on which Manafort's untruthful responses may themselves be of evidentiary value, or to provide Manafort's explanations for certain events, even when we were unable to determine whether that explanation was credible.

sition periods stem from his consulting work for Deripaska from approximately 2005 to 2009 and his separate political consulting work in Ukraine from 2005 to 2015, including through his company DMP International LLC (DMI). Kilimnik worked for Manafort in Kiev during this entire period and continued to communicate with Manafort through at least June 2018. Kilimnik, who speaks and writes Ukrainian and Russian, facilitated many of Manafort's communications with Deripaska and Ukrainian oligarchs.

i. Oleg Deripaska Consulting Work

In approximately 2005, Manafort began working for Deripaska, a Russian oligarch who has a global empire involving aluminum and power companies and who is closely aligned with Vladimir Putin.[843] A memorandum describing work that Manafort performed for Deripaska in 2005 regarding the post-Soviet republics referenced the need to brief the Kremlin and the benefits that the work could confer on "the Putin Government."[844] Gates described the work Manafort did for Deripaska as "political risk insurance," and explained that Deripaska used Manafort to install friendly political officials in countries where Deripaska had business interests.[845] Manafort's company earned tens of millions of dollars from its work for Deripaska and was loaned millions of dollars by Deripaska as well.[846]

In 2007, Deripaska invested through another entity in Pericles

---

[843] Pinchuk et al., *Russian Tycoon Deripaska in Putin Delegation to China,* Reuters (June 8, 2018).

[844] 6/23/05 Memo, Manafort & Davis to Deripaska & Rothchild.

[845] Gates 2/2/18 302, at 7.

[846] Manafort 9/20/18 302, at 2-5; Manafort Income by Year, 2005-2015; Manafort Loans from Wire Transfers, 2005-2015.

Emerging Market Patiners L.P. ("Pericles"), an investment fund created by Manafort and former Manafort business partner Richard Davis. The Pericles fund was established to pursue investments in Eastern Europe.[847] Deripaska was the sole investor.[848] Gates stated in interviews with the Office that the venture to a deterioration of the relationship between Manafort and Deripaska.[849] In particular, when the fund failed, litigation between Manafort and Deripaska ensued. Gates stated that, by 2009, Manafort's business relationship with Deripaska had "dried up."[850] According to Gates, various interactions with Deripaska and his intermediaries over the past few years have involved trying to resolve the legal disp ute.[851] As described below, in 2016, Manafort, Gates, Kilimnik, and others engaged in efforts to revive the Deripaska relationship and resolve the litigation.

ii. Political Consulting Work

Through Deripaska, Manafort was introduced to Rinat Akhmetov, a Ukrainian oligarch who hired Manafort as a political consultant.[852] In 2005, Akhmetov hired Manafort to engage in political work supporting the Party of Regions,[853] a political party in Ukraine that was generally understood to align with Russia. Manafort assisted the Party of Regions in regaining power, and its candidate, Viktor Yanukovych, won the presidency in 2010. Manafort became

---

[847] Gates 3/12/18 302, at 5.

[848] Manafort 12/16/J 5 Dep., at 157:8-11.

[849] Gates 2/2/18 302, at 9.

[850] Gates 2/2/18 302, at 6.

[851] Gates 2/2/18 302, at 9-10.

[852] Manafort 7/30/14 302, at 1; Manafort 9/20/18 302, at 2.

[853] Manafort 9/11/18 302, at 5-6.

a close and trusted political advisor to Yanukovych during his time as President of Ukraine. Yanukovych served in that role until 2014, when he fled to Russia amidst popular protests.[854]

iii. Konstantin Kilimnik

Kilimnik is a Russian national who has lived in both Russia and Ukraine and was a longtime Manafort employee.[855] Kilimnik had direct and close access to Yanukovych and his senior entourage, and he facilitated communications between Manafort and his clients, including Yanukovych and multiple Ukrainian oligarchs.[856] Kilimnik also maintained a relationship with Deripaska's deputy, Viktor Boyarkin,[857] a Russian national who previously served in the defense attaché office of the Russian Embassy to the United States.[858]

Manafort told the Office that he did not believe Kilimnik was working as a Russian "spy."[859] The FBI, however, assesses that Kilimnik has ties to Russian intelligence.[860] Several pieces of the Office's evidence—including witness interviews and emails obtained through court authorized search warrants—support that assessment:

---

[854] Gates 3/16/18 302, at 1; Davis 2/8/18 302, at 9; Devine 7/6/18 302, at 2-3.

[855] Patten 5/22/18 302, at 5; Gates 1/29/18 302, at 18-19; 10/28/97 Kilimnik Visa Record, U.S. Department of State.

[856] Gates 1/29/18 302, at 18-19; Patten 5/22/18 302, at 8; Gates 1/31/18 302, at 4-5; Gates 1/30/18 302, at 2; Gates 2/2/18 302, at 11.

[857] Gates 1/29/18 302, at 18; Patten 5/22/18 302, at 8.

[858] Boyarkin Visa Record, U.S. Department of State.

[859] Manafort 9/11/18 302, at 5.

[860] The Office has noted Kilimnik's assessed ties to Russian intelligence in public court filings. *E.g.,* Gov't Opp. to Mot. to Modify, *United States v. Paul J Manafort, Jr.,* 1:17-cr-201 (D.D.C. Dec. 4, 2017), Doc. 73, at 2 *("Manafort (D.D.C.) Gov't Opp. to Mot. to Modify")*.

- Kilimnik was born on April 27, 1970, in Dnipropetrovsk Oblast, then of the Soviet Union, and attended the Military Institute of the Ministry of Defense from I 987 until 1992.[861] Sam Patten, a business partner to Kilimnik,[862] stated that Kilimnik told him that he was a translator in the Russian army for seven years and that he later worked in the Russian armament industry selling arms and military equipment.[863]

- U.S. government visa records reveal that Kilimnik obtained a visa to travel to the United States with a Russian diplomatic passport in 1997.[864]

- Kilimnik worked for the International Republican Institute's (IRI) Moscow office, where he did translation work and general office management from 1998 to 2005.[865] While another official recalled the incident differently,[866] one former associate of Kilimnik's at IRI told the FBI that Kilimnik was fired from his post because his links to Russian intelligence were too strong. The same individual stated that it was well known at IRI that Kilimnik had links to the Russian government.[867]

---

[861] 12/17/16 Kilimnik Visa Record, U.S. Department of State.

[862] In August 2018, Patten pleaded guilty pursuant to a plea agreement to violating the Foreign Agents Registration Act, and admitted in his Statement of Offense that he also misled and withheld documents from the Senate Select Committee on Intelligence in the course of its investigation of Russian election interference. Plea Agreement, *United States v. W. Samuel Patten,* 1:1 8-cr-260 (D.D.C. Aug. 31, 2018), Doc. 6; Statement of Offense, *United States v. W. Samuel Patten,* 1:18-cr-260 (D.D.C. Aug. 31, 2018), Doc. 7.

[863] Patten 5/22/18 302, at 5-6.

[864] 10/28/97 Kilimnik Visa Record, U.S. Department of State.

[865] Nix 3/30/18 302, at 1-2.

[866] Nix 3/30/18 302, at 2.

[867] Lenzi 1/30/18 302, at 2.

- Jonathan Hawker, a British national who was a public relations consultant at FTI Consulting, worked with DMI on a public relations campaign for Yanukovych. After Hawker's work for DMI ended, Kilimnik contacted Hawker about working for a Russian government entity on a public-relations project that would promote, in Western and Ukrainian media, Russia's position on its 2014 invasion of Crimea.[868]

- Gates suspected that Kilimnik was a "spy," a view that he shared with Manafort, Hawker, and Alexander van der Zwaan,[869] an attorney who had worked with DMI on a report for the Ukrainian Ministry of Foreign Affairs.[870]

Investigative Technique

b. Contacts during Paul Manafort's Time with the Trump Campaign

i. Paul Manafort Joins the Campaign

Manafort served on the Trump Campaign from late March to August 19, 2016. On March 29, 2016, the Campaign announced that Manafort would serve as the Campaign's "Convention

---

[868] Hawker 1/9/18 302, at 13; 3/18/14 Email, Hawker & Tulukbaev.

[869] van der Zwaan pleaded guilty in the U.S. District Court for the District of Columbia to making false statements to the Special Counsel's Office. Plea Agreement, *United States v. Alex van der Zwaan,* 1:18-cr-31 (D.D.C. Feb. 20, 2018), Doc. 8.

[870] Hawker 6/9/18 302, at 4; van der Zwaan 11/3/17 302, at 22. Manafort said in an interview that Gates had joked with Kilimnik about Kilimnik's going to meet with his KGB handler. Manafort 10/16/18 302, at 7.

Manager."[871] On May 19, 2016, Manafort was promoted to campaign chairman and chief strategist, and Gates, who had been assisting Manafort on the Campaign, was appointed deputy campaign chairman.[872]

Thomas Barrack and Roger Stone both recommended Manafort to candidate Trump.[873] In early 2016, at Manafort's request, Barrack suggested to Trump that Manafort join the Campaign to manage the Republican Convention.[874] Stone had worked with Manafort from approximately 1980 until the mid-1990s through various consulting and lobbying firms. Manafort met Trump in 1982 when Trump hired the Black, Manafort, Stone, and Kelly lobbying firm.[875] Over the years, Manafort saw Trump at political and social events in New York City and at Stone's wedding, and Trump requested VIP status at the 1988 and 1996 Republican conventions worked by Manafort.[876]

According to Gates, in March 2016, Manafort traveled to Trump's Mar-a-Lago estate in Florida to meet with Trump. Trump hired him at that time.[877] Manafort agreed to work on the Campaign without pay. Manafort had no meaningful income at this point in time, but resuscitating his domestic political campaign career could be financially beneficial in the future. Gates reported

---

[871] *Press Release -Donald J Trump Announces Campaign Convention Manager Paul J Manafort,* The American Presidency Project - U.C. Santa Barbara (Mar. 29, 2016).

[872] Gates 1/29/18 302, at 8; Meghan Keneally, *Timeline of Manafort's role in the Trump Campaign,* ABC News (Oct. 20, 2017).

[873] Gates 1/29/18 302, at 7-8; Manafort 9/11/18 302, at 1-2; Barrack 12/12/17 302, at 3.

[874] Barrack 12/12/17 302, at 3; Gates 1/29/18 302, at 7-8.

[875] Manafort 10/16/18 302, at 6.

[876] Manafort 10/16/18 302, at 6.

[877] Gates 2/2/18 302, at 10.

that Manafort intended, if Trump won the Presidency, to remain outside the Administration and monetize his relationship with the Administration.[878]

ii. Paul Manafort's Campaign-Period Contacts

Immediately upon joining the Campaign, Manafort directed Gates to prepare for his review separate memoranda addressed to Deripaska, Akhmetov, Serhiy Lyovochkin, and Boris Kolesnikov,[879] the last three being Ukrainian oligarchs who were senior Opposition Bloc officials.[880] The memoranda described Manafort's appointment to the Trump Campaign and indicated his willingness to consult on Ukrainian politics in the future. On March 30, 2016, Gates emailed the memoranda and a press release announcing Manafort's appointment to Kilimnik for translation and dissemination.[881] Manafort later followed up with Kilimnik to ensure his messages had been delivered, emailing on April 11, 2016 to ask whether Kilimnik had shown "our friends" the media coverage of his new role.[882] Kilimnik replied, "Absolutely. Every

---

[878] Gates 1/30/18 302, at 4.

[879] Gates 2/2/18 302, at 11.

[880] *See* Sharon LaFraniere, Manafort's Trial Isn't About Russia, but It Will Be in the Air, New York Times (July 30, 2018); Tierney Sneed, *Prosecutors Believe Manafort Made $60 Million Consulting in Ukraine,* Talking Points Memo (July 30, 2018); Mykola Vorobiov, *How Pro-Russian Forces Will Take Revenge on Ukraine,* Atlantic Council (Sept. 23, 2018); Sergii Leshchenko, *Ukraine's Oligarchs Are Still Calling the Shots,* Foreign Policy (Aug. 14, 2014); Interfax-Ukraine, *Kolesnikov: Inevitability of Punishment Needed for Real Fight Against Smuggling in Ukraine,* Kyiv Post (June 23, 2018); Igor Kossov, *Kyiv Hotel Industry Makes Room for New Entrants,* Kyiv Post (Mar. 7, 2019); Markian Kuzmowycz, *How the Kremlin Can Win Ukraine's Elections,* Atlantic Council (Nov. 19, 2018). The Opposition Bloc is a Ukraine political party that largely reconstituted the Party of Regions.

[881] 3/30/16 Email, Gates to Kilimnik.

article." Manafort further asked: "How do we use to get whole. Has Ovd [Oleg Vladimirovich Deripaska] operation seen?" Kilimnik wrote back the same day, "Yes, I have been sending everything to Victor [Boyarkin, Deripaska's deputy], who has been forwarding the coverage directly to OVD."[883]

Gates reported that Manafort said that being hired on the Campaign would be "good for business" and increase the likelihood that Manafort would be paid the approximately $2 million he was owed for previous political consulting work in Ukraine.[884] Gates also explained to the Office that Manafort thought his role on the Campaign could help "confirm" that Deripaska had dropped the Pericles lawsuit, and that Gates believed Manafort sent polling data to Deripaska (as discussed further below) so that Deripaska would not move forward with his lawsuit against Manafort.[885] Gates further stated that Deripaska wanted a visa to the United States, that Deripaska could believe that having Manafort in a position inside the Campaign or Administration might be helpful to Deripaska, and that Manafort's relationship with Trump could help Deripaska in other ways as well.[886] Gates stated, however, that Manafort never told him anything specific about what, if anything, Manafort might be offering Deripaska.[887] Gates also reported that Manafort instructed him in April 2016 or early May 2016 to send Kilimnik Campaign internal polling data and other updates so that Kilimnik, in turn, could share

---

[882] 4/11/16 Email, Manafort & Kilimnik.

[884] Gates 2/2/18 302, at 10.

[885] Gates 2/2/18 302, at 11; Gates 9/27/18 302 (serial 740), at 2.

[886] Gates 2/2/18 302, at 12.

[887] Gates 2/2/18 302, at 12.

it with Ukrainian oli archs.[888] Gates understood that the information would also be shared with Deripaska. ▇Grand Jury▇

▇▇▇ [889] Gates reported to the Office that he did not know why Manafort wanted him to send polling information, but Gates thought it was a way to showcase Manafort's work, and Manafort wanted to open doors to jobs after the Trump Campaign ended.[890] Gates said that Manafort's instruction included sending internal polling data prepared for the Trump Campaign by pollster Tony Fabrizio.[891] Fabrizio had worked with Manafort for years and was brought into the Campaign by Manafort. Gates stated that, in accordance with Manafort's instruction, he periodically sent Kilimnik polling data via WhatsApp; Gates then deleted the communications on a daily basis.[892] Gates further told the Office that, after Manafort left the Campaign in mid-August, Gates sent Kilimnik polling data less frequently and that the data he sent was more publicly available information and less internal data.[893]

Gates account about polling data is consistent ▇Grand Jury▇

▇▇▇▇▇▇▇▇▇▇▇▇▇▇▇▇▇▇▇▇▇▇▇▇▇

▇▇▇▇▇ [894] ▇▇▇▇▇ with multiple emails that Kilim-

---

[888] Gates 1/31/18 302, at 17; Gates 9/27/18 302 (serial 740), at 2. In a later interview with the Office, Gates stated that Manafort directed him to send polling data to Kilimnik after a May 7, 2016 meeting between Manafort and Kilimnik in New York, discussed in Volume I, Section IV.A.8.b.iii, infra. Gates 11/7/18 302, at 3.

[889] Gates 9/27/18 302, Part II, at 2; ▇Grand Jury▇▇▇▇▇

[890] Gates 2/12/18 302, at 10; Gates 1/31/18 302, at 17.

[891] Gates 9/27/18 302 (serial 740), at 2; Gates 2/7/18 302, at 15.

[892] Gates 1/31/18 302, at 17.

[893] Gates 2/12/18 302, at 11-12. According to Gates, his access to internal polling data was more limited because Fabrizio was himself distanced from the Campaign at that point.

[894] ▇Grand Jury▇▇▇▇▇

nik sent to U.S. associates and press contacts between late July and mid-August of 2016. Those emails referenced "internal polling," described the status of the Trump Campaign and Manafort's role in it, and assessed Trump's prospects for victory.[895] Manafort did not acknowledge instructing Gates to send Kilimnik internal data, Grand Jury [896]

The Office also obtained contemporaneous emails that shed light on the purpose of the communications with Deripaska and that are consistent with Oates' s account. For example, in response to a July 7, 2016, email from a Ukrainian reporter about Manafort's failed Deripaska backed investment, Manafort asked Kilimnik whether there had been any movement on"this issue with our friend."[897] Gates stated that "our friend" likely referred to Deripaska,[898] and Manafort told the Office that the "issue" (and "our biggest interest," as stated below) was a solution to the Deripaska-Pericles issue.[899] Kilimnik replied:

> I am carefully optimistic on the question of our biggest interest.

> Our friend [Boyarkin] said there is lately significantly more attention to the campaign in his boss' [Deripaska's] mind, and he will be most likely looking for ways to reach out to you pretty soon, understanding all the time sen-

---

[895] 8/18/16 Email, Kilimnik to Dirkse; 8/18/16 Email, Kilimnik to Schultz; 8/18/16 Email, Kilimnik to Marson; 7/27/16 Email, Kilimnik to Ash; 8/18/16 Email, Kilimnik to Ash; 8/18/16 Email, Kilimnik to Jackson; 8/18/16 Email, Kilimnik to Mendoza-Wilson; 8/19/16 Email, Kilimnik to Patten.

[896] Grand Jury

[897] 7/7/16 Email, Manafort to Kilimnik.

[898] Gates 2/2/18 302, at 13.

[899] Manafort 9/11/18 302, at 6.

sitivity. I am more than sure that it will be resolved and we will get back to the original relationship with V.'s boss [Deripaska].[900]

Eight minutes later, Manafort replied that Kilimnik should tell Boyarkin's "boss," a reference to Deripaska, "that if he needs private briefings we can accommodate."[901] Manafort has alleged to the Office that he was willing to brief Deripaska only on public campaign matters and gave an example: why Trump selected Mike Pence as the Vice-Presidential running mate.[902] Manafort said he never gave Deripaska a briefing.[903] Manafort noted that if Trump won, Deripaska would want to use Manafolt to advance whatever interests Deripaska had in the United States and elsewhere.[904]

iii. Paul Manafort's Two Campaign-Period Meetings with Konstantin Kilimnik in the United States

Manafort twice met with Kilimnik in person during the campaign period—once in May and again in August 2016. The first meeting took place on May 7, 2016, in New York City.[905] In the days leading to the meeting, Kilimnik had been working to gather information about the political situation in Ukraine. That included information gleaned from a trip that former Party of Regions official Yuriy Boyko had recently taken to Moscow-a trip that likely included meetings between Boyko and high-ranking

---

[900] 7/8/16 Email, Kilimnik to Manafort.
[901] 7/8/16 Email, Kilimnik to Manafort; Gates 2/2/18 302, at 13.
[902] Manafort 9/11/18 302, at 6.
[903] Manafort 9/11/18 302, at 6.
[904] Manafort 9/11/18 302, at 6.
[905] Investigative Technique

Russian officials.[906] Kilimnik then traveled to Washington, D.C. on or about May 5, 2016; while in Washington, Kilimnik had pre-arranged meetings with State Department employees.[907]

Late on the evening of May 6, Gates arranged for Kilimnik to take a 3:00 a.m. train to meet Manafort in New York for breakfast on May 7.[908] According to Manafort, during the meeting, he and Kilimnik talked about events in Ukraine, and Manafort briefed Kilimnik on the Trump Campaign, expecting Kilimnik to pass the information back to individuals in Ukraine and elsewhere.[909] Manafort stated that Opposition Bloc members recognized Manafort's position on the Campaign was an opportunity, but Kilimnik did not ask for anything.[910] Kilimnik spoke about a plan of Boyko to boost election participation in the eastern zone of Ukraine, which was the base for the Opposition Bloc.[911] Kilimnik returned to Washington, D.C. right after the meeting with Manafort.

Manafort met with Kilimnik a second time at the Grand Havana Club in New York City on the evening of August 2, 2016. The events leading to the meeting are as follows. On July 28, 2016, Kilimnik flew from Kiev to Moscow.[912] The next day, Kilimnik wrote to Manafort requesting that they meet, using coded lan-

---

[906] 4/26/16 Email, Kilimnik to Purcell, at 2; Gates 2/2/18 302, at 12; Patten 5/22/18 302, at 6-7; Gates 11/7/18 302, at 3

[907] 5/7/l 6 Email, Kilimnik to Charap & Kimmage; 5/7/J 6 Email, Kasanof to Kilimnik.

[908] 5/6/16 Email, Manafort to Gates; 5/6/16 Email, Gates to Kilimnik.

[909] Manafort 10/11/18 302, at 1.

[910] Manafort 10/11/18 302, at 1.

[911] Manafort 9/11/18 302, at 6.

[912] 7/25/16 Email, Kilimnik to katrin@yana.kiev.ua (2:17:34 a.m.).

guage about a conversation he had that day.[913] In an email with a subject line "Black Caviar," Kilimnik wrote:

I met today with the guy who gave you your biggest black caviar jar several years ago. We spent about 5 hours talking about his story, and I have several important messages from him to you. He asked me to go and brief you on our conversation. I said I have to run it by you first, but in principle I am prepared to do it. . . It has to do about the future of his country, and is quite interesting.[914]

Manafort identified "the guy who gave you your biggest black caviar jar" as Yanukovych. He explained that, in 2010, he and Yanukovych had lunch to celebrate the recent presidential election. Yanukovych gave Manafort a large jar of black caviar that was worth approximately $30,000 to $40,000.[915] Manafort's identification of Yanukovych as "the guy who gave you your biggest black caviar jar" is consistent with Kilimnik being in Moscow—where Yanukovych resided—when Kilimnik wrote "I met today with the guy," and with a December 2016 email in which Kilimnik referred to Yanukovych as "BG," Grand Jury [916] Manafort replied to Kilimnik's July 29 email, "Tuesday [August 2] is best . . . Tues or weds in NYC."[917]

Three days later, on July 31, 2016, Kilimnik flew back to Kiev from Moscow, and on that same day, wrote to Manafort that he needed "about 2 hours" for their meeting "because it is a long caviar

[913] 7/29/16 Email, Kilimnik to Manafort (10:51 a.m.).

[914] 7/29/16 Email, Kilimnik to Manafort (10:51 a.m.).

[915] Manafort 9/12/18 302, at 3.

[916] 7/29/16 Email, Manafort to Kilimnik; Investigative Technique ; Grand Jury

[917] 7/29/16 Email, Manafort to Kilimnik.

story to tell."[918] Kilimnik wrote that he would arrive at JFK on
August 2 at 7:30 p.m., and he and Manafort agreed to a late dinner
that night.[919] Documentary evidence—including flight, phone,
and hotel records, and the timing of text messages exchanged[920]—
confirms the dinner took place as planned on August 2.[921]

As to the contents of the meeting itself, the accounts of Manafort
and Gates-who arrived late to the dinner—differ in certain respects.
But their versions of events, when assessed alongside available documentary evidence and what Kilimnik told business associate Sam
Patten, indicate that at least three principal topics were discussed.

First, Manafort and Kilimnik discussed a plan to resolve the
ongoing political problems in Ukraine by creating an autonomous
republic in its more industrialized eastern region of Donbas,[922] and

---

[918] 7/31/16 Email, Manafort to Kilimnik.

[919] 7/31/16 Email, Manafort to Kilimnik.

[920] Kilimnik 8/2/16 CBP Record; Call Records of Konstantin Kilimnik Grand
Jury   ; Call Records of Rick Gates Grand Jury
    ; 8/2-3/16, Kilimnik Park Lane Hotel Receipt.

[921] Deripaska's private plane also flew to Teterboro Airport in New Jersey on
the evening of August 2, 2016. According to Customs and Border Protection
records, the only passengers on the plane were Deripaska's wife, daughter,
mother, and father-in-law, and separate records obtained by our Office
confirm that Kilimnik flew on a commercial flight to New York.

[922] The Luhansk and Donetsk People's Republics, which are located in the
Donbas region of Ukraine, declared themselves independent in response
to the popular unrest in 2014 that removed President Yanukovych from
power. Pro-Russian Ukrainian militia forces, with backing from the Russian
military, have occupied the region since 2014. Under the Yanukovych-
backed plan, Russia would assist in withdrawing the military, and Donbas
would become an autonomous region within Ukraine with its own prime
minister. The plan emphasized that Yanukovych would be an ideal candidate
to bring peace to the region as prime minister of the republic, and facilitate
the reintegration of the re aine with the support of the U.S. and Russian
presidents. As noted above, according to Grand Jury   the written
documentation describing the plan, for the plan to work, both U.S. and

having Yanukovych, the Ukrainian President ousted in 2014, elected to head that republic.[923] That plan, Manafort later acknowledged, constituted a "backdoor" means for Russia to control eastern Ukraine.[924] Manafort initially said that, if he had not cut off the discussion, Kilimnik would have asked Manafort in the August 2 meeting to convince Trump to come out in favor of the peace plan, and Yanukovych would have expected Manafort to use his connections in Europe and Ukraine to support the plan.[925] Manafort also initially told the Office that he had said to Kilimnik that the plan was crazy, that the discussion ended, and that he did not recall Kilimnik askin Manafort to reconsider the Ian after their August 2 meeting.[926] Manafort said ███Grand Jury███

██████████ that he reacted negatively to Yanukovych sending—years later—an "urgent" request when Yanukovych needed him.[927] When confronted with an email written by Kilimnik on or about December 8, 2016, however, Manafort acknowledged Kilimnik raised the peace plan again in that email.[928] Manafort ultimately acknowledged Kilimnik also raised the peace plan in January and February 2017 meetings with Manafort ████████ Grand Jury ██

████████████████████████████████████ [929]

Russian support were necessary. ██Grand Jury██ 2/21/18 Email, Manafort, Ward, & Fabrizio, at 3-5.

[923] Manafort 9/11/18 302, at 4; ██Grand Jury██

[924] ██Grand Jury██

[925] Manafort 9/11/18 302, at 4.

[926] Manafort 9/12/18 302, at 4.

[927] ██Grand Jury██ Manafort 9/11/18 302, at 5; Manafort 9/12/18 302, at 4.

[928] Manafort 9/12/18 302, at 4; ██Investigative Technique██

[929] ██Grand Jury██████ Documentary evidence confirms the peace-plan discussions in 2018. 2/19/18 Email, Fabrizio to Ward (forwarding email from Manafort); 2/21/18 Email, Manafort to Ward & Fabrizio.

Second, Manafort briefed Kilimnik on the state of the Trump Campaign and Manafort's plan to win the election.[930] That briefing encompassed the Campaign's messaging and its internal polling data. According to Gates, it also included discussion of "battleground" states, which Manafort identified as Michigan, Wisconsin, Pennsylvania, and Minnesota.[931] Manafort did not refer explicitly to "battleground" states in his telling of the August 2 discussion, Grand Jury [932]

Third, according to Gates and what Kilimnik told Patten, Manafort and Kilimnik discussed two sets of financial disputes related to Manafort's previous work in the region. Those consisted of the unresolved Deripaska lawsuit and the funds that the Opposition Bloc owed to Manafort for his political consulting work and how Manafort might be able to obtain payment.[933]

After the meeting, Gates and Manafort both stated that they left separately from Kilimnik because they knew the media was tracking Manafort and wanted to avoid media reporting on his connections to Kilimnik.[934]

---

[930] Manafort 9/11/18 302, at 5.
[931] Gates 1/30/18 302, at 3, 5.
[932] Grand Jury
[933] Gates 1/30/18 302, at 2-4; Patten 5/22/18 302, at 7.
[934] Gates 1/30/18 302, at 5; Manafort 9/11/18 302, at 5.